LIVING THE
DREAM
ON AMERICA'S TEAM

To Brett,

Best wishes

to a sports fan

Larry Cole
 # 63

L A R R Y   C O L E

Fulton Books, Inc.
Meadville, PA

Published by Fulton Books 2021

ISBN 978-1-63860-838-7 (paperback)
ISBN 978-1-63860-839-4 (digital)

Printed in the United States of America

To aspiring young athletes,
that they find their unique talent
to define what success looks like for them.
This is how I define my success and the journey I took
to make my dream a reality.

CONTENTS

PROLOGUE

Let me introduce myself. I am Larry Cole. I played football for the Dallas Cowboys for thirteen years, and I think a lot of people would be interested in my perspective on how I made my journey to become a player for America's team and how it happened to an average guy with average talent but a desire to succeed in whatever he attempted to achieve.

"Excuse me, who did you say you are?" he asked.

"I'm Larry Cole, number 63, who played for the Dallas Cowboys from 1968 to 1981."

"Oh, well, I've never heard of you."

I told him that I played one year with Don Meredith as quarterback, all of the Roger Staubach's eleven years, and one year with Danny White. I played in five Super Bowls, winning two of them, and eight conference championships, winning five, and when I retired, I had the NFL record for most playoff games at twenty-six.

He said, "Really? Who knew!"

Recently, I was talking to a subcontractor who told his young workers that I used to play for the Dallas Cowboys. They didn't believe it. They looked at me, and I said, "Yes, that's true." They still were skeptical. My subcontractor then said to them, "Google it." They did, and their faces lit up as only younger faces can do.

Why are all the stories only about the great players? What about average guys who did their jobs, were good team players, and at times made big plays? Don't more people identify with those people? When I played, my fans were the average working class of people who worked their jobs, adjusted to failures and disappointments in their lives, and moved on. They weren't the flashy guys. They enjoyed the escape of watching pro football and identified with different players.

Most had some lesser-known players, like me, they cheer for along with the stars. Today I am receiving three to five fan mails a week from all over the country, more than when I played. I think many people are very interested to know what things were like in those days. How we all had to prepare for work after football was over. I feel like I witnessed and participated in the most exciting period of the NFL and the Dallas Cowboys. We were the team of the seventies. I was part of the Doomsday I and Doomsday II Defenses. I played seven years with Bob Lilly, and six years with Randy White. Both of these guys are in the Hall of Fame. I will share with you the inside stories of living the ups and downs of pro football and my own development to be part of it.

I am now fully retired from the residential development and construction industry. I am wondering what to do next. I have a lot more time for reflection, and I marvel at my life and all I did with it. I was a shy, timid, sensitive young boy who grew up on a farm in rural Minnesota. I had white hair (not blond) and very light skin, especially during the Minnesota winters.

In this book, I will tell you a story of what being the youngest of four children growing up on a farm was like and what that taught me about how to work and compete. I will share with you my family's heritage. I will write about my development as a high school basketball and football player and my experience as an Air Force Academy cadet and football player for two and a half years. Then, my detour on the road, how I went from the University of Houston to the University of Hawaii and was then drafted by the Dallas Cowboys in the sixteenth round out of seventeen draft picks. Along the way, I discovered something about myself that all the great ones, like Tom Brady, Aaron Rodgers, and Drew Brees, and so many more are challenged by, this single thought: "Tell me I can't do it and I will prove to you that I can." This isn't just reserved for the great ones; average players can become good players and more if they are so motivated.

I played in a unique era of pro football, where the game replaced baseball as the national pastime. I grew up watching Jim Brown, Johnny Unitas, Gale Sayers, Dick Butkus, Raymond Berry, Bart Starr, and many more who carved out their contribution to the game. Joe Namath won the Super Bowl my rookie year, which sealed the merger of the AFL and NFL. I witnessed the advent of Monday-night football with Howard Cossell, Frank Gifford, and Don Meredith. They would set the stage and open the game with the roar of the local crowd proud of their city. Each city that hosted the game was highlighted, adding to the friendly competition between the teams and their cities, and gave the television audience what it might be like to live in those places. I have witnessed the evolution of the game through the innovation of coaches, from Paul Brown, George Halas, Vince Lombardi, Don Shula, Tom Landry, Bill Walsh to the current coaches. I witnessed the rise of the Super Bowl to effectively become a national holiday. I have written this book as if I were sitting down with you and having a conversation about, first, what it is like to play in the NFL. Who the best players and coaches were. What people had the biggest impact on the game? Who the best players I played against were. What it was like playing in that era. How much we were paid and what happened to change all that. The seventies were an exciting era in pro football, and I was there for all of it. Are you interested in hearing my story and my opinion on what was happening in the NFL each step of the way?

I was around for a lot of history and seemed to be that other guy in the background that didn't get a lot of publicity, nor did he want too much of it. Thus, the Zero Club was formed. Find out what that was all about. I want this to be a different kind of book that will inform, entertain, and put you in the moment as each year progresses. I will write this book for my version of the American dream and the impact the NFL had on my life. I will share with you my feelings at that time, my assessment of what was happening with the team, and how all this happened while I was raising a family and running a business. I am giving you the inside story of how we climbed the mountain to win our first championship, how we won our second championship, and how we fought to be in the hunt every year. I will share with you snippets of all the personalities that were there during my time. Grab the book and take yourself back in time. Enjoy!

CHAPTER 1

OUR HERITAGE AND LIFESTYLE

I grew up on a farm in Southwest Minnesota. In winter, Minnesota can get cold, actually *damn* cold! Many days at twenty-five degrees below zero. In the summer, it can get hot and humid. We had to deal with all the elements. In 1858, Minnesota became a state. In 1862, Abraham Lincoln signed the Homestead Act with the intent to settle the western territory. If you worked at least 40 acres of the land and inhabited the land, you could acquire ownership of 160 acres of land from the government after a period of five years. My dad's side of the family came from Norway, while my mom's side of the family came from Germany. In 1869, my dad's grandfather, Lars Cole, and his wife, Johanna, immigrated to Wisconsin from near Gjøvik, Norway. He lived on a 40-acre farm located on Kollstopen. Yes, the 40 acres were located on top of a hill. I have been there. It was a beautiful place. In Norway, only 3 percent of the land is suitable for agriculture. It was the tradition then that the eldest son would inherit the family farm. That wasn't in the cards for my great-grandfather. With the word out about the Homestead Act in America, others from that area did the same thing.

Lars and Johanna stayed in Rio, Wisconsin, for three years and came to Minnesota by covered wagon in 1872. He worked odd jobs around Redwood Falls. In 1876, he homesteaded eighty acres on a farm about three miles south of Hanley Falls. My grandfather Lewis Cole, son of Lars, was born and raised on this farm along with two brothers and two sisters. They were all able to get side-by-side farms.

My grandfather Lewis got two hundred acres. His son Ordell, my uncle, ran the farm for many years. To this day, his son, my cousin Lauris, owns and runs this farm. On June 21, 1899, Lewis married my grandmother Hannah Hagen. Coincidentally, I got married seventy years later on the same date. My dad was the fourth eldest of eleven children born in 1905. He grew up speaking Norwegian until he was six years old, when he went to school and learned English. His mother, Hannah, came to America when she was six. She was Hannah Hagan, and she was born in Vardal, Norway, and came to America along with her brothers and sisters. They all homesteaded farms, too, in the same area.

About seventeen miles away, my grandfather Gotlieb Kelm came to America in the 1880s at the age of eighteen along with his parents and settled in the Boyd, Minnesota, area. He was one of twelve children born near Ranchin, Germany (now part of Poland). All but three of his siblings moved to America. My grandmother Elsie Zietlow was born near Springfield, Minnesota. She was one of eight children. Their house burned down in Springfield, after which they then moved to Tyro Township, just west of Clarkfield, Minnesota. They rented the Tosten Hansen farm while they were getting ready to buy an eighty-acre farm. This area was settled by mostly Germans. My grandfather Gottlieb Kelm died at the age of thirty-eight. He had liver cancer. This happened when my mother was twelve years old. Her mother, Elsie, was pregnant with her last baby at that time. Eight days after the funeral, she gave birth to her youngest son, Melvin. She was a widow with five kids at the age of thirty-two. When she was thirty-nine years old, she would remarry to Otto Bohn. He died ten years later, and she would be a widow again and never remarry. Mom was the only girl. She had four brothers. They would not be able to buy that eighty-acre farm, so they had to leave the Tosten Hansen farm. Grandma's dad, Herman Zietlow, gave them forty acres of land with no buildings. They built a chicken house and lived in it the first year before they could build their house. They then dug out a basement and had an old existing house moved over onto that basement. Mom got various homekeeping jobs until she met and married my dad in 1936. Then life got better for her. She was fortunate to have married into a very special large family after what she had been through. It gave her more stability.

The children who lived in this area of southwestern Minnesota spoke English with a Norwegian or German accent, while their parents gradually picked up the language, learning from their children. There were also other immigrants from other northern European countries. These people brought their traditions from their respective country. The Norwegians were primarily Lutheran. They built the Hanley Falls Lutheran Church in 1892. My dad was born in 1905. All the religious holidays were observed here. The farm kids cleaned up Saturday night and came to Sunday school on Sunday morning, followed by the main service. The kitchen was in the church basement, next to the gathering room. This was where we had "potluck suppers." We seemed to have at least one every month, and all the ladies would bring their specialty hot dishes. At Christmas we would have lutefisk and lefse. Lutefisk was an inexpensive fish, and lefse was a tortilla-like potato wrap with butter and sugar inside. Norwegians always like their coffee in a cup with a saucer. Most like to add cream to their coffee, and they would use the saucer to cool down the hot coffee. Bringing out a tray of sweet desserts was always customary. Most Norwegians were teetotalers. On the German side, they were opposite. Germans were also Lutheran, but a lot were Catholics. For food, they like sauerkraut, bratwurst, German chocolate cake, and a whole lot of beer.

As time went on, the Germans and Norwegians started marrying one another and the traditions merged.

My parents' life was centered on ten towns that were within a thirty-mile radius: Hanley Falls, Cottonwood, Wood Lake, Hazel Run, Clarkfield, Boyd, Montevideo, Granite Falls, and Renville. They lived their entire life there.

My dad was born in 1905. He grew up using horses to do the farm fieldwork. Eventually, he was able to get his own car. My mother was born in 1918. She met my dad when she was eighteen, and my dad was thirty-one. She completed her eight years of education and then went to work in Clarkfield. When she met Dad at eighteen, she had already been on her own for three or four years.

They met at a Cole party, where they played progressive whist, a card game. My mother was partnered with Dad's brother Art. They were able to keep their seats and won the tournament. After playing cards, they all would dance. My dad played the accordion and the mouth organ as he sat on the steps. Mom was more attracted to Dad. Eventually they got married, and her mother, Elsie, now a widow, got remarried and got on with her life. She got remarried to Otto Bohn. Ten years later, he would die from a heart attack. Grandma Bohn was a widow again. Dad had ten brothers and two sisters. His parents were a very kind and giving people. During the Depression, they would feed people that came by and were hurting. To this day, we still have the annual Lewis and Hannah Cole family reunion. Our social life was built on interacting with our cousins. Our family always had a good sense of humor and love of children. When Dad was growing up, he would play the accordion at neighborhood parties.

We got together not only with our family but with other families also. We had the Cole-Nelson picnic too. The Nelson family was almost as big as the Coles. Eventually, we had to split into separate annual picnics. We would have a picnic, play softball, and for the older men, play horseshoes. My uncle Harold wrote a segment for the annual Lewis and Hannah Cole picnic. He was the second youngest of the twelve children. He wrote, "I was taught to be happy, appreciative, and confident and not give up. We learn by mistakes. But it is how you are molded early in life that gives you the strength to overcome."

In the fifties and early sixties, each town had their own school, basketball and football team, and marching band. Mostly every town had some type of festival. Montevideo would have their annual Fiesta Days. There was a carnival that came to town, and there would be a parade as well. Marching bands from all the area towns would be represented no matter how small they were. Granite Falls had the annual Rodeo Days. There were car races and stunt driving in Canby, and Hanley Falls had the annual Threshing Show to display how all the old forties technology worked to transform the advancement of modern-day farming.

Most towns had a baseball town team. This was primarily for those past high school players who wanted an activity to compete in after they graduated. My dad took me to Cottonwood, Wood Lake, and Granite Falls to go to these games. Evenings in the summer in Minnesota were usually very pleasant, as long as that area had been sprayed for mosquitos. All the games were at night, which gave a glow to the baseball field. Of course, as a kid I couldn't keep still, so we played outside the ball diamond. In Granite Falls, we could go to a popcorn stand that is still there now. They use white kernels and have a secret butter ingredient that makes their popcorn special.

The high school kids who most recently got their driver's license would drive around and around, "scooping the loop." The cars were quite interesting, as some would jack up the rear wheels, while some would repaint the cars with a raked dull surface. They had "ducktail" haircuts and black leather jackets. This era was captured by the movie *Grease*, starring John Travolta and Olivia Newton John.

Most people in the area like sports and support their local teams. Volstead Field in Granite Falls is still the same as when I played there. The field has enough seats for three hundred people, all on one side. The field is right next to the high school and across the way to the Bert Raney Elementary School. In between is a playground mound that is filled with evergreen and pine trees. During my brother's games, we could run in the woods and use the elementary school playground equipment. I found the football games to be boring as little happened on each side because nobody had a decent passing game. My brother was a lineman. In those days, people played both ways. I don't remember much about his games except one of his teammates, Wally Knutson, got severely injured when he ran into the bottom of the down markers and caused a wound deep into his chest. Those markers were metal spears at that time. It happened all over the country. That is why they now only have rubber underneath the ball of the pole and the marker holders drop the pole when a runner gets near them. In any event, my brother must have been good, because he got a scholarship to the University of Nebraska.

By late October, it got cold and sometimes snowed, so everyone was ready to go inside to watch basketball. That was much more popular. The season was over in February. The tournaments started, and the state champion was crowned by the middle of March. There was only one class for the tournament at that time. My brother was on a very good team, but they didn't get past the regional tournament. Later in 1960, the little town of Edgerton, population one thousand, won the state championship with four brothers and one cousin.

That team, the Flying Dutchman, is a legend in Minnesota.

In the spring, my brother threw the shot put, did the pole vault and the high jump, and ran high hurdles. He was fairly good at it. He would practice at home, and I would help, though I had no interest in doing any of that. He also played first base in baseball, for which I would have to go to all his games. One game, he missed the ball and it scratched the side of his cheek, which immediately turned to blood. After that, I didn't have any interest in at least playing first base. Roger was a four-year letterman in football, basketball, baseball, and track.

We were the Granite Falls Kilowatts. What a cool mascot! In 1952, Northern States Power Company opened a power plant on the Minnesota River on the edge of town. Their logo was Redi-Kilowatt, a cartoon-type character. We adapted the same. The plant closed in the eighties, and the school district merged with Maynard, Hanley Falls, and Clarkfield. It was then changed to Yellow Medicine East, and the mascot became the Sting, some kind of bumblebee. Really, this was the negotiated name for the Hanley Falls Cyclones, the Granite Falls Kilowatts, and the Clarkfield Cardinals. They first changed it to the Kilo-Cards, but that didn't stand.

My family and other immigrants developed a new society in Minnesota and surrounding states. They had nothing coming to America. The intent of the Homestead Act was to establish stable societies in the Midwest. You had to be hardy to handle the harsh winters. They were coming from northern Europe and the Scandinavian countries, so the cold weather didn't bother them that much. This area became the "breadbasket" for the country. These farmers played a crucial role during the world wars to feed the troops. Germans and Norwegians were both good on building cities and towns that would be self-sustaining. I am proud to be a son of this community, as are my twenty-seven cousins and my three siblings.

CHAPTER 2

HOME ON THE FARM

I am the youngest of four children of Rudy and Vi Cole. I was born in November of 1946. We lived on a 160-acre farm between Clarkfield and Granite Falls, Minnesota. Our address was Hazel Run, population 200. We went to church in Hanley Falls, population 350. We went to school in Granite Falls, population 2,800. I was born in Clarkfield, population 1,200.

Farm aerial view.

Access to our farm was off a county gravel road. There was a big hill just before reaching our driveway halfway down the hill. As you entered the narrow eight-foot-wide driveway, you had to travel up a steep hill that had a big cottonwood tree next to it. When you got past the hill, you would then be on level ground and could see the red-painted grain storage building with an outhouse next to it. On the left was the chicken coop, which housed about thirty chickens and banty roosters. We would buy pullets (baby chickens) and raise them until they could lay eggs themselves in their nests. One of our chores was to gather the eggs twice a day by just feeling under the chicken. Most of the time, it was just fine, but eventually one of the chickens would use its beak to take a stab at the top of my hands. That would hurt! That was just the way it was, and as a farm kid, we just moved on. The driveway took a bend to the right, and straight ahead was a yard light. As a little boy, I called it a "lard light." To the right was our house. It was a two-story house with a basement. You walked into the mudroom, where coats and overalls with manure on them were hung. It was a room about five feet wide by eight feet long with a door. Why the door? Because the manure smell from talking care of the pigs and cows would smell up the kitchen. As you entered the kitchen, the sink and cabinets were on the right. My sister would wash the dishes, and my job was to wipe them. There wasn't any dishwasher in those days. We were it. To the left was the oil burner. This appliance provided heat for the whole house. We would leave open the door to the upstairs to let some heat to the upstairs bedrooms. In the wintertime, sometimes we had to put two blankets on us in our beds as the temperature would fall to the fifties. In front of the kitchen was our chrome kitchen table with six chairs for all six of us.

I remember we had to eat our vegetables before we could leave the table. I hated green vegetables. I liked sweet corn. I was more of a meat-and-potatoes guy. A treat was to have a bowl of ice cream on Sunday night with bread, butter, and sugar. That was our meal. We never lacked for food because we grew every conceivable fruit and vegetables, and we raised our own hogs and cattle.

We had nine cows that needed to be milked every day. In the time it took me to milk one-and-a-half cows, my brother and dad had done the rest. I never had to get up early to milk the cows, but my brother and dad did that. In the evening, I would milk my one and one-half cows and then fall asleep on a stack of straw with my dog, Snooky. When it was time, around 8:30 p.m. for my bedtime, my dad would wake me up and tell me to go to the house to go to bed. I ran by the "lard light" and headed for the house. As I got closer to the house, the light got dimmer. I was always concerned that the bogeyman would get me before I got to the door. He would be coming from the darker right side of the house, I thought.

Off the kitchen was the living room. There was room for a couch, a couple of chairs, and a piano. In the back of the oil burner was where my parents had their bedroom. There was no indoor plumbing in 1953. Behind the kitchen table was access to the upstairs stairway. It was a narrow L-shaped stairs. At the top of the stairs was an alcove where there was room for a crib and a small bed. Straight ahead, the best room in the house, which was for my sisters. They had a bay window, which made the room seem bigger. The walls went up about four feet and then followed the roofline. To the left of the stairs was my bedroom, which I shared with my brother. We had a regular-size bed. As the youngest, I was on the inside. The roof was about two feet above me. When it rained, the sound of the raindrops hypnotized me to sleep or kept me awake when it hailed. The room was about nine feet by nine feet. My brother, Roger, was a big basketball fan. We had a radio in the room. We listened to the broadcast of the Minneapolis Lakers with George Mikan. That was before they moved to Los Angeles. On Sunday nights, we would listen to the crime drama with Johnny Dollar as a private detective.

Our house couldn't have been more than eight hundred square feet, with about five hundred of that on the first floor, plus a basement. The basement was where we kept the potatoes under the steps. We would harvest them and store them over the winter. They would grow stems in the box. That was weird to me.

We also stored jams and jellies from our garden. My favorite was strawberry jam. We also kept a "deep freezer" there. That was this newfangled device that would work without constantly storing ice when plugged into the electrical outlet. We also made our homemade ice cream in the basement. It was fresh and very tasty. It was our Sunday-night treat.

Sibling step picture.

So how did we live without running water? First, we had a well about twenty feet away from the house. We called it a cistern. We had a crank pump, where we would draw water and then take a pail of water into the house and then warm it up by adding boiling water to the water we collected in a stainless steel tub that was five feet long and two feet wide. We kept it in the mudroom, where coats and overalls were kept. In order to save time and money, we would have our entire family of six bathe in that tub. I was about six at that time. My sister Barb was eight. We would bathe first together, then my sister Marlene, who was fifteen at that time, then followed next was our mother, then my brother, Roger, who was twelve at that time, and last was our father. I never thought anything about this until at a family reunion we had in 2007, when my brother mentioned how soiled the water was when it got to him and Dad. I didn't know that. Well, that was the way it was. So you may be asking, How did we tend to number 1 and number 2? As for number 1, it was easy. We would just go behind the barn. It was a little harder for our women, but you could squat and lean against the building. Most of the time, we would go to the outhouse. In the wintertime, we didn't want to walk in the snow that far to the outhouse. We would just urinate in the snow outside the front door. It was about fifty feet away from the house. We had a "two-holer," complete with Sears catalog and, later, this newer luxury, toilet paper. For number 2, once one of the holes was filled up, we would block that off and use the other. Then when both were filled up, we would dig a new hole and move over the outhouse about six feet. Then we would put about a foot of dirt on it. Grass grew faster at that spot.

In 1953, we got running water to our parents' bathroom and the kitchen. I was seven years old. We all took a bath Saturday night to be clean to go to church Sunday morning. In 1956, we got a television. What an amazing device! We had a "rabbit ears" antenna. When we watched the networks from Minneapolis, the picture started out clear and then got very snowy. The antenna on the roof needed to be moved every fifteen minutes. At that time, we watched *I Love Lucy*, *The Jackie Gleason Show*, and *The Steve Allen Show*. They were all professionals as they were experienced in live performances. We found humor in so many ways in those days. The only station that was reliable was the broadcast from Alexandria, Minnesota. They mostly covered local news and didn't have the feed of NBC, CBS, and ABC. Later, the city of Granite Falls built a booster station, and by the late fifties, we could watch a clear picture of all the networks for a monthly fee.

Meanwhile, back on the farm, about fifty feet from the "lard light" was the barn. It was the traditional red barn with a second floor to store the bales of hay. On the first floor we had a room for our cream separators. After milking the nine cows, we would pour the milk into the machine to separate the cream from the skim milk. We would drink the skim milk with our meals, use the cream for cooking, and give the cats a plate of the cream. The rest we would sell to the market. The younger heifers had their gated area across from the cows. In the back of the cows was an eight-inch-deep hole twelve inches wide and twenty-five feet long. Quiz: What's that for? Yep, manure. Every day that manure had to be cleaned out and thrown in the back fenced yard behind the barn, where the cows spent most of their day. You couldn't avoid getting manure on your overalls. Once the manure built up at the backyard of the barn, we would shovel the manure into a manure spreader wagon. Then after harvest, we would distribute the manure with a rotary blade to about a six-foot-wide path and drive up and down the harvested cornstalks and also over the oat, soybean, and barley fields. In those days, we rotated each year with soybeans and oats one year, then corn the following year, and vice versa.

In the back of the barn, about twenty feet was the hog barn. Let's put it this way: pigs lie in their own feces and don't pay much attention to hygiene. Amazingly, their meat hardly ever has health issues, and with low fat, it is a good source of protein. The hog barn is smelly; the outside yard, even more smelly. If you want to clear an area, they eat almost anything. There wasn't a blade of grass in their back pen. When they were fattened up, we took them to market in Hanley Falls.

My older sister, Marlene, liked ducks. Those ducks were in the hog barn. They would have their ducklings. They were so cute to have watched grow and walk behind their mother. We used some of their eggs for Easter.

In front of the hog barn was the pump house. This was where Dad kept his tools. As a kid, I liked to hang out there and discover what all the tools were for. Here was where I got my first nickname, Grease Monkey. Outside the building were our gas pumps to fuel our tractors. I was intrigued with the tractors. They were rated by how many bottom plow they could pull. We had an F-20 tractor that was a crank start and could only pull a one-bottom plow. We had an International Harvester H tractor that could pull a two-bottom plow. That tractor would become a big part of my life when I was nine to eleven years old. Our immediate neighbors had M tractors, and they could pull a three-bottom plow. We would park the tractors by the gas pumps to fill them up in the morning. In the back of them were our implements. We had a combine to harvest the oats, soybeans, and flax. We had a disk to till the ground. We had a two-bottom plow, a mower, a drill to seed the barley, oats, and flax, a mower to cut the alfalfa hay, and a corn picker.

In the back of them was the pasture for the cows. The cows needed to graze and eat regular grass. Farmers use dogs to direct the cows to the barns, and this was a job for our dog, Tippy. She was a collie and known as Marlene's dog. When I was five, we got a cocker spaniel dog that was cute but not much good for anything but to hug and love. This dog was a male. When Roger held that dog in one arm, his penis would start sticking out as he felt so comfortable.

I would curl up with him on the straw pile, and when I wanted to be alone, I would crawl into the doghouse with him between the barn and the hog house. When Tippy died, we got another dog, named Corky. She was a female. One day, I found Snooky and Corky stuck together. I panicked and ran to my mother to get help. She looked outside and saw the dogs and just smiled. I was agonized that my mom didn't seem to care. I was furious! They separated eventually, and we moved on. It wasn't until a few years later that I figured out what really happened. Oh well. I say, when you are country boy, you are curious about everything.

Marlene, Larry, and dogs.

Next to the pasture were the woods and our orchard. We had peach trees, apple trees, crab apple trees, raspberry bushes, and a plum tree. Our mother was a good cook. She made peach and apple pies and canned a lot of fruits. We also had a vegetable garden, where we grew cucumbers, radishes, cantaloupes, strawberries, watermelon, beets, string beans, carrots, potatoes, sweet potatoes, and celery. We would all pick the strawberries, put them in boxes, and then sell them to the general public. I think we sold each box for fifteen cents. What vegetables she didn't sell, she would can and we would eat later. We were an almost totally self-sufficient farm.

Next to the hog barn was the grain storage. Here was where we stored enough grain to feed the pigs over the winter months, and also the heifers and steers from the harvest before they went to market. What was left was taken to the local grain elevator in Hazel Run.

Out in the far corner, on about eight acres of land, we grew alfalfa hay for the cattle. We would mow the alfalfa and give it a few days to dry. Then get a tine to get the alfalfa to gather in a roll about two feet wide and as long as a row would go. Then we sent in the hay baler to bound up the hay with twine to make a bale of hay. We would rig up a trailer following behind the baler so we could stack the bales on the open trailer and haul them to the barn. We would use an elevator to get the bales of hay up to the big barn door on the second floor. Then we would stack them as high as we could reach. So in the winter, we would take a couple of bales and drop them in a scuttle hole in front of the trough area for the cows to eat while they were being milked.

My brother, Roger, loved to play basketball. In Minnesota, it is too cold in the winter to play basketball outside. Roger figured out that if we stacked the bales a little higher on half the area, we could use the rest of the area for a basketball court with two baskets about thirty feet apart. Dad was okay with this if we did all the work and did our chores. In this part of the country, farms were about half a mile apart. Most families had at least three or four kids. We would get together with our neighbors and some cousins a few miles away to have games at one another's places. We thought ours was the best. I remember vividly during Thanksgiving weekend in 1955, when Roger was a freshman in high school, his coach, Les Espeland, brought out a new, shiny orange basketball. The ones you could buy in the store weren't like that. Most of the guys that played were Roger's age. I was the little brother that would tag along. They would let me play, too, but didn't guard me too closely. Roger went on to be a starter at center for four consecutive years, from ninth to twelfth grade. I don't believe anyone has done that since.

In the spring we would prepare to seed the crops. After harvest the previous year, we plowed the soil to prepare for the next year. On land that was used for oats, barley, and flax the previous year, we would use a disk to till the soil. The same disk is used today with a lot more technology. The spiral blade loosens up the soil enough to allow it to accept seed. After we disked, we then used a drag to smooth out the soil. A *drag* is like a big tine rake. Then we brought out the drill, which was about twelve feet wide and had boxes where seed was stored and then released. We would drive the tractor up and down the field. We then prepared the soil in the same manner to plant the soybeans and corn seeds. To do that, we used another machine, a corn planter. These two crops were planted in rows. The purpose was to not overuse the soil. That was why they rotated crops in those days, soybeans one year, corn the next year. This was in the days before the wide use of fertilizer and now GPS technology to provide for healthy soil. We had a two-row planter. We would use wire from the start to the end of the rows to make them straight. For soybeans, the seed was let out sequentially from the seedboxes. For corn, the planter would let out three seeds every eighteen inches by having a loop in the wire to trip the seedbox every time it moved eighteen inches. When this was completed, the crops would grow, but also so would get the weeds.

After the plants came out to about eight inches tall, we installed a cultivator on our H tractor. They were V-shaped blades, about six of them, that cut through the dirt when the blades were lowered hydraulically after finishing a row and turning around. Since the corn was seeded in pods eighteen inches apart, the cultivator would need to go through the field sideways. To remove those weeds, this was done twice from June to early July, once each direction. My brother, Roger, would do this work. Dad tended to the cattle and the shop, where old machinery always needed a lot of repair.

In June of 1956, my brother wanted to make some extra money and go to work for another farmer, Gerald Velde. He was married to

Dad's cousin Harriet. Roger was a good student in math and science. He wanted to go to college to become a civil engineer. My mother was a stickler for education, that we kids grow up to get a good education and do something other than farming. Dad couldn't tend to everything by himself, so at the age of nine, I got the job to do most of the cultivating. Earlier in the spring, I started doing the plowing, disking, and dragging. That didn't require too much skill; it was just repetitious and monotonous.

To do the cultivating required much more concentration and skill. The idea was to remove the weeds. But what if you were daydreaming and you veered off course? You would dig up the new corn or soybeans. It was especially difficult on the hills, where you had to compensate for the lean of the tractor. These were problems that couldn't be corrected. When I crossed the corn, it required having a crank on the steering wheel. Every fourth row I would have to turn the tractor wheels to the right for half a turn and then to the left to go straight again. That was because every fourth row changed because the wire was moved after every round trip of the corn planter. You could drive by and see the bald spot on the hill. My dad was not happy and didn't have a lot of tolerance for errors. He would always call me out when I made mistakes. It was hard at first, but he was taking a lot of responsibility for our family that he believed I could handle the job. Farm machinery can be very dangerous, and in those days there wasn't any OSHA. I had an uncle who lost his hand pulling out a cornstalk from the auger of his corn picker. Being scared of bad outcomes served the purpose: be careful. I did the whole same routine the next summer, when I was ten. We acquired an old 1931 Model A Ford. I got to drive that around the farm. In front of the passenger seat was a choke, where you could add additional gasoline to start it. My brother showed me that if I pulled it out when I came down the hill of the entrance to the farm, it would make a loud pop. I thought that was cool. When I did it, Dad noticed and I got in trouble. Roger just smiled. I got in trouble, not him. Oh, to be the little brother!

When we went to visit Dad's family, he would mention to my uncles that I was doing all the fieldwork. That gave me some pride, that he believed that I could do the job. That probably was my first step in achieving things beyond my expectations.

For the soybeans, we had to keep out the cocklebur weeds and the corn seeds that grew back corn from the previous year. The reason for this was to protect the swather of the combine from breaking with having to swath tall cornstalks. The solution for this was to have the children go through the soybean rows with a curved blade to remove the cornstalks and cut or pull the cocklebur weeds. We would usually have about fifty acres of soybeans, so it took about two to three weeks with ten-hour days for two or three people to get this done. With all the plants, there were a lot of bugs and mosquitos, so we wore straw hats with a cloth screen held by the hat to below our necks to protect us from the mosquitos.

Larry's 11th Birthday

By late July and early August, it was time for harvesting the grain. In those days the neighbor farmers got together and did the harvest together at one another's farms. It was usually about three to four farmers with their children workers. It turned into a work and social occasion. We would get an afternoon lunch with Kool-Aid, sandwiches, and plenty of sweet desserts. We had the combine drivers, the tractor and trailer drivers, and those who ran the elevator to put the grain into the grain elevator. These social occasions lessened the drudgery of doing hard work. In September, we would be back in school, so to harvest the soybeans, we would have to work after school until sunset. We didn't store the soybeans, so we took them straight to the market elevator at Hazel Run.

In late October and early November, we picked the corn. This time was one of my favorite memories of my family and our lifestyle. We all worked together. My mother grew up on a farm and was capable of doing almost anything. We installed the corn picker on the H tractor. It had rotating metal augurs that tore off the stalk with the corncob in it. A conveyor belt would advance the corncobs into a wood trailer with sides on it and that was pulled behind the tractor. She would go row after row until full. Then my brother would bring her an empty wagon to switch out and take out the full wagon to the corncrib, next to the pasture. Dad was there, operating the elevator, moving the corncobs to the top of the corncrib. He would unload the wagon with a tine fork in as much as the elevator could handle. Then when the corncrib got filled unevenly, my sister Barb and I would be in the corncrib and, using our bodies, kick the corn over to level the corn and to use the full capacity of the corncrib. While this was happening, my older sister, Marlene, would be preparing supper, which we ate after dark. We, as a family, had done a day's work and were proud of it.

CHAPTER 3

MY LIFE IN GRANITE FALLS

In late 1957, our mother informed us that she would be taking a job as a nurse's aide at the hospital in Granite Falls. She said she would put her work times on the calendar so we could see when she would be gone. Her hours were seven to three, three to eleven, or eleven to seven. This meant we would have to help more around the house as she would be gone. I didn't think much of it at that time. In March of 1958, she told me that we would be moving to Granite Falls and leaving the farm. I loved the farm and was not happy about it. She said I could then ride my bike to see my friends in town and that we were moving into an almost-new house. We had been renting this farm and would have to move because the farm was sold without our knowledge. We had to move. We then had an auction to sell all our equipment. Most of it was old equipment. We priced the equipment as high as we could with the help of an auctioneer. Friends and relatives came to the sale and bought stuff they really didn't need to just help us out. This was very humiliating to my dad. But as the saying goes, "he handled it like a man." Many times in my life, I remember how he handled setbacks. He handled it without becoming bitter. My mom, to her dying day, knew that when they had a chance to buy the farm before World War II, my grandfather, my dad's dad, advised them not to take on any debt. That was a missed opportunity. With the help of Mom's stepdad, they could have bought it. As the war carried on, grain and cattle prices skyrocketed. They could have paid off the debt in five years.

My grandma Bohn cosigned an FHA loan so we could buy this house at the western end of Granite Falls. Dad would be getting a new job but didn't have one yet. Mom said I could play baseball that summer with the other kids. It was sounding better. She said I would have to give up my dog, Snooky, because she couldn't take care of him and didn't want a dog in this new house. I was devastated. She said that our family friends Noreen and Helen Albach had agreed to take Snooky. They had three children that I knew well from church, so I finally said it was okay. I would later visit after two months. Snooky was very happy to see me. After six months, Snooky wasn't all that enthusiastic to see me. He had now bonded with their family.

We moved into the house in March. It had two bedrooms and a large laundry room. Roger and I took one bedroom, Barb had her own bedroom, and Mom and Dad slept in the laundry room. It was about nine feet by nine feet. Mom did make Barb share her closet. Dad took over the basement, where he had a shower and a work sink. That was good enough for him. He could remove his overalls and take a shower before dinner. We moved the washer downstairs and the deep freezer. Dad also set up a small workshop. Marlene was long gone and was married that spring. She and her new husband would settle into an old house in a settled neighborhood in Minneapolis.

Dad talked to Marvin Just, who lived in the neighborhood behind us. He had a construction company, and Dad asked him for a job. Dad was fifty-three at that time. He would do the bricklaying all day and come back home physically spent. It was a tough job for a middle-aged guy who was used to being the boss. It was a hard adjustment. He helped build the Granite Motel. A couple of years later, my dad took me to basketball practice at night. He also picked up my friend Tim Prenevost. His dad was the county engineer. My mom asked me to see if he had any open jobs for my dad. I asked him, and he told me to have my dad come by his office to talk to him. Dad got the job, which was to mow all the county ditches in the summer and in the wintertime. Then he would work with the sanding crew to keep the roads open. That part of the job was hard in cold weather. He would have to shovel the sand out of the truck in all weather conditions, which included many days at below zero. His face would get red, but he really didn't mind doing it as he felt it was a service to his fellow citizens, many of whom were relatives. In the summertime, the "mowing ditches" gig was a cushy job. He could do the mowing in the time allotted, and he even had plenty of time to stop in for coffee at area farms. He loved to talk. He was a truly unselfish guy who loved people. He was a cheerful man, something I have tried to emulate. He did that job for twelve years, then retired when he could get his social security. In retirement, he would mow the yards of many of the neighborhood widows. They offered to pay, but he wouldn't accept payment. He said he would keep a record in his little flip-top notebook, but he never did bill them.

Roger got his football scholarship to go to the University of Nebraska. After he graduated in May, he took a job in South Dakota for the summer. While there, he got encephalitis. It was caused by a bite from a tsetse fly. He was weakened and couldn't come home because it was contagious. But he recovered by the end of August and headed off to Lincoln, Nebraska.

I was now free to play sports with the other kids. I could go bowling, play pickup basketball, and play baseball. I had never really played baseball, but I thought I would give it a try. I was left-handed, and it wasn't convenient to play first base. I wasn't skilled enough to play the infield, so I was placed at left field. When the ball was coming my way, I would either overplay it or underplay it. I had no depth perception. So I was on the bench most of the time. I was scared of getting hit by the ball when I was at bat. Other than that, I was great. When we did a scrimmage, I was among the last to be picked for the team. I enjoyed the comradery, but I realized this was not my sport.

I got a call from my sister in Minneapolis. She wanted to know if I wanted to spend the rest of the summer with her and her husband. He needed help painting this old house. I agreed to go there and do the painting. But I found out it was more than painting—it was removing all the old caulking and scraping the wood window frames. We sanded and applied two coats of paint. At first, I thought this was much better than doing farmwork, but as time went by, when we had finished the windows and inside walls and I thought we were done, her husband, Jim, decided we should paint the entire outside lap siding. That also needed scraping and sanding. By the time we got to that, I hated the messiness and smell of painting. I liked to cover a lot of area. Jim liked to take his time to make it perfect. I wasn't that way at all. I just wanted to get it done as soon as possible. When I accidentally spilled a gallon of paint on the roof, Jim was ready to end my help. We joked a lot about it later.

I experienced a lot when I lived there for about a month. It was a culture shock to see how other nonrural people lived. The next-door neighbor was a devout Catholic who had statues all over his backyard. In the back of the alley were Jewish people. Their Sabbath was on Friday dusk to Saturday dusk. I got to know them quite well. And it all broadened my horizon.

I got back home, and I would now be entering seventh grade. They wanted all kids to play both football and basketball in that grade. I didn't want to play football. I didn't like playing outside in the Minnesota weather in October. But my brother gave me a call and talked me into it. The seventh graders were at the bottom of the totem pole. They got the hand-me-downs. I remember the football pants I got. They were too big, and the thigh pad holder was ripped apart. I was to take tape and wrap it around my thigh. My helmet was leather with no guard bars. The older kids were starting to get them. But we didn't. The school was trying to make room for the seventh graders, so they cleared a vacant area across from the elementary school. There was a mound of granite rock next to it. The field had all kinds of jagged-edged rocks that would cut our skin on the hands, arms, and legs. After parents complained, they moved us to the grassless general-purpose field next to the varsity football field. It wasn't much better but had fewer rocks. We were learning how to tackle, but it hurt when we hit the ground.

Finally, the season was over and we could go to basketball indoors. I was five feet, four inches when I entered seventh grade, shorter than a lot of kids; however, I wore a size 12 shoe. That was supposed to be an indicator that I had a lot more growth ahead of me. When school was out, I was offered a job to live with my second cousins on a farm near Hanley Falls. These were Gerald and Harriet Velde and their three children. Vonnie was one year younger than me, Tim was three years younger, and Colleen was six years younger. Gerald wanted some help with his farming as Roger was now off to college. I thought this might be interesting as I had no interest in trying to play baseball again. I would come for the week, and they would take me home to my family for the weekends.

Gerald had a new 560 International Harvester Tractor that could pull a four-bottom plough. That would be where I would spend most of my time on during the summer, on the cultivator. Farmers had figured out how to add a radio to place on top of the engine so they could listen to music while tending to the hypnotic hum of the tractor running all day. I still remember the song I liked that year. Its lyrics started like this: "In 1814, I took a little trip down the Mississippi to the Gulf of Mexico. I took a little bacon, and I took a little beans. And we caught the bloody British in the town of New Orleans." I would listen to the radio for about three hours. I would get up at the break of dawn and have breakfast at 7:00 a.m., then go out to the field until noon, then have a big lunch and take a thirty-minute nap. Then back to work. In late afternoon, one of the kids would bring me an afternoon lunch with a sandwich, cookies, and Kool-Aid. Then I would finish up about five thirty, have supper, play with the kids, go to bed, and do it all over again the next day.

Later, the soybean rows needed to be weeded and the corn removed. Vonnie and Tim would help for about three hours, and I would need to continue until it was done. Gerald wanted me to also rake out the thistle. That was a big job.

One job I did like was building a new grain storage building. Gerald ordered these arched wooden beams that would curve down to the foundation. His brothers helped build it. We dug the grade beams for the foundation, set the steel, and then used our own mixer to make the concrete. We placed the anchor bolts in the foundation and then raised the frames. We could shingle the entire length from the foundation, across the top, and back down to the other side. I found construction fascinating and later would find that was a big part of my life.

After this, we did the harvest with Gerald driving the combine, and I was supposed to drive the truck at the same speed as the combine without spilling any grain. That was really hard to do. When I didn't get in sync with Gerald, the grain would spill, as I needed to adjust to the same speed. Damn, that was tough to do! Gerald had a quick temper like my dad. He got mad, but he would get over it. This was one of the steps in my life where I needed to be on my toes. I was good enough to have high expectations, but I needed to come through consistently.

When I agreed to spend the summer with the Veldes, there wasn't any agreed price. I really didn't think Gerald thought he would have to pay anything. My mother got Dad to bring up the subject when he dropped me off at home after the last day of work. Gerald asked me what I wanted. I said I didn't know. Whatever was fair. That would be the last time I would ever say that to an employer. Gerald asked Dad if $60 was okay. Dad said okay. I was shocked, but I didn't want to say anything. Later on, I figured I was getting about $0.05 an hour. I wouldn't make that mistake again. Nevertheless, I enjoyed living there. They took me to a rodeo with their family in South Dakota, and that was my first outing out of the state.

The summer was over, and it was now time for eighth grade. The equipment got better, and we all received real helmets. Linemen were able to get two bars across the face. That was a big improvement, as making a tackle wouldn't then risk the face and teeth as much. We also got mouthpieces. I was able to get a little more aggressive. I still didn't like playing football, but I was expected to play by my friends.

The season was over, and we moved on to basketball. I was still short, about five foot six, and not as tall as the Italian and Polish, kids who had started puberty two years earlier. I was skinny with a big frame. The season came and went. Spring was here. I was offered a summer job to work for Kermit Velde, Gerald's cousin. He had a farm about two miles from our previous home, where he and his wife, Bernice, lived with three daughters and one son, Paul, who was off in college. So Kermit needed help. He would pay me $0.75 per hour. Wow! That was a lot more.

Bernice would pick me up Monday morning unless it was raining. I would stay there all week, unless it rained again, and she would bring me home. That was nice, because I was the only kid living there. Kermit had diesel tractors, and they could do a lot of work.

I did my usual cultivating and cutting weeds in the soybean fields. Kermit didn't have a lot of soybeans, so it was nice not to spend all summer doing that. The Minnesota soil is black glacial till with various layers of granite rock underneath. The soil would usually be about ten feet deep before we got into rock. After the crops were rotated and the dirt was plowed under, several large rocks would be exposed. They could damage machinery, so they needed to be removed. Kermit thought that would be a good thing for me to do. I would drive a tractor with a flatbed trailer to pick up the rock. I would take about thirty feet wide up and down the field. I would pick up the rock with gloves on, then carry it to the trailer. For the big ones, I would drive next to it and pull it up. For the really big ones, I got help from Paul, his son, when he came home from college. I cleared the entire 160 acres. I was proud of what I had done.

It was time to get back to school for my ninth-grade year. I had a little more confidence in myself as I was starting to get stronger, especially my back, with all that rock lifting. I started to like football. As part of the B team, I had to line up for the varsity offensive line and give them the look of the team they would play next. I remember the offensive guard, Lowell Halverson. He gave me a "forearm shiver" that dropped me to the ground. Lowell was about five feet, nine inches and was a stalky guy about 175 pounds. Some of the varsity guys started laughing, and it was then I started to return the favor and enjoy physically taking on my opponent. Years later, I told him that was the hardest I got hit in high school.

We both chuckled.

It was now time to start basketball. Coaching was a lot better as Don Bentzen came to town. He was very patient with me and saw my potential. I was still getting shots blocked, but I was learning how to use my body to block out. I was getting better at shooting free throws too. I wasn't a starter on the B team, but I was learning.

The season was over, and spring had arrived. Kermit wanted to know if I wanted to work after school. I said sure. I would ride the bus to their place and immediately get on the tractor once I arrived. Bernice would take me home after supper. She was a good cook. By that time, Dad had to do most of the cooking for me. He doused everything with salt and pepper. He would squeeze the fat out of the hamburger in the pan until it lost its flavor. God, was it great the days when Mom could do the cooking!

As the summer rolled around, I went back to work driving tractors. I found out that Kermit had bought the Alton Erie farm right next to his. We cut down a lot of the trees to put more land into service. The house was removed. The rest of the buildings would be used to store grain. Kermit did not have any cattle, so he converted all his hog and cattle building into storage sheds. The government would pay the farmers money not to farm some land. Grain had to be dry, so the building had blowers installed to keep the grain dry. This summer, I would drive his truck to the elevator in Hazel Run. I took the back roads as I was only fourteen years old at that time. I had to drive the truck into the elevator and lift the hydraulic trailer bin and dump the grain into a grate on the floor. Then I would go back for more.

Kermit was a very successful farmer. He drove Cadillacs. He never had a pickup truck. He would just drive the Cadillac into the wheat fields and think nothing of it. Next year, he would get a new one. Finally, I had to remove the fencing and clear the brush from the trees. I also had to remove rock. This farm wasn't as bad for rock, but it still was a thankless job.

In the mornings, Kermit would get out his Bible and read a few lines of scripture and then say a short prayer. I had all the Christian upbringing, but my parents didn't do that. At first, I was a little uncomfortable, but I learned to enjoy it. He had a great voice and had a daily radio program at an area radio station. His opening line was, "This is the day the Lord has made. Let us rejoice in it and be glad." I always liked that passage.

It was time to get back to school again, this time for tenth grade. I was fully in puberty and felt strong. I played with the B team and started to get noticed in a couple of games. At the end of the season, I suited up for varsity. On offense, I played tight end. On a game we won handily, I caught a ten-yard pass in the flat on the three-yard line and took in to score. That felt good, but I knew my future was at offensive and defensive tackle.

The season ended with snow on the ground, and I was ready to get inside to play basketball. I had grown about four inches since the last year and was starting to fill out. I was getting better at shooting with a nice touch, and I was getting to be a good rebounder. We did a lot of jump roping in warm-ups. I wasn't very good at hook shots, but I developed my own fadeaway jump shot. The coaches hated it because I couldn't follow up my shot. That usually didn't work from ten feet or more. As I made more shots, the coach got over it. I was able to suit up for the varsity. I didn't get much playing time, but I would next year.

The season came to an end, and I once again worked for Kermit in the spring. He was in his fifties but still could do the work of a twenty-year-old. I marveled at how fast he worked and the endurance he had. I thought I was young and strong. How could he keep up with me? He was always patient with me, and I really developed a respect for him. I didn't aspire to be a farmer, but if I did, he would be the first one I would seek advice from. The summer came, and I did the usual. He always had one more job I could do. I was now getting $0.85 an hour, and I had money in my pocket. I worked hard for him, but I never felt used. During the summer, Kermit built one of those storage buildings like Gerald built. I got a chance to work on that and did the siding and shingle work. I liked doing construction.

At the end of the summer, it was time to take the grain to market. Kermit got the trucks lined up, and I ran the auger. When we started, it was easy to shovel the grain into the auger. When we got down to the bottom of the pile, it was a lot harder. I shoveled all day. When I was done, I went to football practice in full pads. At the end of the day, I was very tired, but I realized I was really in good shape.

I was now ready for my junior year, and we had a new coach, Jim Miller. It took a while for the players to buy into his program. The previous coach, Curt Holt, left his job and became an FBI agent. He was a people person and had a soft-handed approach to coaching. Jim Miller was more blunt. That didn't bother me, but some of the players rebelled against him. I spent most of the time with Coach Dick Hammond. He was just the right coach for me, firm but patient. We started out fast with wins over average teams. When we go to play the big one, Madison, on homecoming, we made too many penalties. Of course, we felt the refs were unfair, but it didn't change the score. On offense I played right tackle. Mike Minelli was our running back. Our main play, buck left, dive right, and vice versa. We ran a T-formation. The defense didn't know which one would get the ball. We didn't have much success running outside, so the game was straight up the gut. I was the right tackle. I was getting stronger and was able to move the defensive player back and make a lane for Mike to run. He would always give his all even if there wasn't a hole. In those days, we wore cleats to run on the grass. He could sustain drives with four- or five-yard runs to move the chains. When there wasn't a hole, Mike would just run over me with his cleats cutting into my back. I jumped on him to watch where he was going. He said, "Well, if you opened the hole better, I wouldn't need to run you over." That pissed me off. So what did I do? I drove off the snap harder, and the holes opened up again. He must have figured out how to motivate me. On defense, I was beginning to get noticed by Dave Putnam, the sportswriter for the *Granite Falls Tribune*, and Willmar's Lefty Reinweiler, who was a legendary writer. He covered the entire southwestern Minnesota area. He came to practice one day and introduced himself. I was impressed. I was built with a low center of gravity. I was bowlegged and lanky. I was six foot four and weighed 190 pounds. I was skinny, but strong. I could shed blockers and quickly get into the hole to make a play. I played a lot by instinct.

I made one of Lefty's Area Team of the Week. That was a big move. But we finished second in the conference, which was a big disappointment. We felt we had the team to win it all. After the end of the year, I was chosen by the coaches to receive the Gary Petersen Lineman of the Year Award. Carlton Werner, one of our captains and our center and tackle on defense, was expected to win the award as he was a senior. This was very emotional for me. Earlier in the year, I was a pallbearer at Gary Petersen's funeral. He had been become a very close friend of mine. But he got mononucleosis and died at the age of sixteen. He was one year younger than I was and a very strong and promising offensive guard and defensive tackle. He was a likable guy and a little brother like I was. His nickname, lovingly, was Melonhead. His big brother was Doug Peterson, a good football player that had graduated from high school the year earlier. He would get on Gary for something, and we all laughed at how Gary responded in his good-natured way. I had to go onstage to accept the award from our coach at a school assembly. I was nervous and stunned, but honored. I felt bad for Carlton. Well, not that bad. He had more tackles than I did. Both Doug Peterson and Carlton Werner would later become friends of mine.

Gary Peterson Award.

Basketball season started. I would be competing with John Hamre for starting center. He was a senior. He was big with broad shoulders and was about six foot five and weighted about 220 pounds. He had a lot of discipline problems in school with run-ins with teachers and coaches. He had some talent but didn't show it consistently. The varsity basketball coach was Dick Neilson. He was a good coach, with the right amount of patience and firmness in discipline. The year started. Dick liked to run a double-post offense, which was two centers. John Hamre was one, and Butch Berg was the other. Bruce

Haugland was the power forward and our best player. The guards were John Knutson, also a junior like me, and Wink Lundell, the other senior guard. The offense wasn't working as smooth as Coach Nielson wanted. They weren't in sync. By the fifth week, Coach Nielson gave me the start. I am not sure if it was because of an injury to John or if he just wanted to make a change. On January 4, 1963, I got my first start against Redwood Falls. I played against their star player, Gary Munson. We both scored points, but I outscored him. On offense, my shots were falling. I had fifteen points and shot 40 percent. We won the game. When I got home, I was so excited I couldn't sleep. This was the realization of a goal I had had since I was in the fourth grade. We had a game the next night against Pipestone. My emotions had died down. I played good enough, scoring nine points, but nothing outstanding. I stayed in the starting lineup. Butch Berg and I worked well together, setting screens for each other. My biggest skill was as a rebounder. I followed up many of Butch's shots with a tip in. He and I flowed well together. Bruce Haugland was a great passer. He did a lot of give-and-go, where he would feed me the ball and run by me as I gave him back the ball or turned around and took my fadeaway jump shot. We synced good together. Wink Lundell was a good ball handler, though he didn't take many shots. John Knutson, the other guard, was good at feeding me the ball at the free throw line. I would get the ball, turn around, and take the shot or drive to the basket.

By the end of the season, we were winning most of the games. Then, against Ortonville, the favorite in the conference, I shut down their star player, Pete Hanson. He only scored seven, but he won the scoring title for the conference, just edging Butch Berg. He was six foot six and could shoot the fifteen-foot jumper from anywhere. I almost totally shut him down on defense at the beginning of the game as I stripped the ball from him many times. I had quick hand-eye coordination, a skill I didn't know existed until years later. We won the game 57–42 and won the District 11 championship. We hoisted Dick Neilson on our shoulders. We felt we could win the state championship. We went on to the regional tournament at Gustavus Adolphus College in St. Peter, Minnesota. This was the big time!

Junior picture.

We won our first game easily against Fairfax, 72–56, as Bruce Haugland and Butch Berg dominated the game. We then advanced to the regional championship game. We would play Marshall, a city thirty miles south of Granite Falls. They didn't have any tall players but had an outstanding guard named Terry Porter. He was one of those cocky and confident players. We believed we had more talent than that team. As the game started, we got off to a decent start. Bruce was making his shots, and Butch Berg made his moves, made a number of shots, played aggressively, but then started to get in foul trouble. Before the end of the first half, the coach decided to rest Butch and play John Hamre to make sure he didn't get any more fouls. John and I hadn't really played together. Without Butch, he didn't do so well, and nor did I. We started the third quarter with Butch, but he soon fouled out. The whole town felt the officiating was bias toward Marshall. By the end of the game, they would foul me and I would go to the line. I was feeling the pressure. I missed most of the shots, so they kept on fouling me. In ultimate humiliation for me, I totally missed the basket on one of the shots. I felt so bad for my team. We had come so far. No one expected Butch to foul out of the game. That hadn't happened all season. When Butch went out of the game, I wasn't ready to pick up the slack, nor was John Hamre. He hadn't fouled out all season. We lost, 52–47. We thought the game was stolen. Marshall went on to win the state championship. They were a whole lot better than we gave them credit for. They were great on defense and great under pressure. Something I would learn for future performances down the line.

Earlier in the season, before I was a starter, I got an infection on my little toe that spread to my lymph system. That was a life-threatening disease. In those days, we wore canvas tennis shoes. We had no ankle support. We would get an ACE bandage to wrap our feet before every practice and game. We also painted a gummy material called Tuf-Skin on the bottom of our feet to try to prevent blisters. I have always had wide feet. My little toe got inflected, and by the time I went to the doctor, he immediately sent me to the hospital. I had lymphangitis. I was there all week. They injected me, and I mostly had to just rest. I had a roommate in my hospital room. His name was Clarence Moss. He had gone to school at the Colorado School of Mines. I had never heard of it, but you had to be pretty smart to go there. Clarence was kind of an underachiever, but a guy with a lot of depth. He was about forty-five at that time. He had broken his kneecap. That took a lot of therapy. We had a lot of downtime to talk. We started to bond well together. At the hospital was—guess who—my mother, the nurse's aide. She was there. How many kids get to have their mom tend to them at a hospital? She would assist Clarence in taking him to therapy. I asked Clarence where he worked. He told me he worked at the BMC lumberyard. I asked a lot of questions on what all he did. Later, he said he could get me a job there for the summer. I asked him what I would do. He said I would build Gehl box trailers. They were used to catch the grain harvest attached to the newer combines. We would build the floors and sides out of wood and attach them to the steel trailer frame. I had enjoyed working on the storage buildings for both Gerald and Kermit, so I was open to the idea. I recovered within a week and was back at basketball practice by the end of the week.

I heard back from Clarence, and he said he would get me an appointment with the manager. He said they would pay me $1.15

an hour. On Saturdays, we would work until noon, and then off the rest of the day. Wow, that was huge! I told him I would take the job. I let Kermit know that this was what I wanted to do. He offered to match that salary, but he knew I had already made up my mind. He was one of many people who had a big impact on my life. I learned a lot from him.

After the last day of school, I started work. The work was more constructive, and I enjoyed making things. I would start work at 7:00 a.m. I lived two blocks away, so I could walk to work and back home. At around nine o'clock, we would go to the coffee shop and throw dice to see who would pay for the coffee and doughnuts. There were four of us. I was the kid. We took an hour break and got paid for it. What a concept! I had to do some boxcar unloading of lumber, but not very often. On Saturday, after the lumberyard closed, the guys pulled out a bottle of whiskey and had a drink together before going home. I drank Sun Drop (like Mountain Dew) in a bottle. Clarence would spike the bottle with a shot glass of whiskey. My pure blood system had an immediate reaction to relax me. My aches and pains from a week's work evaporated. I would walk home with a little buzz in my head. My mother asked me why I was in such a good mood. I think she knew, but she never said anything.

In high school, we were told that if we wanted to go to college, we needed to take Latin as an elective. I took shop. That was one of the best decisions I could make. Our teacher was Dick Hammond, also my defensive coach. He taught us drafting, woodworking, leatherworks, metalworks, soldering, and plastic works. I learned a lot that I would later use in my life. Dick was an excellent teacher and coach, for that matter. During the summer, I used the lumberyard's table saw and router to build myself a desk for my room. I would build it in my downtime. I cherished that desk for many years, even after I left home.

In the spring, I was told that a recruiter from the Air Force Academy had talked to my coaches. He said they were interested in recruiting me to play football at the academy. I didn't know what to think about it. He wrote me a letter and asked to meet with my parents and me to make his pitch for me to enter the academy. I had not even thought about any of the service academies. He came to the house, and he said I would have to achieve a certain threshold level with my SAT scores. He also said that I would have to pass a physical and a physical fitness test to see if I could handle the physical challenges ahead of me to be a cadet. All cadets were appointed by congressmen and senators. He said they would arrange for a congressman from California to make my appointment. The athletic department arranged for this to happen. They wanted to build a strong football program. Apparently, my local congressman already had made his decision for whom he wanted to appoint. I didn't commit at that time. I said I would think about it. Everything was paid for, and if I didn't make it in football, I would still get my education paid for. I wouldn't need to get a part-time job. That sounded appealing to me. On top of it all, we got paid an allowance of about $200 a month for incidental expenses. Still, I parked the idea in the back of my mind.

Football preseason began in August. This was my senior year. Mike Minelli, Steve Carlson, and I would be the tricaptains. We had some good players, and we had high expectations with some good players coming in from the junior class. We fell short the year before, and as in all seasons, we were hopeful. We had a lot of positions to replace.

I had a good game in the third week and got named to the WCCO Team of the Week. In Minnesota, this was a big deal because Sid Hartman, an icon sportswriter, was behind it. After that week, I got a letter from Murray Warmath, head coach from the University of Minnesota. He had taken the Gophers to the Rose Bowl the previous year, so he was an accomplished coach. One of our players from Granite Falls was the center for the Minnesota Gophers, Paul Benson. In Murray Warmath's letter, he invited me to stop in if I was in town. No bus ticket, hotel reservations, campus visit, or meetings with assistant coaches. Then I never heard another word from them. The Air Force Academy was the only college team I had heard from. My good friend and teammate Bruce Haugland talked to the football staff at Gustavus Adolphus College. He had enrolled that fall. They would give me a partial scholarship for playing both football and basketball. They would pay for the tuition and food, but not boarding. I tossed that idea around for a while, especially being able to also play basketball; however, I dismissed that as not adequate. I started to think more about the Air Force Academy. I couldn't get excited about the small colleges like St. Cloud State and Mankato State, where a lot of my friends enrolled. I wanted to do something different. We finished the season with a 6–4 record. I made all-conference and the all-area team. It was not a very satisfying season. We finished lower than the previous season.

In the meantime, I was starting to think about what I would major in at college. I liked math and science. I liked physics and chemistry. And I had zero desire to be a doctor. I liked shop. My brother had just graduated from the University of Nebraska with a civil engineering degree. I decided I would do that too. My brother was a huge influence in my life. He spent so much time with me, showing me how to make things and play basketball with him and taking Barb and me to the movies in Clarkfield on Sundays. Tickets were $0.15 apiece. When he met Susie Haugland, sister of my friend Bruce, my time was over. They got married that spring. I was best man.

In my senior year, I was on the student council and was vice president of the class. I also had a cameo appearance in the school play, but I had zero talent in acting. I think I was more comic relief. The rest was football and basketball. It was now time for basketball practice. We had high hopes of finally getting to state after the devastating loss to Marshall. Johnny Knutson and I were the returning starters. From the junior class, we had two big centers, Doug Agre and Tommy Lewis, coming in that had talent. Then Billy Richter and Weldon Reiten at guards.

As the season was getting underway, Johnny Knutson was kicked off the team because his girlfriend got pregnant. She was a sophomore. They sent her to the "School for Unwed Mothers" a hundred miles away from her family. It was a devastating loss for her, us, and him. Johnny was a popular guy. He was one of my best childhood friends. He dropped out of school and went to Minneapolis to go to college. I saw him once a couple of years later in Minneapolis. He never came back for any of the reunions until he showed up at the fiftieth anniversary. Everyone was so happy to see him.

The season got underway. Weldon Reiten played guard a whole lot differently from Johnny Knutson or Wink Lundell. So did Billy Richter. They both liked to shoot the ball rather than set up plays. I spent most of the time getting my points from rebounds and tip-ins. My shooting percentage went down, but my points were up. The most I remember from that team was that during warm-ups, I could now dunk the ball.

Dunking picture.

I averaged fifteen points a game, but only a 35 percent shooting percentage. I made the WCCO Radio All-State Team of the Week on February 20, shortly before the playoffs. We just barely beat Maynard, a small town eight miles away, by two points in the first round. We were favored by a bunch. We then lost to our rival, Montevideo, in the second round by around ten points. That was it for me, a fourteen-month basketball career. One of my best friend's dad told me I should stick to football instead of basketball. Half-insult, half-compliment. But he was right.

I finally made my decision on where I wanted to go to college. I wanted to do something other than go to a local small college. I wanted the challenge. After the season, I went to Offutt Air Force Base in Omaha, Nebraska, to do my physical fitness test to qualify to enter the Air Force Academy. It was very comprehensive, but I passed all the tests. They showed us what all the officers did. It was overwhelming and exciting. I was a big John Kennedy fan. He said in his inaugural speech, "Ask not what your country can do for you. Ask what you can do for your country." I was influenced by his message. I had to agree to serve five years in the Air Force upon graduation or commit six years to serve in the enlisted ranks if I left the academy. That meant if I left the academy, I would be in the active or inactive reserves until six years expired, which included time at the AFA. I was recruited by Captain Joswiak. He grew up in Minneapolis and went to DeLaSalle Catholic High School. He played football for the first Air Force Academy graduating class of 1959. He was also recruiting Mike Rengel from DeLaSalle High School. He arranged for Mike and me to visit the grounds of the academy before we enrolled. This was in April. They flew us to Denver and then picked us up at the airport. I was impressed by their interest. Mike was as big as I was, but a little taller. He was dressed in his cranberry sweater with his penny loafer shoes, a fad going around Minneapolis. That hadn't come to Granite Falls yet. I was dressed in traditional small-town blue Levi's and long-sleeve shirt. Mike's dad was a fire department executive, and Mike lived his whole life in the city. I was just the opposite, being first a farm kid, and then a small-town boy. We hit it off and soon became friends. We had different kinds of personalities, but we complemented each other. We were both sensitive about some things, but we also could take a lot of teasing. He was a bright guy and had a lot of opinions. I agreed with some, and with some I didn't. We stayed at a motel off campus where the team stayed the night before home games. We toured the academy. The first time we saw it, it was breathtaking, with all these aluminum buildings nestled up against the backdrop of the Colorado Rockies. That shouldn't influence us, but I think it influences a lot of people.

This looked first-class to me.

Then we met the coaches. They seemed like ordinary football coaches. Some were in the Air Force, but when we played football, rank didn't matter. They all felt it was a sanctuary from all the disciplined things we had to do as cadets. We could be proud of going to school that few could qualify for. We both decided to commit so we would see each other later. I kept in shape and prepared to enter the Air Force Academy on June 29, 1964, at the age of seventeen. Later, I found out that I had to go through a background check by the FBI. They didn't speak to my parents; instead, they talked to my schoolteachers and Kermit Velde, my first employer. Kermit gave me a good recommendation.

We had our senior prom, and then the graduation ceremony. I had my first public speaking assignment as vice president of the class. I did okay and impressed myself that I could do this. I will always remember the theme song of the ceremony, "Climb Every Mountain." We were so fortunate that we had city leaders, ministers, and teachers who prepared us for the real world.

In early June, my parents and my sister Barb and I took our first vacation. Times for our family were tough but improving. My parents wanted to see the Air Force Academy before I reported on June 29. We had never taken a vacation as a family before. We drove to Deadwood, South Dakota, and saw all its history, and then on to Rapid City, where we saw the phenomenal vista of Mount Rushmore. Then we drove to the Air Force Academy. What an awesome sight with all the chrome and glass buildings built with the same colors as airplanes! We toured the campus, where very few cadets were there as they had just graduated the class of 1964. We went to the visitor center, where Mom bought some of the souvenirs. I still have some of them.

We then drove to Kansas to visit my sister Marlene and her husband, Jim. They had recently moved there from Minneapolis as it was better for Marlene's health. She had a bad case of rheumatic fever when she was in high school, and so they needed to move to a drier climate. Jim was a music teacher in North Newton, Kansas, where Bethel College was located. Marlene was the church secretary for many years.

We then moved on to see the Royal Gorge with this bridge over it. When we looked down, we could hardly see the bottom! Barb and I enjoyed the amusement park there. We then moved on to Kansas City, where Roger and Suzie lived. They had gotten married in 1963. Roger worked as a civil engineer, and Suzie was a music teacher. As kids, we did things one way, but it was interesting to see how we children had so much common history but were so different with how we did things in our adult lives.

We got back home, and I continued to work out to be ready for basic training. During that spring, the county opened up a technical school walking distance from our house. Mom decided that she and I would partition off rooms downstairs, and she would use the bedrooms for guests but also to rent out to students and also single high school teachers. I had a month to work before I went off the Air Force Academy. We built two nine-by-nine bedrooms. We framed it, sheathed it, and painted it. On top of it all, we added a bathroom. That was huge. Having two bathrooms instead of one was a big deal then. We lay the floor with twelve-by-twelve VATs (vinyl asbestos tile). Little did we know that the asbestos was a hazard. Those tiles have since been removed. We got about 80 percent complete before I left for the academy. It was now time to get on with my own life as a single adult.

CHAPTER 4

MY LIFE AT THE AIR FORCE ACADEMY

On June 29, 1964, at the age of seventeen, I had my second plane ride. I flew on a plane from Minneapolis to Denver. It was a transition time, where planes were moving over from propellers to jet. This one was a combination of both. It was called a propjet. In those days, we had stewardesses in their formal uniforms and hats. During the flight, we got a full meal served with china. I thought, *Wow! Isn't this luxury?* When I got to Denver, I had to transfer to a DC-3 on our way to Petersen Field in Colorado Springs. It was a WWII-era plane, a C-47. It was all propellers. In the mountains, there were a lot of changes in the airstream. The flight was only thirty minutes long, but I threw up three times on the way to Colorado Springs. I got off the plane, got my bearings, and started to think. *So I'm here to get my education before going off to flight training school? Hmm! Oh well, this must be an aberration.*

I got on the bus for a seven-mile ride to the grounds of the Air Force Academy. The first place we went was to the infirmary. They gave me a complete physical, then administered shots with a handgun. Damn, that hurt! They weren't too concerned what I thought. We then went to the tailor. Tailor? Yep, we got measured for our formal uniforms, our parade uniforms, and our everyday dress. We had to wear a tie tucked in to the top two buttons on our shirts. Our pants had to be a precise fit, and a belt that could be adjusted. We got issued boxer shorts. No briefs allowed. Then a shower robe and a razor and box of soap. Then it was boots, shoes, and slippers. We had dress shoes and combat boots, with fatigues for military drills. Then athletic shorts with T-shirts with the USAFA logo. We all looked alike. We got issued our laundry bag. And we were done. Well, not quite. We went to the barber. Some barber. He shaved all our hair off and took a picture for our ID card. We would get paid $200 a month, but all those clothes were deducted from that account. It would be a while before I would have any cash for discretionary spending.

We could now go to our rooms, which were quite nice. We each had a single bed and desk and shared a closet and a gun rack. Gun rack? Yeah, though it was only for marching in parades. It was an M-1 without a firing pin. Air Force airmen showed us around and answered questions we had. They showed us where the showers were, then took us to Arnold Hall, which had a movie theater, bowling alley, and formal room for dances. This was where we could meet with guests, since guests were not allowed on the cadet grounds. Tourists could watch us over the wall about twenty feet higher than the cadet area. This was why fellow cadets called this place the Blue Zoo. The athletic facilities were awesome, with basketball, volleyball, wresting, handball, squash, and tennis courts. Even officers used the facilities to play handball or squash and could run a circular track indoors. Next to the athletic facilities were acres of athletic fields where they played dodgeball, lacrosse, rugby, baseball, and football. The field house was about fifty feet below the cadet area. This should really be great to do all these activities. The airmen were with us for about three days, at which time they took us to the Mitchell Hall, our dining hall, a separate building for all the meals.

They lined us up in rows, called elements, and three across was a column. They showed us how to march and react to commands. Left turn, march. Right turn, march. About-face (put one foot back of the other foot and pivot 180 degrees), then column left and column right, where each cadet would go to the front line and turn left ninety degrees. We would walk and run in columns. They told us that on Thursday, July 2, they would end their orientation and the cadet first classmen would takeover. They gave us all a *Contrails* book. We were to read it and be prepared to memorize passages that were shown in bold print. It was first classmen's job to train the incoming fourth classmen, or doolies, as they were called. The definition in the *Contrails* book of *doolies* says, "That insignificant whose rank is measured in negative units; one whose potential for learning is unlimited; a fourth classman."

The airmen did a good job and were so helpful. They told us to keep our sense of humor. I am not sure what that meant. They marched us over the dining hall. At twelve noon, the cadet wing commander took over and gave this order. "Fall out and make corrections!" That was when the shit hit the fan! The upperclassmen got in the face of each doolie. "Stick your chin in. Squat. Roll back your shoulders. Tuck in your elbows." Some guys smiled because we were told to keep our sense of humor. "Wipe that smile off you face, smack!" They would ask us why we enrolled at the academy, telling us we were the worst class ever to show up and we weren't good enough. As each cadet started to answer, they would say, "What is the answer to a why question? 'Yes, sir,' 'No, sir,' or 'No excuse, sir.' Put your eyes down!" They showed us how to properly salute, with second and third finger against our eyebrows and then a straight forearm. They did this for about ten minutes. Then they marched us into the dining hall with our chins in and our eyes down. My nervous system was in hysteria mode. What did I get myself into? I realized they were just doing their job, but damn, this was going to be tough. Then we sat down at these tables that held eight people. At each end there was a first classman. These tables had tablecloths and a very formal setting, with silver serving containers. We were to sit in our chairs with our shoulders back, our eyes down, and our heads straight ahead. We could not turn to the left or right. We were then to use our peripheral vision to accept the silver tray and take our allocated portion. We had to wait until all were served. While we were eating, the table commander told us he would be asking us questions from the *Contrails* book, telling us we better start reading in our free time. My nervous system was starting to settle down. Finally, we got to our room to escape behind our doors. Then, after thirty minutes, we had to take a shower. We needed to line up in the hall. We put on our shower robes and our foot clogs and took a bar of soap in a plastic box to the shower room. After the shower, we had to report to the upperclassmen. We would salute them and say, "I have showered, shaved, and had [or had not had] a bowel movement in the last twenty-four hours." Then, finally, a little peace in our rooms to reflect on the day and fall asleep. Lights were out at 10:30 p.m.

The next morning, we were up at five o'clock to do our morning run. We would run in ranks for about 1.5 miles. This was when we heard for the first time the word *hyperventilation*, when you get tired and gasp for air, and you didn't get enough air to refresh yourself at this altitude. You had to slow down your breathing, breathe through your nose, and get back slowly. After a couple of weeks, most people adjusted to this. It was very scary the first time as we didn't know what was happening to us. Then, we would come back, take a shower, put on our blue slacks, blue shirt, and blue tie. It was time to line up in ranks and then march to the Mitchell Hall for breakfast. Then we would go to Vandenburg Hall, where the classrooms were, and hear lectures and see movies of military history. Upperclassmen were standing in the aisles to catch anyone who fell asleep. If a cadet did, he would have to stand for the balance of the class. Most of us would learn to semisleep with our eyes open. Then it was time for lunch, eat a little, and then recite military knowledge from the *Contrails* book. When it came to military planes, I had no clue. Unlike many of my classmates, many of them military brats (children of military families), I was not around many people who served in World War II. My family was made up of farmers who did their jobs to feed the troops. After a few days, there weren't many doolies smiling anymore—so much for that sense of humor! This was serious stuff. In early afternoon, we would go to gun class and learn how to shoot a rifle, take it apart, oil it, and make it ready for inspection. Sometimes we would run with the rifles. We mostly walked with them at parades, and we were taught how to present a rifle at an angle with the chamber open for inspection. The inspecting officer, a military officer, would grab the rifle quickly with his right hand, take a look in, and hand it back. He then made a comment to a nearby upperclassman, who would mark in his notebook whether the inspection passed or not. He would write it down.

In late afternoon, we would go to the athletic field and play dodgeball. It was strenuous as each side pushed the ball to exhaustion. Only one side won. We were training for the final week of basic training. We would go through Hell's Half Acre, an obstacle course located back in the woods. First, we had to learn some skills. We needed to climb over a ten-foot wooden wall. I had a hard time with that. We were so active physically that I lost about ten pounds! My upper body was not as strong as the rest of my body. I would run at the wall and take a step toward it. Then I would need to get my hands on the back of the wall and lift my body up to the top and then jump down. I would try, and I would disappoint my upperclassman, who really was a kind, patient guy. He would show me the technique again, and I failed repeatedly. He was built like the ideal soldier size, five foot nine and about 165 pounds. He told me that unless I could do this, I wouldn't be able to pass basic training. That added to my stress level. I tried again. This time, I hooked my hands over the back and tried to just pull instead of lifting myself over. It cut both of my wrists. I was despondent, and he knew I really tried. Other upperclassmen saw me bleeding and sent me to the nurse. They bandaged my wrists up, and then a counselor came in to speak to me. I had no idea what she wanted to talk to me about. She was investigating whether or not I tried to commit suicide. My God, no! Well, after all that, I finally figured to use my momentum to push up on the front part of the top, using my weight to propel me up. Damn, was I relieved that I could do it!

Gradually, all of us were learning to take orders. When you take the oath, you agree to be under the laws of the Uniform Code of Military Justice. That is not the same rights as an ordinary citizen. It states that if you fail to follow a lawful order, you are subject to a court-martial. We were totally subservient to the first classman during basic training. It lasted for six weeks before school started. At dinner, they would play "The Star-Spangled Banner" in front of the dining hall. I was beginning to feel like I was training to be a soldier. I was proud of myself and started dealing with the question of, Would you be willing to die for your country? I would get goose bumps, feeling patriotic. By the end of the summer, I was able to say yes. This is what the military relies on. Unfortunately, politics and leadership decisions make it harder, as it did during the Vietnam War. I was being trained to be a soldier if the country needed me.

During the summer, we took a bus to Denver in order to give us all a chance to ride in the back seat of a T-33 training plane. I was all excited about it. That sounded so cool! I got in, put on my helmet and mask, and was ready for takeoff. Once we got in the air, the pilot wanted to show me some of his moves. My stomach started to ache, and sure enough, I threw up again. The next time I went up again, I didn't throw up, but I felt very woozy. How in the world could I fly the plane when all this was happening to me? The nervousness of going through basic training added a lot to it.

The most enjoyable training was survival in the mountains. We would be gone for a week. I was ready to get out of the Silver Womb, as we called it. We were issued a minimum amount of MREs (meals ready to eat). We would hike and then set up camp. We pitched a tent and built a fire. There was a nearby stream to get water. We boiled it and put a pill in it to make it potable. We were allowed to hunt for rabbits if there were any around. One of our guys caught one. We skinned it and shared it. I got one of the legs. That was tasty. Having real food was nice. The air was so fresh too. It got cool at night, and the days were around seventy degrees and sunny. Finally, at the end of the week, it rained. Now I was ready to get back to civilization.

We then went to the firing range building, where we learned to fire a pistol. I had fired a shotgun before, hunting pheasants on the farm, but never a pistol. I was amazed at what a kickback a pistol could have. We learned how to breathe and squeeze the trigger. Then we could see how close we came to the target. It was a lot tougher than many of us thought it would be. It was now time to go to Hell's Half Acre to run the obstacle course. I was able to get to the first wall, then crawl under posts and netting on arms and feet, roll over a wall, drop into a puddle of muddy water, then sprint to the pole climb, shimmy my legs up, do that, run over a hurdle, and go to the finish line. It was over. I passed. I would never have to do this again. This was a major accomplishment in my life. I learned I could do things that I didn't think I could do.

Classes began. I liked the fact that there were only about twelve people in the class. The classes were very interactive with the teachers. Mostly, all the teachers were Air Force officers, some graduates. They were lieutenants, captains, and majors. Some never really had a degree in teaching, but they did the best they could in the time allotted. Our entire day was scheduled for us. We would be active from six in the morning to ten thirty at night. There was little free time during the week. On Saturday, we would have a parade in the morning. We would have to put on our full dress formal parade uniform. On Saturday afternoon, we could go to Arnold Hall and go to a movie or go bowling. That fall, the James Bond movie *Goldfinger* came out. It is still my favorite movie, because at that time, it took my mind totally away from the grunt of being a doolie and of being locked in. We weren't allowed off campus the first year unless we were in intercollegiate athletics.

After that, we could go off campus. My high school friends and teammates Tom Thorkelson and Wink Lundell came to visit me after basic training. It seemed like years ago I lived their lifestyle. I got a little homesick, shook it off, and then moved on, knowing that I would be home for Christmas vacation to see them and all the hometown guys at that time. That was something to look forward to. I called my parents every Sunday. They also got a letter from Captain Joswiak, who told them I was doing just fine, a very thoughtful thing to do for all the moms of the cadets he recruited. The first few weeks were tough, but now I had more positive things to say. I was making new friends. I was coping.

Now it was time for football season. I was not at all excited about that. My body had lost ten pounds. I felt weak and didn't really want to hit anyone. I got off to a slow start. I was fifth team offensive tackle for the first two weeks. I was more concerned with classes and the other responsibilities, and I slowly started getting better and stronger. I decided that one good reason to play football was that football players were at the training tables. We could sit at ease and didn't need to deal with all that military knowledge stuff. The food was better, and more of it. That in itself was enough to have a reason to play football. Playing on the team would allow us to get off the campus. As fourth classmen, we were allowed only one off-campus visit per semester. This did not include the football trips out of town. I started getting my strength back and found my way on defense to make the starting lineup. We had a trip to BYU in Utah and one to the University of Houston. When we played the University of Houston, we played against Warren McVea, the first Black athlete on their team. When we lined up on defense, I threw my usual forearm shiver to stand up the tackle and slide off to make the tackle when the running back hit the hole. I did that. I went after McVea to make the tackle, and just like a jackrabbit, he darted right past me into the secondary. He darted all over the field. He gained about 150 yards that day. We lost. He was quicker than anyone I played against, certainly up to that date. We finished the season on a positive note, with an 8–2 record. We knew our recruiting class was the best class in the history of the AFA, the twelfth year after the founding of the academy.

I was in Fifth Squadron. Captain Dick Abel was our AOC (air officer commander). He was also an assistant football coach. He was in charge of our military training. With all four classes, we had about eighty people. We all marched together to dinner. My roommate was Chuck Yoos. He was a good roommate. He helped me with things that I would forget to do. He wasn't brought up in a military family, but he was very organized and exact. He, Carl Steiling, and I would go to movies together at Arnold Hall, get some snacks, and did some bowling also during our doolie year.

On the last day of the season, the entire cadet wing went to the University of Colorado game. They were our perennial rival. I decided to take that weekend as the one I was allocated. I went to a Colorado fraternity. It felt so normal and natural. We would have freedom until 1:30 a.m. Sunday. We were supposed to wear our uniform as doolies, but we changed into civvies and didn't get caught. Sometimes military rules clash with common sense. It was great relief to interact with people outside the AFA. Now, I was so looking forward to Christmas break.

Four weeks later, Christmas vacation came. I got a "hop" on a military plane to St. Paul, Minnesota. My parents were there to pick me up. We stayed overnight at my uncle and aunt's home in St. Paul. Alfred was a photographer, and Mom wanted to get my cadet picture.

Cadet picture.

It was nice to feel the warmth of family. I was looking forward to seeing all my family on Christmas Eve. On Sunday before Christmas, my mother asked if I would wear my full dress uniform to church. I didn't want to, but my mother was very proud of her cadet son. I did that and saw everyone. When I say *everyone*, I mean almost everyone. When I got home, I put on my civvies (civilian clothes) very quickly.

There was a New Year's Eve party at the house of one of my friends. I was told my old girlfriend would be there. I broke off with her just before I left for the academy. I was in a party mood. There was a lot of drinking going around. In Granite Falls, the guys didn't do any drinking until their sports years were over. They would get kicked off the team if they got caught. We all loved to get together for parties. This was the first time for all of us to be back home. Some went to the U (University of Minnesota), Mankato State, St. Cloud State, St. Olaf, or Gustavus Adolphus. I had a little too much to drink, and then I saw her. I was just locked into her. We had never really broken up. I enjoyed being with her that night; however, I did not want to have a long-distance relationship. That was the last time I saw her.

Vacation was over, and it was time to get back to the AFA. The first Sunday back, I started to reflect on how much fun all my friends were having being away from home, and here I had to live the life of AFA doolie. I was back to living this subhuman life until recognition week in May. I got busy and moved on.

Later in the spring, Mom and Dad came out to the academy for a spring football game. There they met Mike Rengel's parents (his dad and stepmother) from Minneapolis. We all socialized together. Mom took a couple of pictures commemorating their trip to the academy. They had a great time experiencing something new.

Cadet room.

Mom and Dad cadet picture.

In the previous year's fall's classes, I felt like I was ahead of the other kids in math and science. In the second semester, we were covering new material. I still did fairly well in the science classes, but when it came to business economics, that was harder for me to zero in on the details. The one class I just hated was literature. I had to read all the Greek and Roman classics. Who cared about Greek goddesses, Shakespeare, and Roman emperors? I would start reading, and my mind would wander. At the academy, we had very little time to study in our room. When classes were over at 3:00 p.m., everyone had to participate in intramural sports if you were not in varsity sports. The only study time was between 7:30 p.m. to 10:30 p.m. It so clashed with engineering: define the problem, find the facts and measurements you can use, apply the formula, and get the answer. I really didn't care what the classics really meant when they said it. I took that attitude all the way to the finals that spring. I flunked the class. I was a B+ student in high school, and the first semester here, I maintained that, but not in the second semester. I was now a B- student to a C+ student. English was a three-credit class. If you flunked any class in that semester, you would have to stay another three weeks of summer school to pass the class. They also had another option. I could take a "turnout exam." I focused on reading this stuff for a week and got myself prepared enough to take a shot at the turnout exam. I didn't want to have to stay behind and not go home for three weeks. There were seventeen of us who took the exam. Only two of us passed. I was relieved, and I could now go home.

I went home for the early summer. I caught up with the guys, but most had a job during the day and there wasn't much for me to do. We would get together in the evening, play cards, and meet at Slette's Taproom, a small bar and pizza joint. We would also go to the Tiptoe Inn and play pool and had our twenty-one-year-old friends buy the beer. After three weeks, I was ready to get back. When we got back, we would head out on our ZOI (zone of the interior) trip. It was the most memorable summer of my life. We traveled all over the country! Other than the family trip before entering the academy, I had never been out of the state of Minnesota. The academy wanted to show us cadets what the Air Force, Army, and Navy were all about. Our first stop was Hill Air Force Base in Utah. They showed us what air traffic controllers do. They monitor all planes in the sky with radar. They showed us how they would use electronics to locate and communicate with the pilots what was around them when in flight.

The most memorable part of the trip was the dance they had for us. In those days, they stressed that there were many formal occasions for Air Force officers and that we cadets needed to be civilized with proper, formal manners. They arranged for girls from BYU and other nearby schools to come to the dance. They required that each cadet get matched up with a girl that was, at a minimum, shorter than the guy. If they ran out of girls, we could go in to the party alone. That was what most of us wanted. This was a lousy way to put two people together. What they did was have an officer on one side of the wall with the boys, and a woman chaperone on the side with the girls. They would let the line run in order until there weren't any tall girls matching up with short guys. Some guys would drop out of the line when they got closer and then went to the back of the line. When we were getting close to the end of the line, there were more girls than guys. Larry Cook, always the rebel, went into the bathroom stalls and lifted his feet off the ground so he wouldn't be noticed. The officer in charge looked under the stalls, and he said, "I can see you, Mr. Cook.

Come on out." He then put him at the front of the line. Since I was now six foot five, they would match me and other tall guys with girls that were six foot two tall or more. I just wasn't attracted to tall girls, and I had to spend the next two hours with her. She was a nice girl, but I had little in common with her. She had facial hair on her chin too. Sorry, I was fickle in those days. I'm sorry, but I couldn't handle that.

That summer, the Beach Boys came out with the song "California Dreamin'." It was playing all the time on the radio. Our next stop was Travis Air Force near San Francisco in California. I looked so forward to going to California. At Travis Air Force Base, they housed a lot of the transport planes, cargo planes, and refueling planes that flew west over the Pacific Ocean. This was the first time I saw the immense beauty of the Monterey Bay and the Golden Gate Bridge.

We then went south to Vandenburg AFB. That was where they launched missiles and did a lot of testing into space and on the nearby deserts. This was the most intriguing part of the trip, for us to find out what all they were working on. This was before the moon launch in 1969. Then it was time for a break in our military indoctrination. They took us to Santa Catalina Island. At that time, there was a popular song with that namesake. It was just beautiful there. It took about thirty minutes to get there from Huntington Beach on a boat. We played golf, went on dune buggy rides, and flirted with the girls at a beach party. Many had their mothers there, so they did some of the screening for their daughters. One thing I learned then was, women who learn to flirt never give up the need to flirt with any guy at any age. Wasn't this the home state of Mrs. Robinson of *The Graduate* fame, anyway? Since we had so little time, we were not a threat to their daughters. It was fun to spend time with them. As a male institution at that time, we missed the company of women in our lives with normal relationships.

We then moved on to San Diego. We got on an old Navy ship. It wasn't very functional, but it was good enough to give us an idea what life on a ship was like. I didn't like it. They took us out to sea to show us how they navigated. It was interesting, but I didn't like the up-and-down, back-and-forth motion. I didn't throw up but felt woozy by the end of the trip. I was glad I didn't go to the naval academy.

We then got on a C-124 Globemaster cargo plane. Many of the soldiers called it the Barfmaster. We did not travel in luxury. This plane was the workhorse of the Air Force until 1974. The interior was a big noninsulated cabin that had camping-like seats lined up on the walls. There were about twenty of us on this plane. It was loud and noisy; no way could we take a nap. When we flew over the Grand Canyon, there were air pockets. Of the twenty, only two guys didn't throw up. We were never happier to land.

Cadet Picture without hat

We were now at Cannon Air Force Base near Clovis, New Mexico. They specialized in reconnaissance operations. This place was out in the boondocks. The soil was red. I had never seen that before. It would stick to our pants and shoes. This base concentrated on intelligence, surveillance, and reconnaissance. They also trained attack dogs. They demonstrated what a dog could do. They asked for a volunteer to fight the dog. My fellow cadets volunteered me. I put on this big jumpsuit and a helmet. It had padding to protect me from the dog. I got out in the arena and took on the dog. The dogs were formidable. They put on a good fight. I held my own. The only unprotected area of my suit were my lower ankles. The dogs started to snipe there. I was ready for my time to expire. I got some kind of recognition for my performance. I would remember this moment when I would line up against some of the bigger football players I would play against.

We then moved on to Fort Benning, Georgia, the primary training headquarters for the Army. They trained the infantry and conducted jump school for all the branches of the government. I remember how hot and humid it was there in July, with no air-conditioning at that time. It was hard to get to sleep. I also remember being able to pull the trigger of a machine gun. I touched the hot part of the gun and lost control. No one got hurt, but I was thankful my supply was spent.

We then flew on to Pease AFB in New Hampshire. It was home to the B-52 bomber at that time. It played a major role in WWII. It is now a joint base with other branches of the service. It was so beautiful with all the tree-lined golf courses. I played golf when I was there and discovered that those trees weren't so beautiful when you sliced your driver shot. I lost about nine balls that day.

We now went to our final stop of the trip, Wright-Patterson AFB, just east of Dayton, Ohio. This AFB is home to the National Museum of the US Air Force. It is the largest museum of planes in the world. Currently, they have 360 planes. It was very interesting to finish the trip. These trips gave us an overview of the whole Air Force. The AFA doesn't do this anymore, for budgetary reasons. It was the most memorable summer of my life. We got to see different parts of the country and experience how vast this country really is. Now it was time to head back to Colorado Springs and the AFA. Our trip was complete.

After a few days, it was time for training camp for the football season. We headed out to Oxnard Air Force Base near Oxnard, California. We would be there for a week. We did our practices at Camarillo High School, about ten miles away. The base was right on the Pacific Ocean. The beach was nowhere near the beauty of the beach we saw near Vandenburg AFB. We would get on a bus and drive the rural roads to Camarillo. This was an agricultural area. We would pass by the Mexican workers doing their work in the field. They were working to provide for their families, to give them a step up the ladder on the American dream, just like my parents did for me. The soil looked so dry and depleted because there was very little rainfall; however, with irrigation, everything seemed to grow. The soil was gray, with a lot of cracks. They had been at work since sunrise. We were on our way to practice at about 8:00 a.m. We had two-a-day practices. We mostly did individual groups in the morning, working on fundamentals in small groups. Joe Moss was my defensive coach. He was a no-nonsense kind of guy. He would let you know what he thought of your effort and effectiveness. He was really hard on a couple of my teammates. After having worked for my dad and Gerald and Kermit Velde, I was used to this. I found him to be good at teaching the fundamentals. His main emphasis was what we called a forearm shiver. I was now totally playing defensive tackle. When we took our first step, we would thrust our forearm at the blocker with enough power to neutralize his forward motion. On the second step, we would use the other forearm. Then we would pull back our arms and slide to either side to be in position to make the tackle. Since I have long arms and shorter legs, I have a lower center of gravity. That helps when you are trying to stand up the blocker. At noon, we would go back to the base and jump into the swimming pool for a half-hour before we had lunch. After lunch, we would have a meeting in an auditorium with auditorium seats. My hamstrings would start to cramp up. It was painful. I would lie down in the aisle to stretch out my legs. That didn't help. Before practice, we were offered salt pills. I didn't take any. It didn't get that hot in California, so I didn't think I needed them. I was wrong. I then began to take two or three pills before every practice. The cramps didn't go away, but they were less severe. Two years later, Gatorade was invented in Florida. That solved the problem.

We completed our training camp after a week and flew back to the AFA campus to start my sophomore year. I was now a third classman.

As cadets, we have plenty of time together. We started with approximately 1,000 cadets in the class of 1968, spread over twenty-four squadrons, when basic training started, and a year later, we were down to approximately 750. Everyone had their name tag on them with their ID number. I was Cole, L. R., 54612. All the names were posted outside their room door. We got to know a lot of our fellow cadets. We were very busy, but we still had a lot of downtime together because we were not allowed off base until Saturday afternoon and evening until 1:00 a.m. We always made the most of the free time we had. As with all athletic guys, we all teased one another to provide comic relief. The nicknames came. I became Lurch, which I hated. Then Granite. I liked that name because it represented a tough, strong guy from Granite Falls, Minnesota.

There were a lot of positions available on the football team. There had been a cribbing scandal the previous spring whereby a couple of cadets broke into Vandenberg Hall. They stole tests from their files. They then sold them to various cadets. The OSI (Office of Special Investigation) got involved and found those who had participated. Some were on the football team. They resigned. Even though we didn't have the experience, we felt we had talent. Our first game would be against Wyoming. Joe Moss, our defensive coach, told us that they were installing another digit on their scoreboard. We needed to work very hard to keep from embarrassing ourselves. We really didn't think that was possible, but we had no idea how good or bad we were. For our class, this was our first varsity game. We heard this message for two weeks. We didn't know what to expect.

By game time, we were apprehensive. We held our own. We stopped their running game in the first half and kept the game close. On offense, we didn't have much of a running game with our undersized offensive lineman. It wasn't their fault. Larger bodies would not pass the physical in most cases. Paul Stein, our quarterback, got most of the yards by himself. He wasn't that big. He was quite a competitor. He was a charismatic character. He also was the Third Squadron commander. Wyoming pulled away in the fourth quarter. We lost the game 31–14. Since our measuring stick was less than one hundred points, we exceeded expectations.

The next week, we played Nebraska. They were a perennial power. After the first quarter, we were behind by 21–0. Then our resolve and the altitude got the best of their bigger lineman. We came back and lost 27–17. "Close, but no cigar." We called it a moral victory. The following week, we played Stanford toe to toe and lost by one point, another moral victory. We then played California and lost 24–7, a step backward.

The next opponent, we played Oregon at Multnomah Field in Portland, Oregon. We fought them to an 18–18 tie. That was progress. The most memorable aftermath of the game is that Oregon had painted the field yellow before the game. This wasn't their home field. After the game, we had to throw all our uniforms out because the yellow stain did not come off our pants or jerseys. The next week, we won our first game. We beat the University of Pacific, 40–0. It was a small college near Stockton, California. We were not sure what to think about it all. Were we good or not? The next week, we hosted UCLA. They were a rated team. They were led by Gary Beban, the future Heisman Trophy winner. Mel Farr was the running back. Our defense was starting to gel. We shut them down for most of the game. We lost 10–0. It was another moral victory.

The following week, we would play Army at Soldier Field in Chicago before fifty-five thousand fans. This was the biggest game of my life. I had suffered an ankle sprain the week before and didn't know if I could play or be effective. My parents, my brother Roger and his wife, Susie, and sister Barb and her husband, Ken, came down from Minnesota and Wisconsin for the game. This was the big time. I warmed up before the game and put pressure on my ankle for the first time. My ankles were taped, and I was hopeful I could be effective when the game started. I started the game tentatively, and as the game proceeded, I got more confident. I made a number of tackles, stopping many of Army's offensive drives, as did my cohorts. We won the game 14–3. This was historic because this was the first time Air Force beat Army in history.

We went to Arizona the next week. As we were players for a service academy, our away games were such a treat to get off campus. We didn't need to wear our uniforms; instead, we traveled with team shirts and slacks. It was a really relaxed atmosphere. The coaches understood and let us have as much freedom as possible. The night before the game, we would bring a rented comedy movie, many of which were Jerry Lewis movies. We would laugh and throw bundled napkins at the screen. We just loved being together. We beat Arizona 34–7. The most memorable part of that weekend was, when we were taking off on the plane for the return flight, we looked outside the windows shortly after takeoff and saw one of the engines on fire. I remember the look on Coach Kendall's face—he was in panic! The rest of us were apprehensive but young enough to think this was something not unusual. We landed the plane. The coaches announced that we would be laid over an extra day to have time to fix the plane. Well, for us, that was great! Many of us went to Nogales, Mexico, to see that lifestyle. Wow, was that different! We went to see a bullfight. That was gruesome. Some of my teammates took in the nightlife. One of them had a rendezvous with a young senorita. It was his first time for sex. He fell in love. He wanted to take her back with us. When he sobered up, he got lots of ribbing from the guys.

The next week, we played our nemesis, the University of Colorado. We lost 19–6. We still felt good about the season. We would be returning a lot of starters, so we were looking forward to the next season. It was now time for the off-season. I started to lift weights for the first time. I weighed about 225 pounds, but I needed more strength in my upper body. I played a little pickup basketball in the gym. I had grown an inch in high school. I could easily dunk the ball and move but knew I wasn't good enough for the varsity. I also had mandatory PE classes with wrestling, boxing, tennis, and squash. I was never in better shape. We also had a class in "unarmed combat." This was very useful to me. I would learn how to do a side parry, where you place your forearm at a ninety-degree angle and then use the other hand to turn the knife or gun back toward the aggressor. This was useful stuff. I sure hoped I would never need to put this technique into action.

We then started spring football. It was brutal for running backs. We linemen would come out of our stance, slide off the blocker, and then run over three beanbags ten feet apart, and then when we got to the third beanbag, the freshman running back started running and we would knock the crap out of him. Not fair, but that was the way it was. That spring, I got in a squabble with an up-and-coming offensive player. He didn't like me, nor did I like him. He was what we called an off-season all-American. He had a nice build but wasn't much of a football player. I embarrassed him on one play. Then when the play ended and after a couple of minutes, he blindsided me and hit my neck when I was relaxed and not prepared for a hit. Ever since, I have had a tight neck with a neck twitch, not involuntary, but annoying. Some injuries don't entirely heal; you just learn to live with the dull pain. We then had our intersquad spring football game. We played seven quarters. I had no backup. We had new quarterbacks. The coaches felt they needed more film. I was exhausted. I just needed to take a shower, have a quick drink, and get on the road to Denver for our night out to celebrate the end of spring football. We couldn't afford to go barhopping. That would cost too much. So we decided to crash a wedding party. We kept getting that puzzled look from the guests wondering who those guys were. We had our civvies on, but with our short haircuts, it wasn't hard to figure out who we were. Finally, we had to confess that we just wanted to go to a party. They understood that we had rigid lifestyle and just wanted some normalcy, so they let us stay for the whole party.

School was out, but before we got on with leaving the cadet grounds, we had to participate in the Jack Valley Campaign. This was meant to simulate wartime conditions for a real ground war. We spent a week in the woods on the campus grounds known as Jack Valley. They set up prison camps for those who got captured. For those who got killed, they were taken out of the games and just held there until it was over. We had simulated war games with officers refereeing the battles, with us firing blanks. We would hide behind trees with our M-1s. Most attacks would be at night. I would hear in the background when the officer would holler, "You're dead!" and then I heard from one of the participants, "Bullshit!" He moved on and kept in the fight. The referee couldn't find him. This was kind of like a *M*A*S*H* episode. The smart guys hijacked the food truck. They ate well. That left their opponents with only MREs. Since there was intimidation but no real-life torture at the prison camp, it was hard to simulate real-life warfare. I think the leadership decided to leave that training to the professionals at Fort Benning, Georgia, and to the escape-and-evasion trainers at Alaska.

It was now time for our summer activities. We would participate in what was called Operation Third Lieutenant. There isn't such a rank; however, the AOCs got together and assigned our fellow classmen to go to an Air Force base around the country. My roommate, Ron Benson, and I were assigned to Luke Air Force Base in Phoenix, Arizona. We would be there for three weeks. Our job was to help schedule the training times for pilots around the world. Most were from NATO nations. We had German, French, and Australian pilots during the time we were there. Our work wasn't very significant. Most of the time, we would go to the officer's club and play pinball. They had a bunch of machines. Pilots had a lot of time to kill waiting on their planes. They needed some recreational activities. The highlight of the trip was riding in the back seat of an F-104 plane. The pilot practiced dive-bombing, and then he revved up the engine so we would be traveling at Mach 2 (twice the speed of sound). No, this time I didn't get sick, and I actually enjoyed it. I was able to take over the stick so I could feel how the maneuvers felt.

When the pilot got right near Mach 2, the plane started shaking. I told him, "I'm good." He signed a certificate that I traveled at Mach 2. Actually, it was 1.93. I still have that certificate. This was the first time I lived in a hot climate. Damn, it was hot! Most days were 102 to 110. Ron and I met some girls who let us spend Sunday with one of their families. We went to a lake with no trees around it. That seemed strange. We did some boat riding, and the locals did some waterskiing. Dipping in the lake didn't cool us off. It was warm. We also drove for about two hours with her convertible, top down. At that time, the Lovin' Spoonful had a popular song on the radio. It went, "Hot town, summer in the city. Back of my neck getting dirt and gritty. Bend down. Isn't it a pity? Doesn't seem to be a shadow in the city. All around people looking half-dead, walking on a sidewalk hotter than a matchhead." That song was appropriate for those people who didn't live there every day. I remember how drained I felt at the end of the day.

We had three more weeks of summer vacation before training camp started. I went back home to Granite Falls. That summer, a national pipeline was being built just outside the city. The company was from Texas. A lot of college kids traveled to Minnesota to take jobs for the summer. They were still hiring local kids. They paid $2.85 per hour. Wow! Most of my friends were working there, so I decided, if I wanted to see them, I would do the same.

Each morning we would be there at seven o'clock and then waited for a crew to pick us up. Most of the work was tedious and boring. We would guide each pipe in place as the crane lowered it to the ground. We stacked lumber to hold each end of the pipe for those pipes not ready to get in the ground. Then when that section was ready to be lowered, they could get the lift belt easily under the pipe and lower it into the ground. We still had plenty of time to go out for a beer or two at Slette's Taproom. We met a couple of guys from Stephen F. Austin College in Southeast Texas. They had a Texas drawl. They were from Carthage, Texas. They pronounced it "cathage." We were fascinated by how they pronounced their words. They would take so long to say their words. Once television became more accessible, the national accent seemed to move to California language. All our accents were Norwegian, German, or Swedish. Most of our parents maintained their native accent. Those of us my age didn't. The Texas guys could party with the rest of us. Summer was over. I made a few bucks. It was now time to get back to school and report to training camp for my second varsity year.

We headed back out to Oxnard in early August. We were very optimistic that we could compete with anyone. The previous year, we held our opponents to less than twenty points for seven games. The other three were twenty-four, twenty-seven, and thirty-one points, against California, Nebraska, and Wyoming. We knew the class of 1968 had a great recruiting class, and now we had experience. We played on a national stage with our schedule against UCLA, Stanford, and Colorado. We made history as the first AFA team to beat Army. We would miss quarterback Paul Stein, who graduated, to lead us on offense, but we had a strong-arm passer in Sonny Litz, who gave us great expectations to lead the offense. In the AFA Press Book, they listed Neal Starkey and me as all-American candidates. Neal was tough-hitting defense back, and he also did punt returns. He was a great leader. I played the most number of plays on defense and was considered a durable, reliable player with a "nose for the ball." We had a very good defensive line with Jim Hogarty and Gerry Wynguard at the defensive ends, Mike Rengel and I at tackle, and Ken Zagzebski at nose tackle. We had good backups with Al Burchett, Ken Medlin, and Jack Hanning. Our linebackers were Cocaptain Lloyd Duncan, Bob Hinson, Dave "Sluggo" Allen, John Hayden, and Clay McGee. Our defensive backs were Neal Starkey, Steve Roseman, and Tom Zyroll.

We lost the opener against our nemesis, Wyoming, 13–0. We just couldn't get our offense going.

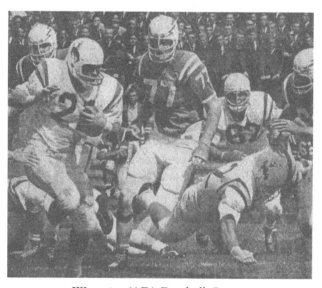

Wyoming/AFA Football Game.

The next week, we beat Washington 10–0. The following week, we beat Navy 15–7 for the first time in school history. We out-field-goaled them. The following week, we blew away Hawaii, 54–0. We were now 3–1 and getting nationally ranked. Then the wheels fell off the wagon. We lost five out of the following six games. Moral victories didn't matter anymore. Our offense stumbled. Jim Schultz was a standout at tight end. He would make the tough catch in the crowd and take a beating. He had very good hands. Larry Cook was our main running back. Mike Guth and Ralph Kaspari were the fullback tandem. Scotty Jackson, team cocaptain, was a very good blocking guard, as well as Don Heckert. The consistency wasn't there. We didn't have a scrambling quarterback, so most drives broke down that left the defense on the field too long. Jim Schultz and I made honorable mention all-American, but it wasn't very satisfying. With a winning record, we would have had a better chance.

During the season, as part of our military training, I was required to take "flight indoctrination." On Sunday nights during the football season, every three weeks, I would need to fly in the back seat of a fighter plane traveling from Colorado Springs to Amarillo, Texas. It was a long boring trip with no maneuvers, just the pilot speaking to me about what they needed to do to operate the plane. Fighter pilots have injection seats that, when activated, will eject the entire seat and parachute. In the back seat, the room was so confined that it was very uncomfortable to attach the seat belt. My back was killing me after I recovered from a football game the previous day; I just decided to take off the seat belt so as to give my back relief. The reality of whether I wanted to be a pilot was setting in. The pilot said, "Isn't this great?" I kind of mumbled, "Yeah, sure." I couldn't wait to get off that plane.

With my size, I would be limited to cargo or bomber planes, anyway. I just wasn't that motivated anymore. I just never felt comfortable in the air. The semester ended. I was now three semesters away from graduation. What would I do as an Air Force officer?

That fall, the classes that I took were aeronautical engineering, surveying, electrical engineering, differential equations, vector engineering mechanics, and introduction to law. I majored in civil engineering. We needed to take an introduction to all the engineering fields before we got to the specifics for that field. I figured that if I did graduate, I would be working as a civil engineer. I could do that as a civilian.

Rumors started to spread that there was a "ring" going on in a couple of squadrons. My roommate shared that information with me. Some of the cadet football players were rumored to be flunking out, so their fellow cadets helped them out. I didn't know if it was true, but it was my responsibility to report this to my squadron honor rep. Under the Air Force Academy honor code, it is stated, "We will not lie, steal, or cheat, nor tolerate among us anyone who does." I did not solicit this information, nor did I want to know. Under the honor code, I was required to turn in my roommate with this knowledge. I thought about it, but I just couldn't do it. I was brought up with all the traditional values my family and community aspired to be. Turning in my roommate wasn't one of them. The term back then was being a *tattletale*, or a *snitch*. I just didn't think it was my responsibility to determine his future. That moment passed, and we just moved on. About six months later, at the start of the second semester in 1967, I found out that other cadets knew I had knowledge of this, and if this "ring" got exposed, I would be included as part of it. That was very depressing.

The academy policy was that tests would be the same for all cadets in each elective. By sharing verbally what the questions were on the previous day or that same morning, it gave the cadet a step up on knowing what to expect for the upcoming test. At first, it was to help a few cadets with failing grades, but it then grew into a kind of a in-the-know society. Many good or average students decided to share the information with one another. By doing so, they wouldn't have to spend as much time studying and could watch a little more television or just socialize in the dorm rooms of cadets from other squadrons in the evenings rather than taking the whole time to study. This was beginning to become a burden on all of us. There was paranoia setting in. I finally succumbed to taking the shortcut on studying and getting the information on the tests. It didn't really improve my grades, but it did allow for more free time, which is a valuable quantity at a service academy.

The situation was beginning to be depressing. Then in the middle of all this, one of my best friends, Jim Schulz, fellow football player, decided he wanted to quit the academy in January 1967. Jim was coming off a good football season for ability to make the clutch catches. Jim was a free spirit and just was worn out with all this disciplined routine. He went to his squadron commander to ask him to let him quit. He refused or wasn't allowed to, so Jim decided to turn himself in for an honor violation. He didn't want probation; he just wanted out. For him to do that, he would need to identify other cadets who he knew had cheated. He identified a couple of players who had already resigned. This was devastating news to me. I was looking forward to our senior season in hopes that we could finally have a winning season and a national ranking. Without him, our chances would be nil. Then I heard our starting quarterback, Sonny Litz, and our main running back, Larry Cook, also decided to turn themselves in.

Word was getting out that a number of cadets were starting to turn themselves in. Many were my friends. I just couldn't handle being at the academy without my friends and teammates. I started to think it over. If I left, I knew I could get a scholarship elsewhere. I knew what the consequences would be if I turned myself in. I dreaded telling my parents what had happened. I realized this would put a blemish on my record. On the other hand, I just couldn't be motivated to remain a cadet and graduate. I decided it was too much for me to handle. I turned myself in for an honor violation. I had to name a couple of people that had shared information to me. Those cadets had already turned themselves in by then. I went before the honor committee and admitted to not just the toleration but also cheating and violating the honor code. There was no evidence for any of this. I could have got probation if I only admitted to toleration. I just couldn't do it, and by then I just wanted to leave. They voted to expel me, so it was time to get on with the rest of my life. I called my parents and told them I was leaving, that I would be home within a week and tell them what happened then. They were disappointed but wanted to see me and hear everything firsthand.

All this tension was relieved when the processing to be discharged began. On our college transcript, it would say HV on the bottom, which stood for honor violation. It didn't have any significant consequences for the places I considered to continue my college education in. When we left, we would be assigned to the Air Force Reserve as an airman second class for the remainder of the six-year commitment for which we signed upon accepting our nomination to the Air Force Academy in 1964. This would last until June of 1970. So when I checked out of the academy, I received approximately $2,000 in back pay, two and a half years of free education, an honorable discharge, and I was assigned to the reserves. The Vietnam War was raging by 1967. We were fortunate to not be assigned to report there.

Seven of us decided that we would take a trip to New York and Daytona Beach for spring break. Before we did that, we would all go home to face our parents. We headed out to our homes.

Some parents didn't take it very well, which caused a rift for many years. They disowned their own son, which was a big scar on their relationship. Others, like my parents, took the news with acceptance. They had experienced many disappointments in their life; they could handle it. I am forever grateful to what that meant to me. My mother was so proud of her son, the cadet. I explained the whole story to them. They quietly just listened and asked questions. They understood my reasons for not turning in my roommate but were disappointed I fell into the ring. When most of your friends are involved, it's hard to remain independent. My mother asked me to promise her one thing, that I would finish college. I agreed I would. The academy would later drop the toleration clause of the honor code. Also, they changed tests from one class to the next so they weren't the same, eliminating the temptation. Approximately fifty-five cadets would be leaving the academy. Most had gone on to successful careers. Two of my teammates went on to graduate and become generals. Our class invited us nongraduates to the thirtieth reunion of the class of 1968. It was great to see everyone. We shared stories of our different lives and still enjoyed being together. Our coach, Ben Martin, stopped by to see us also. A group of about six to ten of us get together every three years to this day, for over twenty-five years now. Some graduates, some not. We share a very special experience together that has shaped our lives. The Air Force Academy is a very special place, and I don't regret going to the Air Force Academy. I learned so much about self-discipline and doing things I didn't think I couldn't possibly do. I have the highest respect for those who graduated and served their country. For me, I am also glad I left so as to allow myself to take a different path to my future.

CHAPTER 5

THE TWO MOST SIGNIFICANT YEARS OF MY LIFE

After getting the face-to-face meeting with our parents, explaining what happened at the academy, we were now ready to experience our newfound freedom. We were ready to blow off some steam and explore new places on our own. We also wanted to check out some of the schools along the way, to see if they would give us a scholarship. I drove one of the cars, my 1961 Chevrolet Delta Dart. Ralph Kaspari had his 1958 Buick, known as the Growler.

I set off from Granite Falls and drove to Minneapolis to pick up Mike Rengel. We then drove to Chicago to meet up with Ralph Kaspari and Jim Schultz. Eli Bebout, from Wyoming, met up with us in Chicago. Then we drove to Indiana to pick up Charlie Bensley. After that, we met up with Carl Hite in Michigan. His girlfriend lived there. When we were there, we stopped in at one of the small schools to gauge their interest. Carl was a track star. They were interested in him, so we took time to go on campus. We met the football coach. They didn't have much to offer in real scholarships, but we wanted to hear they had some interest. That didn't happen. From there we went to New York City to pick up Scotty Hughes. He lived in Queens. He had that full New York accent. Ralph, Carl, and Eli took the northern route through a portion of Canada and back to northern Pennsylvania. This was a shorter route. Mike, Jim, Charlie, and I took the southern route through lower Pennsylvania. While we were on the road, a snowstorm happened. Being from Minnesota, I was used to driving in the snow, but at a lower speed.

Ralph, Carl, and Eli had to stop for about four hours going through Canada because the snow was coming down so hard. They then resumed. We arrived at exactly the same time at Scotty's house within one minute. What a coincidence! This was the first time most of us had seen New York City. As we approached New York City, things grew bigger and bigger. It was exciting for a small-town boy. We went downtown to see some of the sights. While we were there, my car started to make a tapping noise on the engine. Oh, crap! I took it to a mechanic in downtown New York City. He said it would cost $250 to fix. Damn, I didn't have $250 I wanted to spend. I really didn't trust the mechanic. I decided that since it still ran, I would drive it to Daytona Beach, where we planned to stay for a week. Then I would look into it. We left New York after a couple of days and headed for Daytona Beach. When we got to North Carolina, the engine was sounding worse. I reduced my speed to about forty-five miles an hour just to get there. Ralph was starting to have problems with his car too. But we finally got to Daytona Beach, where we then started to look for a motel. Most were sold out. However, we were able to find a motel at a reasonable price on the beach. We had arrived. We had a kitchenette for one of the rooms. This was where Ralph took apart his carburetor and put on the kitchen table. Ralph was a strong guy for his size. At the academy, he played football and also did the still rings in gymnastics. He had a very strong upper body. He was a man's man. He took apart his carburetor on the kitchen table and cleared enough room to have a hamburger. He took a bun and put raw hamburger meat on it. Yuck! After he fixed his car, I asked him to take a look at mine. He did and said I just needed a new tappet. We went to a junkyard and bought a tappet for $2. He changed it out, and the car went back to working fine and was ready to go. I'm glad I didn't spend that $250!

We finally arrived at the beach, and I then went out to the ocean and rode the waves. Then a big one came in. I kept going into the ocean to catch the next one. I really didn't learn to swim at the academy, just on my back. I got in over my head and couldn't feel my feet on the ocean's surface. Thank God Mike Rengel was there to rescue me from getting dragged out any farther! We enjoyed the nightlife, too, met some girls, and partied on the beach. We were allowed to park on the beach in the afternoon. I parked my car, moved on with the party until someone told me some cars were underwater. Oh, crap! Luckily, the water had only gotten up to the bottom of the fenders and didn't ruin my brakes. I drove it out of there and breathed a sigh of relief.

A couple of our guys stopped in a shop and got interested in buying a diamond. It was big. The vendor was willing to sell it for only $200. He said it was worth $1,000. They wanted all of us to chip in. Four of us chipped in. We could then make enough money to pay for the trip. We took the ring and showed Scotty what a good deal we made. He was from Queens and was more street-smart than the rest of us. He suggested we take it to a different jeweler and put it under the microscope to see if there were any flaws. We did and found that there were flaws all over and, at best, it was worth about $150. We were pissed off and decided to all go together and demand the vendor give us our money back. We were all big football or basketball players, and we walked in a show of force. They ended up giving us our money back. We were quite naive falling for this. Our sheltered life at the academy didn't prepare us for this.

We finished the Daytona Beach segment of the trip and moved on to Gainesville. We then moved on to the University of Florida. Ray Graves, the head football coach, agreed to sit down and talk to us. He said he really didn't have any openings and didn't think he could get us a scholarship. He did encourage us to look around. He said we would find some place. Getting a two-year scholarship for one year of eligibility was not a given. I remember one statement he made. He said he would have to put on his golf shoes with metal cleats and walk on the university president's desk to get a scholarship like this.

We then moved on to Florida State. The four of us football players met with Bill Peterson, head football coach. Carl Hite met with the track coach and secured a scholarship. Eli and Charlie were basketball players and not interested in Florida State. Scotty wanted to just go back to New York. After we met with Bill Peterson, he gave every indication that Jim Schultz and I would be offered a scholarship. We left Tallahassee believing this was where we would be going to school.

We then drove back to Chicago. I wanted to get a decent job to make some money. I decided that I would stay in Chicago before I went off to college in August. Ralph Kaspari's parents were gracious enough to allow Jim Schultz and me to live at their house in the basement. Jim's family lived in the southern suburbs of Chicago, about an hour away. He would go home there on the weekends. Ralph and his family lived in Mount Prospect, a suburb northwest of Chicago. Ralph's dad was an architect. He would catch the train a mile away and go to downtown Chicago every day. He would come home, go to his study, catch up on the news, and spend time with his daughter, Pam. He was a Navy officer who served in WWII. He was a very kind, levelheaded guy who was mostly reserved. Pam was just the opposite. She was ten years old and was very outgoing, like her brother Ralph. They had a brother two years younger than Ralph, Dave. He was quiet like his dad, but very bright. Ralph's mom was a conversationalist. When I got home from work, I would sit down with her for about an hour before dinner. I enjoyed having the female companionship I had missed as a cadet. Ralph was outside, working on his car or talking to his neighborhood friends. They had a small park in front of their house where the guys could play a pickup game of softball or basketball. The Kasparis were living the all-American life in a suburban community, where all conveniences were within reach of where they lived. We could drive to Lake Michigan on the weekend and dip in the water or climb atop the Sears Tower on the 114th floor. What an awesome view of the city and the lake! I had never lived in the suburbs.

This was pretty neat.

We also could take the subways to go to various bars. I was twenty years old at that time. I had a fake ID, a North Dakota driver's license made by a resourceful academy cadet. Jim Schultz had gone to the AFA Prep School, so he was a year older and was twenty-one. Jim loved to barhop and move from one to another. We got to one nightclub that looked really nice. The bouncer asked me for my ID, and I gave him my North Dakota license. He looked at it and said, "It is no ha-ha good!" I asked, "Ha-ha?" He said, "Ha, ha!" I was crushed and embarrassed. Jim and some of his buddies got in. I then figured out how to take the subway, change trains to get back to Mount Prospect. Ralph's friends had a vast range of personalities. It was just like the *Happy Days* television series in the seventies. There were souped-up cars and motorcycles. There were Fonzie, Richie Cunningham, and Ralph Mouth type of characters. It was a great time to be young!

Jim and I got jobs as mailmen at nearby Arlington Heights starting April 1. We got paid $2.65 an hour. It was a great job for us. The downside was getting up at 5:30 a.m. to report to work at 6:00 a.m. We would start by "throwing the mail" into the cubbyholes at our station. We learned to place the mail between our fingers so as to work faster to get each letter into the proper address cubicle for those on our route. We would finish this around 9:00 a.m. to 9:15 a.m. Then we would go out on our route. We used our own cars. We would park at the end of the street, do that portion on one side, and return and then move over to the other side of the street. We had six hours to complete our route. I packed a bologna sandwich and a drink and would eat that in my car. Being young, we finished our route in about four or four and a half hours, with an hour and a half to kill time. Sometimes I would go to the horse races. I did a few times. I would also go back to the house to take a nap if I was out late the night before. Then we would get back to the post office and help get the incoming mail for our route to our cubicle stations ready to sort the next day. There also was overtime, so we could easily get if we worked twelve hours that day. We punched in and out by a card. Ralph took a job delivering Sheetrock. That was a tough job. I helped him out a couple of times. Carrying Sheetrock into a two-story building and turning ninety degrees is hard. Ralph was naturally strong in his upper body. For his size and weight, that was impressive. I was making money and saving money since I didn't have to pay room and board. I paid for my lunch sandwiches. I didn't have to pay for the evening dinners.

By late July, there was a job opening up flagging a street that was under repairs. There was an evening shift, from 5:00 to 10:00 p.m.

That meant I could do my mailman job and this at the same time. The pay was $4.65 an hour. That was hard to turn down. The work was on an unlit two-way road with trees on each side. Our main job was to move traffic through one lane instead of two. This was important at rush time. When it got dark, no one could see us even though we had on the safety vests. The drivers didn't pay attention to us.

We then decided to kill about one and a half hours at a local bar before we punched out at ten o'clock. We did that for about two weeks. That was very lucrative at that wage.

We went ahead and sent our academic transcripts. A month later, I got a letter from the academic adviser of athletics at Florida State saying that their administration just did not want to give a two-year scholarship for playing just one year. I was very disappointed and wrote Bill Peterson a letter telling him how he did not keep his word. He wrote me back saying that his hands were tied and the administration wouldn't budge. He said I was an outstanding athlete and should be able to find a home elsewhere. I appreciated his response. Now I needed to get to work to find a new place to go.

I wasn't highly recruited out of high school, so this was a new experience. I heard from the University of Wyoming, the University of Utah, the University of Houston, and the University of Hawaii. What was different with the University of Hawaii was that the NCAA gave Hawaii a special exemption to help them build their football program. I would be able to go there and play immediately. I considered that but wanted to just play my last year of football with a top 10 team and then get on with my life as a civil engineer. Since I was already acquainted with the University of Wyoming, for we played them the previous two years, I didn't really need to visit that campus. I took a trip to the University of Utah, where Mike Giddings was the coach. They took me around, and it looked like a great place to live and play football. They were not a highly ranked team, but their program was on the accent. I then took a trip to the University of Houston, where they gave me the first-class treatment. They picked me up at the airport and took me to a baseball game at the new Astrodome, at that time known as the "eighth wonder of the world."

This was the first domed stadium in the world. They took me to the club on top of the stadium and fed me whatever drinks I wanted. They used some of their big backers to show me around town and two of their star players to go to the local hangouts and introduce me to some of their teammates. They really did want me. They had no problem offering the two-year scholarship for one year playing. I got back to Mount Prospect. I made up my mind.

Houston was ranked in the top 10. This was what I was looking for. I decided to accept the scholarship at the University of Houston. I finished out the summer and gave my notice to the post office that I would be leaving. Our supervisor was disappointed that we both were leaving. We told him we wanted to finish college. He tried to get us to consider going to postal inspector school. We appreciated his offer, but we were ready to move on to get back to college. Ralph Kaspari, Jim Schutz, Mike Rengel, and Larry Cook from the Air Force Academy had committed to play for the University of Hawaii. I was headed to Houston, Texas. Before I left Mount Prospect, I decided to buy a new car. I would be driving a lot of miles from Chicago back to Minnesota and then on to Houston. I decided to buy a new white English Ford. It was called a Ford Cortina. It was a compact car. It cost me $1,675 with the trade-in for my 1961 Chevrolet Delta. My family had never bought a new car. I liked the idea of starting at the beginning of zero when adding miles.

I went back to Granite Falls and spent the weekend with my parents. Then, I headed out for Houston with my Cortina and was ready to start my future. This time I would be completely on my own. I knew only the people I met a month before. This was my decision, and I would have to live with it. So I got on the road. Once I got to Dallas on I-35, I looked over downtown and saw such a dark-looking city. This was where my favorite president, John Kennedy, had been shot and killed. It was just eerie. From a distance it looked ominous. I continued on the road and got to Corsicana, just south of Dallas. All of a sudden, I heard a big pop in the back of the car. I pulled over and checked to see what happened. My gas tank had a big hole in it. I was screwed! I was close enough to the city that I was able to walk to a nearby auto repair shop. They sent out a wrecker to pick up the car. They said that more than likely, the object that caused the damage was an angle iron from a semitrailer mud flap. They would have to order a new gas tank. In those days, we traveled with traveler's checks. Thank God I had made enough money that summer to pay for the damage—it was about $250! I then checked into a nearby motel room. I had to spend the night there and pick up the car around noon the next day. I was bored, so I watched some television. I remember watching the weather report. The longtime weather anchor was Warren Culbertson. I was now where the Texas accent was strong: "This is Waaarrrenn Cullllllllbeeeerrrtsonnn."

I picked up the car and got moving on to Houston. I checked into my dorm room and worked on getting settled. I didn't have much stuff, but it was mine. My roommate was Billy Bridges. He was very kind and worked to help me blend in with the other guys. He took me along to some of the clubs, where his teammates were celebrating getting back to football season for a new year. That Sunday, they had a golf tournament with the local supporters, players, and staff. I noticed a lot of the players had really nice clothes and cars. I just assumed their parents were more affluent than I was. When we got around to sharing stories, I was finding a cultural gap. Most of them spoke with a drawl, and I couldn't always understand them. When I was at the Air Force Academy, we had cadets from all over the country, so the main accent was like one they did on television. In Texas, the television anchors had the same accent, so I had to learn to speak slower for them to understand me. Anyway, I didn't have a problem with any of them. I just felt out of place. I figured I would adapt just like I did at the academy and move on.

We started our first practice. My god, it was hot and humid! It was ninety-five degrees, with ninety-five degrees of humidity. We started the practice with twenty-five minutes of agility drills. Holy crap! The first few days, I was dying from the heat; however, I noticed that the drills were very effective with my agility and endurance. Once the rest of the practice started, it was the normal routine of drills I was used to. This was when reality set in. Since I wouldn't be playing that year, I was expendable, so I would be on the scout team. One of the old-time football drills was to line up a two-by-twelve wood board and have the blocker and defensive lineman line up against each other. You would usually do your turn and move on to the next blocker and next defensive lineman. The coaches had other ideas. I would line up against the blocker(s), then I would take on the first, then the second, and finally all five linemen! Then I was replaced by a true redshirt freshman to relieve me, and he would do the same. They would then do a second round for each of us. The coaches were very pleased with me as I took on all of them and held them off, including their all-American guard. He was a very good player, but small by today's standards. I would do this again the next day for two weeks. I was establishing myself as a good recruit. I was fitting in on the field.

Finally, it was the weekend, and it was time to go out with the guys Saturday night. On Sunday, I got a call from Ralph Kaspari out in Hawaii. I told him I was doing fine. He filled me in on how well things were going with all the guys. He told me Doug Steeve, Mike Sansone, and Jack Spithill from the academy were also there. They were from the class of 1969. He said they went to the beach that weekend, and of how good everything was going. I told him I was doing well and thanked him for calling. After I hung up, I thought, *Boy, I miss these guys!* We had grown up together at the academy. We knew everything about one another and shared a life challenging experience of the academy.

The next week, started and we were ready for our next scrimmage. It was at the Astrodome. That was where the University of Houston would be playing their home games. The players were getting up for the scrimmage like it was a real game. I had to be on my toes to compete. I played well enough, but the reality had set in. I was a two-year starter in major college football and wouldn't be able to suit up until the next year. That weekend, Ralph called again, and this time I shared with him how I really felt and that I missed the guys so much. I realized I didn't give the ability to play right away at Hawaii enough consideration. I asked Ralph to talk to Harvey Hyde, the coach who recruited me, to let him know I would call him. I had his number from a previous letter. He talked to me and said, "Come on out." He then followed up with a telegram from the coaching staff. Now the hard part. How do I tell head coach Bill Yeoman? I just couldn't face him, especially since I was going through so many emotions about what was happening to me. I decided to just write a letter to him. I left a note to my roommate to give the letter to Coach Yeoman. I rewrote the letter on another sheet of stationery to make sure I knew what I said, in case there would be major repercussions. I got up and left the next morning and drove to San Francisco. I would then ship my car to Honolulu. There wasn't any repercussion from Coach Yeoman. He had coached at West Point. I think he knew where I was coming from and what I was going through.

On my drive from Houston to San Francisco, I had plenty of time to think out my future. I had just given up on playing my senior season with a nationally ranked team. Now I would be playing against small college teams. That didn't seem too challenging. Well, I decided that I needed my friends to transition to a normal, civilian life. I have always made friends easily. I had no idea how much I relied on friends. A lot is going on in your life between living at home and not being married, with a more traditional life. I liked my independence, but I needed friends to confide in that cared about me. These guys cared. I decided I would play this last year of football and get that over with. Then I would go back to the University of Minnesota and finish college and get my degree in civil engineering and start my career.

I got to San Francisco and put the car on the ship to transfer it to Hawaii. I then got on a plane and arrived in Honolulu. The weather was warm, but not uncomfortable like Houston's. The trade winds constantly blew, cooling down the skin. The sun, though, could still do its damage to the skin. I got picked up at the airport by the coaches. They took me to the campus and checked me in. The campus was pretty, but the football facilities were lacking. The offices and dorm were portable buildings. The uniforms were probably ten years old. The jerseys had buttons underneath to keep them from coming untucked in. For me with a long back, that was probably a good idea. I have never seen anything like that ever since. The equipment was quite picked apart by the time I got there. I arrived one week before the first game. I had to play that game in tennis shoes because they didn't have my size, 14E. By the second game, I had new shoes. The younger players were required to live in the portable dorms. Mike Rengel, Ralph Kaspari, Larry Cook, and Jim Schultz got a two-bedroom apartment off campus. They insisted I move in with them, so we had five people. One of us had to sleep out front on the couch. We would rotate that weekly. There were other players in this apartment complex. On Saturday nights, the place got loud. During the week, guys were coming and going. It was impossible to study. I figured out I needed to go to the library to study. I ordered a hamburger. I didn't recognize what they served me. It was a little hamburger with a lot of breading filler in it. It was awful! That was when I discovered ham and cheese sandwiches. The guys got ahold of a porn flick one time and a camera showing the projection on the wall. I walked in to see body parts on the wall. At first, it got my curiosity up. Then it became boring. There was also a gay bar in the next building over, called Yappies. Men with expensive cars would pull up to the curb and park long enough to look for one of the cross-dressers to come over and negotiate a price. The cross-dressers were really good-looking, until they lifted their skirts up and urinated standing up. Oh my!

We had to pay our own rent, but we got a minimal reimbursement during the season only. They paid for tuition and provided one meal a day during the season. This wasn't that much of a scholarship. At the apartment, we had this very nice native Hawaiian from the university who brought us fresh pineapple. It was very good! Some of us decided to make a meal out of it instead of buying other food. We later found that was not wise—we all got diarrhea.

I went to the first practice and saw what kind of team we had. There were many junior college transfers from the West Coast, from Washington down to California. Also, there many players from the major colleges that weren't getting playing time. There were those from UCLA, USC, San Diego State, Washington, and Oregon. I was discovering that we had the ingredients of a pretty good team on defense. On offense, we had a senior quarterback, Dick Hough, who was also in his final year. We had Larry Cook and McKinley Reynolds in the backfield. We called them Thunder and Lightning. Larry Cook was Mudder.

Ralph Kaspari was a strong blocker and could carry the ball when needed. We had Jim Schultz, slot receiver, who was the clutch receiver and downfield blocker. The linemen were mostly junior varsity guys, but they were coming into their own. On defense, I was finding we might have a better defensive line than we did at the Air Force Academy. Mike Rengel was a strong side tackle. I was a weak side tackle, and John Hoffman was the strong side defensive end. He was six-foot-seven and weighed about 260. He came from USC. In addition, we had Dennis Goodrich, a weak side linebacker who was smaller but a very solid, quick player. The other linebackers were Dick Dillehay, a junior college transfer, at middle linebacker and Jack Spithill from the AFA as the other linebacker. After my first practice, the guys took me to Waikiki Beach. This was the first time I had seen it. It was beautiful and so tourist friendly! The backyards of all the hotels were on the beach, with Diamond Head on the horizon. There were beautiful brown-sand beaches. The drinking age in Hawaii was twenty instead of the twenty-one for most mainland states. So I could now buy my own drinks. Turning twenty-one would be a non-event. I walked on the beach barefoot. The breeze was so refreshing! When we left, I had found I had spent too much time in the sun. My shoulders were solid red, but worse, I walked barefoot on the asphalt to the car and developed two silver-dollar-size blisters on the balls of my feet. The next day at practice, it was painful wearing the shoulder pads, and especially my feet running with those blisters. How would I explain that to my coaches without them wondering what an idiot I was? I gutted through it. It got better each day. So much for being a "beach bum." I had the blond hair, but I also had tender white Scandinavian skin. I learned my limitations.

Our first game was against Linfield College. I didn't start, but I got a lot of playing time. The next week, I was a starter against Lewis and Clark, and the third game I was named cocaptain along with Jim Schultz. We lost the first game 15–3. The second game, we blew away Lewis and Clark 34–3, followed by Central Washington 30–7. We were 2–1 and feeling good about ourselves. We only had two away games, so the next week we went to Humboldt State in Northern California. It was located in the redwood forest. I had never seen such a dense and wet place! The field had a big hump in the middle to try to make the water drain to the sidelines. It rained throughout the entire game. Our Mudder, Larry Cook, and Ralph Kasapari got yards, but no sustained drive. On defense, I couldn't get off the blocks because I just sank into the mud. I was not having a good game. I got in an argument with the sideline coaches. I picked up a bunch of mud in my hands and threw it toward them. That was bush league, as we called it in those days. I lost my temper. I apologized to the coaches. That wasn't the real me.

We lost 13–0.

On that weekend, we were taken to San Francisco to see a 49ers game. I don't remember much about the game, but I did remember going to the intersection of Haight-Ashbury. We saw the flower children, the drugs, and the protests. I thought of so many of the people that came there totally rejecting the way of life they were brought up in the Midwest. So sad.

In any event, it was great to get off the island for a change of pace.

The next week, we played Cal State and lost 9–3. We were now 2–3. We weren't scoring points, but our defense was shutting down every team we played. On many plays, John Hoffman and I would meet each other deep in the backfield, causing many TFLs (tackles for loss). Mike Rengel usually got the double team block. He would hold his ground. We finally got untracked on offense and started scoring points while still playing good defense. We won the next four against Idaho State, UC–Santa Barbara, Cal Western, and Fresno State. The final game of the season was against a major college team, the University of Utah. We had become a very confident team and wanted to prove we were in their league. Before the game, our coach spoke to us, telling us, "Did you see them warm up? They are big, really big! I shouldn't have scheduled this game." When Jim and I heard that, we asked Coach King to let us have a few minutes with the team. We told them we had every reason to believe we could win. We fired them up and got on the field and went to work. We played a solid game on defense, and our offense fought for every yard. Our quarterback, Dick Hough, had a great game and kept answering their scoring. The game came down to the ten-yard line. McKinley Reynolds missed a pass over the middle. Then on fourth down, he went to the flat and was wide open to catch the pass for the win. He dropped it. We lost 25–20. That was it, the end of my college career. To this date, the 1967 defense has the school record of only allowing a combined run and pass of only 2.6 yard per carry. Those of us who played on this team feel proud we turned around the program. Mike Rengel, Larry Cook, and I were seniors, and all the others were back the following year to build on our accomplishments. It was the most enjoyable year playing football I had experienced to that date.

After the season, we decided to break up into two different living arrangements. Mike Rengel, Jim Schultz, Charlie Bensley, and I rented an apartment on Date Street, just off campus. Charlie had come over on a basketball scholarship. Ralph Kaspari and Larry Cook got their own apartment.

During the fall, I continued on my path to a civil engineering degree. When I transferred credits for the AFA, some were meaningless to them, like military history, economics of national security and air power, and twentieth-century weapons. I realized that it would take me at least two more years to graduate. That was kind of depressing. The school year began. I liked the more relaxed atmosphere with more downtime than I was used to. The classrooms had three-inch-wide windows that opened up to the outside without screens. The breeze came through the windows, inviting us to go outside. I had a hard time concentrating. In my life, school was in session when it was cool or cold outside. This was different. The quality of the teaching was lacking in communication except for the head of the department. He was from the mainland. He would take time to sit down with us and answer our technical questions and help us with our engineering studies. One of my teachers was such a philosopher that he tried to teach a course in materials science as to what was the intent of the authors of the textbook. In engineering, it is to state the problem, list the items that are known, develop a hypothesis, and then proceed to solve the problem with a step-by-step process that has one outcome, the answer. If that wasn't true, buildings would crumble. I remember one of the professors was a young Canadian guy, about twenty-four, who taught fluid mechanics. He came to class with Bermuda shorts, sandals, and a T-shirt. He would open the class, talk for about ten minutes, tell us to read the following chapters, and we would be tested on it the next class. In the meantime, he would spend his entire afternoon at the oceanography laboratory near downtown Honolulu. I relied on my friend Mike Rengel to tutor me. He was really good at understanding the textbooks. My grade point average was slightly above 2.0. Just after the last game of the season, the average grade point average of the team was approximately 1.75. My eligibility was over. Many of the returning players below 2.0 were put on academic probation for that spring.

Having a new apartment that was a lot quieter during the week helped. My normal routine was to study from eight o'clock to ten, then go to the Blue Goose, a bar adjacent to the campus. I would have my pitcher of beer, go home at around eleven thirty, go to bed, and get up the next day. One of my teammates, Rick Hrdlicka, was a bartender there. He was a good-looking guy, and he would attract a lot of good-looking girls to the bar on weekends.

At the same time after the season, Jim Schultz got a job at one of the bars in downtown Honolulu. He was really good at it. He was a very charismatic guy who was easy to talk to, a trait important for a bartender. Occasionally, we would go downtown and stop by his place. During the week, it was not a good idea. In Honolulu, as the saying goes, "every night is a Saturday night, every day a holiday." This is actually true with tourists from all over the world there during the week. We got to know Don Ho, who performed at a club with the Don Ho Show. For tourists, this was a must stop for their itinerary. He personified what Hawaii was all about. Getting up to go to class the next morning was hard to do. I usually skipped class that next morning. During the day, I would go to the East West Center. Students from all over the world were there. I met a lot of interesting people.

The football season was over on December 2, and this would be the first time I would not be home for Christmas. It was too far to travel and too expensive. Around the third week of December, I got word that I had been invited to play in the Hula Bowl along with quarterback Dick Hough. I was slowly getting out of shape with more time to have a social life. It was easy to blow through money going to the clubs along Waikiki Beach. You could literally walk out to the beach from the bar! At night, when the moon was out, it reflected on the water. You could see the waves glowing with the moonlight. This place was quiet and romantic. The girls loved it, but I decided to not have more than two or three dates with any one girl. I didn't want to get attached; plus, it was expensive. Most of the girls there were from California running away from something.

Hula Bowl

I wasn't that excited about playing in the Hula Bowl. I didn't want to train for it. I liked the honor of being selected to the Hula Bowl, but I didn't want to work out to get ready for it. Having played in Hawaii that year, I was sure that the pro scouts had forgotten about me. Since this would be the first nationally televised Hula Bowl, my family could see me on television for the first and only time this year. This was a weeklong event, where I got to meet the best players in America: Gary Beban of UCLA (the Heisman Trophy Winner), whom I had played against twice; Larry Csonka from Syacuse; Ron Yary from USC; Blaine Nye from Stanford; and Adrian Young from USC, to name a few. The UCLA head coach, Tommy Protho, was our coach for the South. He was his own person. He would wear that fedora hat with his black glasses. He would smoke a lot of cigarettes on the sideline during the game. Duffy Doughtery of Michigan State was the North coach. He was a bear of a guy.

Both were well-established, good coaches. All the guys came to Honolulu for the week. I got to know Blaine Nye. I had played against him twice the past two years, and we developed a friendship and hung out together. Also, Adrian Young of USC hung out with us too. Honolulu did a good job with a number of events. Hawaii liked their football. Their high schools rivaled the *Friday Night Lights* of Texas.

The game came. It was a warm and still day at the stadium. The rules didn't allow either side to blitz. Our defensive line was composed of Blaine Nye, Ron Yary, and myself. The other side had Larry Csonka. That was all they needed. I would neutralize the blocker, slide off, begin to tackle Larry Csonka, and he could drag me five to seven yards down the field. I was embarrassed how bad I did. He was just so strong with his legs. First down, then do it again. He would march them down the field to score. We could have shut him down with a blitz, but that wasn't allowed. Blaine and Ron Yary didn't do much better on the other side. Ironically, those two ended up being all-pro offensive linemen. We lost the game 50–6. After the game, I figured this was it. Any chance of playing pro football would likely be over with my play. I went back to my hotel room. I went to bed at about ten o'clock. The next morning, I was so sore I couldn't get out of bed, literally. I rolled over and just lay there until I felt like getting up about three hours later. In my mind my football career was over.

I got back to my apartment and got back into my normal routine. I was losing my discipline and falling into a depressing pattern of drinking too much and losing interest in school. At that time, the movies *Valley of the Dolls* and *The Graduate* captured the antiestablishment of younger generation. In one of the bars, there was a picture of the poster "Uncle Sam Needs You," with an image of

President Johnson as Uncle Sam pointing a gun at you. The war in Vietnam was putting a real drag on the country. Friends back home were getting drafted. I was fortunate to be in the inactive reserves because all units had been filled in Honolulu. I was just marking time in Hawaii. I was losing my normal motivation. I had always looked forward, but I no longer felt that way. I was in malaise. Both Mike Rengel and I decided to plan to transfer to the University of Minnesota that next fall. I needed to get home to remotivate myself.

Then I was told by the athletic department that an NFL scout who worked for multiple teams said that maybe the Rams or Chargers would be interested in me. I had never heard from them. A few days before the draft, I got a call from the Dallas Cowboys. They asked me who else was interested in me. I told him the Rams and Chargers. He wasn't too impressed because I had no firsthand information for them. It was then I made up my mind that unless I was drafted, I was not going to play pro football for anyone. I gauged that if they were interested in me, they would draft me. On the first day of the draft, news of who was drafted leaked out. They had gone through the fifth round. On campus, one of my teammates told me I was drafted by the Rams. I told him I hadn't heard that from anyone. He then said the Honolulu Rams. Very funny. The next day, I actually got drafted by the Dallas Cowboys in the sixteenth round out of seventeen. In your face, dude! I got a call from the Cowboys that day and confirmed that I was indeed drafted. They told me they would get back to me. They sent me a Dallas Cowboys brochure that was quite well put together for its day. In that package was a full, shiny blue-and-silver brochure telling the story of the Dallas Cowboys. The Air Force Academy believed in this type of marketing too, shiny, first-class-looking brochures. There was a quote from Tom Landry that said, "If you come to training camp and prove that you have the talent and desire to succeed, we will find a place for you." That was actually true. He had converted basketball players like Cornell Green into defensive backs and Rafael Wright from tight end to offensive tackle. He was a young coach in his forties and was a former Army Air Corps bomber pilot in WWII. With my background, I could relate to a guy like that. I was starting to get interested in giving pro football a shot. I owed it to myself to have them tell me I wasn't good enough to play pro football. A month before, Dallas played Green Bay in the Ice Bowl. We watched the game at our apartment. Growing up in Minnesota, I was a Green Bay Packers fan. It was eighty-three degrees in Honolulu, seventeen below in Green Bay, a one-hundred-degree temperature swing. When Green Bay won, I jumped up for joy! Little did I know, a month later, I would get drafted by Dallas.

In early February, I got a letter with an enclosed contract for $10,000 from the Winnipeg Blue Bombers of the Canadian Football League. I hadn't even talked to them. I ignored it. I got a follow-up letter from their general manager on February 16. He wanted to have an answer if I would accept his contract. I called him and told him I would think about it as I hadn't heard back from the Cowboys. He then called me on March 1 to get an answer. He did a follow-up letter that day and told me that if I hadn't heard from the Cowboys by then, then they were not too interested in me. He said the contract was not negotiable and that if I didn't sign it, the price would only go down. Screw that! I finally heard from the Cowboys. They offered me a contract for $15,000 a year if I made the team. They would give me a $2,000 bonus upon signing, and $2,000 more if I made the team. Since I didn't get a part-time job, I needed the money to pay expenses I had in the spring. I got a bank loan on my car to get enough money to finish out the spring. I accepted the offer because as a draft choice, you either played for that team or not at all. They sent me the contract to sign. I signed it and returned it. At that time, no one could make any changes to the contract except the price. It was all or nothing. They then sent me a check for $2,000. That was sweet! I paid off my car loan and pocketed the rest to make enough to make it to training camp.

They then arranged to fly me into Dallas for "rookie orientation weekend." All the draft choices and the signed free agents came in to test us both on and off the field. The Cowboys were a pioneer in using computer technology. They ran us all through the usual forty-yard dash, broad jump, weight lifting, etc. They also had us take a psychological survey to see if we all had the aggressiveness to compete at this level. I went to Dallas and met my fellow draft choices.

I had met Blaine Nye and Ken Kmeic in the Hula Bowl. I met the others that day. I did the athletic tests. I wasn't in shape. I didn't really impress anyone. I also was told later that I failed the psychological test in that I tested out as a "lamb" instead of a "lion." That happened to LeRoy Jordan too, so I wasn't too concerned about that. They didn't know me yet. I felt the test was flawed. I went back to Honolulu knowing what I needed to do before I reported to training camp. I didn't lose confidence in myself. I knew I could compete against the other draft choices.

My roommate, Mike Rengel, had the misfortune of having his mother pass away when he was sixteen. So he learned to cook for his dad and himself. I was weighing about 230 at that time. The Cowboys told me I needed to report to camp at a minimum of 245 pounds in order to compete at this level. Mike had decided to sign a free agent contract with the New Orleans Saints. We decided to start having a healthy diet, eating a well-balanced meal. I bought the groceries, and Mike did the cooking. We then both went to the weight room to get some more strength before training camp. The Cowboys sent me a couple of cases of Hustle, a high-protein drink. This formula worked. By the time we left Honolulu in June, I had my weight up to 245 pounds and I was a lot stronger. In the meantime, McDonald's came to Honolulu in the spring with real meat hamburgers. God, they tasted good! Mike was naturally bigger and didn't need to gain weight, but he did need more muscle. In the meantime, both of us were accepted at the University of Minnesota. If we didn't make the team by August, we could go directly to the University of Minnesota and get on with our lives in pursuit of an engineering degree.

Spring moved on, and by then we had discovered the entire island. A favorite pastime was to going to Makapuu Beach, where we could do bodysurfing. There wasn't much current, and we could catch a ten-foot wave and ride it for about twenty yards. Even a lousy swimmer like me could do it. I did learn to cover up my skin. We also went to the Hawaii Wildlife Center, where the most beautiful plants and birds lived. We drove around the whole island. It took about two and a half hours. By the time we left, we were both ready to get off the island. Mike and I, being from Minnesota, liked the wide-open spaces.

Early in June, we finished our classes and were ready to leave for the mainland. I shipped my Cortina back to San Francisco. We flew there, picked up the car, and were on the road back to Minnesota. We drove through the wide-open spaces of California and Nevada. That felt so good! As we entered Utah, my Cortina started to break down. We drove through a small town of about one thousand population, where we took it to a local mechanic. He said I needed engine work. If I drove it farther, the damage would be irreparable. Instead of paying for a towing service, I then bought a used car for $200. Mike and I towed it about one hundred miles to Salt Lake City. I dropped off the car at the shop in Salt Lake City, and once it was fixed, I paid about $300 for the repairs. Now I owned two cars. Since I was going to Granite Falls and my brother lived in the suburb of Bloomington, I had Mike drive the Cortina to his house. I decided to sell that car. I had a better chance to sell it in the big city rather than in Granite Falls. My brother, Roger, would sell it for me. I drove the $200 car to Granite Falls. I would use that car for the next month.

It was nice getting my bearings back. My parents were happy to have me back home. They knew that if I didn't make the team, I would be back in the fall to enter the University of Minnesota. I started training for camp. I knew I needed to be in shape on day 1 to make an impression. I would go to the Volstead Football Field, where I played my high school games, to work out. They had a track around the field. I was told that when I got to camp, I would have to run the Landry Mile. It was six laps of 440 yards each. If a player didn't do this in the allotted time of twelve minutes, they would have to train until they did. I ran that every day. I would begin my routine with the same agility drills that I learned at the University of Houston. Since the temperature was much lower, it wasn't quite as draining. Those were really good drills. I still wanted to end my workout with pushing myself. I saw the local guys and would go out on the weekends, but I trained during the week. I helped Mom do some more remodel work in the basement to add a new room. That kept me occupied. I signed over the $200 car to my dad and told him to do with it what he wanted. My parents and I drove to Minneapolis and spent the night at my brother's house. Roger had sold the car. I signed the papers, received the cashier's check, and got on a plane to Los Angeles.

After I arrived, I was met by the training camp staff. Our training camp was at Cal Lutheran College in Thousand Oaks, California, about an hour out of Los Angeles in Ventura County. The staff picked us up and put us on a bus to training camp. As we entered the city, the view of the mountains in the background was stunning as we passed through West Lake Village. Thousand Oaks had a population of ten thousand people at that time. There was a lot of open spaces in the hills just off the campus. The climate was about as compatible for me as possible. It was foggy in the morning. The sun came out around noon, then when it got about eighty degrees by 4:00 p.m., a cool ocean breeze lasted until about by 6:00 p.m. The evenings were seventy-two degrees by sunset. Then it cooled down to the sixties overnight and started all over again the next morning. Unfortunately, at the best time of the day, we would be in evening meetings. I knew with this climate, I could give making the team my best shot. We arrived at the campus. We checked into the dormitory. They had typical dorm rooms like the AFA, two single beds, two desks, and two dressers. The coaches were on one wing, and the players on the other.

I ran the Landry Mile in about ten and a half minutes, well within the twelve-minute limit. I was ready for running the forty-yard dash. I ran it in 5.2 seconds, far better than the 5.5 seconds I did at the off-season camp. I was ready to get started.

The Cowboys brought the rookies in early. After two weeks, the veterans would join them. When the Cowboys drafted me, they had me penciled in as an offensive lineman. During the fourteen-day camp for rookies, they lined me up on offense first. Our quarterback was Roger Staubach. He was still in the Navy for another year. He gave up his two weeks of leave to practice with the team. Wow, that was commitment! They liked how I played. The offensive coach was Jim Myers. He was a no-nonsense, tough-love kind of guy. He had coached at Texas A&M. That figured right. I then moved to defense, and they liked my play there too. I came to play defense, not offense. The defensive line coach was Ernie Stautner. He was a Hall of Famer for the Pittsburg Steelers. He was a tough guy but had a very firm but friendly demeanor. I like the fact that he played the game. Ernie wanted me, and he won the battle to keep me on defense.

The veterans came to camp. In those days, they worked in the off-season and didn't report to camp in shape. The starting defensive line were Willie Townes, Jethro Pugh, Bob Lilly, and George Andrie. The backups were Ron East at tackle and Larry Stephens at Defensive End. Larry was a big smoker at that time that he dropped out on the Landry Mile with two laps remaining. I then silently said to myself, I may have a chance to make this team. When I saw the players, there were many that seemed so old. How could they still play football? Football was for younger people, wasn't it? Chuck Howley was over thirty and looked like an old man. The offensive lineman had one or two knee surgeries and lost a lot of their quickness. I wasn't impressed in the early days.

I was now introduced to the flex defense, which was such a novel way of playing defense because I had always gotten off the ball, neutralized the blocker, and slid off. In the flex defense, I would first need to lineup the right way, read the opposing blockers, and take my initial steps to get in position to neutralize a block or make the play. I was kind of astounded that this was the way the Dallas Cowboys played defense. I then watched Bob Lilly and George Andrie execute these moves. Bob was so quick off the ball if the guard in front of him was pulling, he exploded into the backfield. George Andrie was six foot six, 255 pounds of solid muscle. He executed the crash technique with a lot of power. If the guard and tackle both block down that means they are running a trap or a play to the other side. George needed to take him out of the play. The key to the crash technique was to sharply crash down off the block and meet the pulling guard and then turn the forearm ninety degrees. His momentum would push one off to the outside, where he would unintentionally push one off to meet up with a running back and make the tackle or drive the play to the outside for the middle linebacker to make the tackle or the strong safety. When I was in the offset position and they ran the ball straight ahead, LeRoy Jordan, the middle linebacker, would scrap off my back and move outside to make the tackle or drive the ball carrier to the outside. At first, I thought that would be impossible to learn. I then saw Bob Lilly and George Andrie execute that technique flawlessly. I would have to learn how to do that. Bob was such a help in patiently explaining what to do. He had played left end before he moved to right defensive tackle. That was his natural position. Jethro Pugh was left tackle. He was six foot six and lanky, at around 260 pounds. On end runs he would grab the guard as he was pulling out and make the play in the backfield many times. He was an unusual athlete, lanky, long arms and legs, and smart. Willie Townes, the left defensive end, was really good at executing the crash technique, but not as good as George doing all the other moves.

I was a work in progress. First off, I had never played this type of four-man line in college. In this defense, you lined up on the edge of the offensive tackle. I was bowlegged, so Ernie had to work on me to close my stance. It was kind of comical. He would kick my feet over so I could get the feel of a closer stance for the crash move. I would take the first big step and adjust. When the offensive formation was stacked to the right, I would have to line up two and a half feet off the ball and take an initial jab step to the right. Then, if the blocking pattern was straight ahead, I would do a forearm shiver while stepping back to the left. At first, I thought, *You are kidding me, right?* I had a 275-pound offensive tackle coming at me, and I needed my whole body to stop him. I found that he was also put at a disadvantage by having to take an additional step toward me since I was lined up off the line of scrimmage. If he only got a piece of me, I could go inside his block and make the tackle. I needed to hold his block long enough for LeRoy to scrap off my back. Sometimes I could just shrug him off. Each day I worked at this, but it took time.

On the pass rush, I had no idea what to do. Tom Landry was asked about this. He said he had no idea how to pass rush but said Bob Lilly and George Andrie didn't know how to do it when they started their career as well. Ernie worked closely with me to discipline my steps to get to the quarterback. I also got a lot of help from Ralph Neeley, our right offensive tackle. He was a number 1 draft choice from Oklahoma. He was in his fourth year and had just made the all-pro the previous year. He showed me how I could counter different offensive line techniques. He taught me that for every move, there was a countermove changeup. I started to pick them up. In the meantime, the veterans got in shape and my opinion of them changed. Everything happened so quick. We had to make split decisions. I found out Chuck Howley had a "nose for the ball" and could move around very swiftly. He was a playmaker. So much for the old man I thought he was! I remember lining up for scrimmage drill. I forgot what to do on the defensive call. I quickly asked Chuck Howley what I was supposed to do on that call. He said, "I don't care what you do. Just stay out of my way." Until I made the team, I was a nonperson. Gee, that was what it was like at the Air Force Academy basic training. Tradition was that all the rookies had to stand up and sing their school song during dinner as a form of hazing. Hawaii didn't have a school song, so I sang "Tiny Bubbles" by Don Ho. Don Meredith and Dan Reeves just loved that, so I had to sing it many times. At camp we had to put on a rookie show for the veterans at the end of the summer. More creative, acting-type guys set that up. We also had to go get ice for the veterans for them to ice down their knees. Jim Boeke was my veteran. He was an offensive tackle with many knee injuries, so he needed a lot of ice. He was a very nice fellow. He later went on to teach high school and did his stint in acting with many appearances on *M*A*S*H*, *Forrest Gump*, and *Heaven Can Wait*, plus television shows.

We played in the Hall of Fame game in Canton, Ohio, that year. This was the first pro game I played. It was an exhibition game against the Chicago Bears. Across the field was the legendary George Halas. I was on specialty teams. I would line up next to the kicker. I was on the second team on kickoff coverage. John Douglas, a rookie linebacker, was first team. His job was to run down to break up the "wedge" blockers that were composed of Dick Butkus, Ed O'Bradovich, and George Seals, three of the Monsters of the Midway. He went down and got clobbered. They hauled him off the field. Holy crap! Was this harder than I thought? Someone was offside on the play, so we had to rekick. I got into the game scared as hell that this pro game might be tougher than I thought. I went down there, broke up the wedge, and survived. I later got into the game. I got to the quarterback, blocked his arm, causing him to fumble, and recovered the fumble. It didn't seem like such a big deal at that time, but for rookies to get noticed, you had to make plays. The next week, we played San Francisco. I recovered a fumble on the kickoff coverage. On August 16, Bob St. John of *The Dallas Morning News* wrote an article that quoted Tom Landry. He said that I was the best rookie lineman on offense and on defense during the two-week rookie camp. I downplayed the fumble recovery as no big deal. Tom Landry said it was not necessary so. They liked players to be able to make the big play. This was something to think about. I also learned that Tom Landry had talked to Bill Yeoman, head coach of the University of Houston. He told Coach Landry that I was his best defensive lineman when I was there. Wow! By going to Houston before Hawaii, I had enhanced my chances of getting drafted by the Cowboys. Sometimes the stars line up.

Bob Taucher, a rookie offensive tackle from Nebraska, was my roommate. We hit it off well together. On Wednesday and Saturday nights, we could go out on the town. Players huddled at one club and the coaches at another. I liked going to the Rendezvous restaurant. They had an aquarium behind the bar. It was so relaxing to get away from football. Being a Dallas Cowboys was beginning to add to my sex appeal. A guy's being a cadet was appealing to some women, but being a pro football player seemed to have more appeal. This time I had enough money to buy the drinks. We went to Malibu Beach on Sunday. Malibu was about thirty minutes away. I would sun for an hour and then cover up with towels for the next couple of hours while the tan guys played more volleyball and dipped in the ocean.

We had played three exhibition games, and now it was time for the team to start making rookie cuts. The rookies were told to be in their room in the morning before the next meeting. The assistant coach would call the rookie to report to Coach Landry's room and bring their playbook. It was the dreaded call that they didn't want to receive. Some players would survive the first round and live to play another week. My roommate was on the bubble and dreaded it each week. I had been doing good and didn't think too much about it. Just before leaving training camp for Dallas, the Cowboys cut Larry Stephens. That was a big break for me. Of course, Ernie told me it didn't mean anything; I still hadn't made the team. Having dealt with so many coaches, I was pretty sure I had just made the team. Of course, I couldn't show that.

We broke training camp and headed for Dallas. We would be staying at the Holiday Inn on North Central Expressway (Highway 75) and Mockingbird Lane. None of the coaches would stay there. We were on our own. We just had to survive the final cut in the next two weeks. I remember a lady named Dotti who worked there who was like our housemother for a fraternity. She was all Texas, big blond hair, a charming Texas drawl, and a confident assertiveness. We were her boys. She would make sure we would get what we wanted for breakfast and to orient us with what was around the immediate area and how to get to the practice field five miles north of Forest Lane Drive. Some car dealers were willing to provide us cars temporarily. Since I had left my car with my folks, I had no transportation. Three of us used one of the dealer cars to get around. Their motivation was to get us to buy a new car once the season started and we would be getting a game check weekly.

The first weekend back, we played the Green Bay Packers in an exhibition game. The stadium was sellout for an exhibition game. Boy, this was football country! For me, growing up a Green Bay fan, I found it magical to see the green and gold up close. With the evening lights, the Packers uniforms and helmets shone. During the game, I got to Bart Starr twice with pressure. That was a thrill to me as he was one of my childhood heroes. He had spoken to the cadet wing about a year and half ago after winning the NFL championship.

The next week we got on with practices at the Dallas training facilities. August is especially hot in Dallas. Most of the time, it was at or near one hundred degrees but didn't have the humidity like in Houston. The afternoon practice would start later in the day. We no longer had two-a-days. We would have the morning meeting at the Holiday Inn and go out to the practice field at around 2:00 p.m.

for meetings there before practice. We finished the preseason. Bob Taucher did not make the final cut. I felt sorry for him. He survived to the last cut. He left and would never play football again. He wasn't interested in semipro. Over in New Orleans, my buddy Mike Rengel didn't make the final cut, too, but did make the taxi squad. That fall, he played semipro for a team in Orange County, California. He would make the team the next year.

Seven of us draft choices made the team: Dennis Holman, David McDaniels, Ed Harmon, John Douglas, Blaine Nye, D. D. Lewis—all the first six picks. Then it jumped down to me at sixteen. Now that the season started, these guys would bring their wives to Dallas. Almost all of them were married. If Bob Taucher had made the team, I would have shared an apartment with him. All the others were married. So I had to shop around for an apartment. I didn't want to live alone. I found out that an Air Force Academy classmate who also left the academy had a job at Texas Instruments. He was from Houston and had just graduated from Rice University and had his degree. We leased an apartment three miles from his job and five miles away for me to the practice facility. Most of the time, when I was there, he was working a night shift. The arrangement worked out fine. Once a month he would go to Houston to serve his time in the reserves. I was still assigned by the Air Force Reserve in Hawaii that was filled up.

It was now time to start the season. Since I was getting paid, I didn't mind sitting on the bench for a while. After the first week, Blaine Nye and I went to Fort Worth to buy our Pontiac GTO cars. Mine had a triple carburetor and had hideaway lights. I would get really good acceleration. I also got about nine miles to the gallon. Gas was cheap then, so it wasn't a big thing. We drove our cars down I-30 side by side, with big smiles on our faces. I had a car, had an apartment, and was looking forward to not having the pressure of being a starting player. I would be playing on the specialty teams and would see very little action during the game. In those days, starters played the whole game unless they were injured or the game was a rout. Now that the season had started, I had the evening to myself. I didn't have to go to school and study in the evenings. Most of my training camp friends were cut or were married. George Nordgren and Ken Kmeic were signed to the taxi squad, which meant they could practice but not play in the games. They were single, and I hung out with them a few times. Other than that, I was on my own. Being a Dallas Cowboys was a big deal in a football town like Dallas. I could go to any of the local bars and meet some women. I remember dating this girl that was very nice, but we didn't connect enough to have a relationship. At least that was how I felt. She had a three-year-old son from a previous marriage. When he started calling me Daddy, I cut off that relationship. I didn't want a stepson.

I also dated a nineteen-year-old girl that had a lot of spunk. She was very emotional and comfortable to be with, but not someone I wanted to spend the rest of my life with. I wasn't looking for someone to marry; I just wanted companionship. She kept pressing me to say I loved her. I didn't. She kept asking, "When are we going to get married?" Oh boy! I had to break that one off. It seemed at that time Texas girls would get married by seventeen and divorced by nineteen. I wanted no part of that.

The season started. We blew away Detroit, scoring fifty-nine points. They had a rookie quarterback. The second week, we beat the Cleveland Browns. Jim Brown was retired. Then we beat the Philadelphia Eagles and the St. Louis Cardinals. We were 4–0. Willie Townes got reinjured in the St. Louis game. He had had a nagging injury since training camp of a calcium buildup on his thigh. And so the coaches made a decision to start me against the Philadelphia Eagles in week 5. I was playing against Bob Brown, a veteran all-pro offensive tackle. He weighed somewhere just under three hundred pounds. He established himself with the LA Rams and was now with Philadelphia. I was quite nervous going into the game. This was for real, not an exhibition game. On the first play, I was in the offset position, two and a half feet off the line of scrimmage. I read my keys. The play went to the other side, and I trailed in pursuit. On the next play, the blocking scheme was straight ahead. I took my inside step, then moved my left foot up just as required in the flex defense. I forgot one thing: I didn't stay low and straightened up to see what was happening in the backfield. Bob came after me and literally dropped me on my back, not my ass, but my back! *Welcome to the NFL!* I thought. I was so embarrassed. This was what the guys would laugh about during the film session of the previous game on Monday. This was when my second gear kicked in. I was pissed off and determined that would never happen again. I am usually an easygoing guy, but this wasn't acceptable to my pride. The rest of the game, I was in a zone to be on my toes and alert. I made several tackles and even got a couple of quarterback pressures and traps. After the game, Bob Brown came over to me, shook my hand, and congratulated me. That meant the world to me. Coach Landry and Bob Lilly were interviewed after the game. They said that no one had picked up the flex defense that fast. They said I played a good game. That was satisfying. I received the Unsung Hero Award by Oak Farms Dairy. Jethro Pugh received the Outstanding Player Award. Now I had to do it again next week. So much for my "sabbatical" from playing every game!

The next week, we would be playing the Minnesota Vikings at Bloomington, Minnesota, my home state. We were now 5–0 and the talk of the NFL. This would be the year that the Dallas Cowboys would get over the top and win the NFL championship. The team had lost the last two years at the goal line against the Green Bay Packers in the NFL championship game. My entire family came to the game, including my parents, siblings, aunts and uncles, cousins, and second cousins. Gerald Velde and his family came to the game. The folks back in Granite Falls would be watching the game on television.

The game started. Our offense was led by Don Meredith. He was the league's leading passer. He wasn't putting many points on the board in this game, however. On defense, the Vikings had Jim Marshall, Carl Eller, Alan Page, and Gary Larsen, plus Karl Kassulke and Paul Krause in the secondary. They shut down our offense most of the game. Cornell Green and Mike Gaetcher were effective on blocking the Vikings' field goal attempts and getting turnovers. By the fourth quarter, we were leading, 13–7, with an uneasiness that at any moment Joe Kapp, the scrambling Vikings quarterback, would explode and be able to win the game 14–13. During the fourth quarter, Jethro Pugh and I had a stunt for the pass rush we called "the limbo." At defensive end, I would take one step upfield and Jethro Pugh would drive into the offensive tackle and try to bring his blocking guard with him. I would then circle underneath and scrape off his back and take a direct route to the quarterback before the guard could recover. The stunt worked. I hit Joe Kapp just as he was releasing the ball. The ball fluttered to the sideline. Cornell Green diagnosed the play and intercepted the ball. I heard the roar of the crowd, got up, and peeled back to try to give the downfield block to free the runner to take the interception to the end zone. I thought to myself, *Don't clip!* I was able to knock the pursuing offense tackle off his feet and a tight end in one block. They both fell down. Cornell scored, and this put the game away. I couldn't have written the script better. After the game, I was named the AP Defensive Player of the Week and interviewed on national television after the game. Sometimes dreams do come true. I was covered in the papers all over the country. I know because my mom kept a scrapbook and included news articles from Portland, Green Bay, and Chicago sent by relatives.

We were now 6–0, and the Green Bay Packers, the defending champions, were coming to town. The game was a sellout. The stage was set for the Cowboys to finally beat Green Bay. They weren't the team they were when Vince Lombardi was the coach, but they were seasoned vets. Vince Lombardi was up in the press box this year as general manager. The Packers won 28–17. So much for revenge! We didn't live up to the challenge. But we moved on and beat the New Orleans Saints 17–3.

The following week, we hosted the New York Giants. My parents came in for the game. They were excited to see my new lifestyle. They had never been to Dallas. When I picked them up at the airport, they saw the Oak Hill Farms Billboard with my name in full print. They were impressed. They also wanted to meet my new girlfriend. I had met her at one of Craig Morton's parties. He was this handsome backup quarterback from the University of California, and he would attract a lot of good-looking women to his parties. She was a Braniff Airlines stewardess. She also was a singer, performing at some of the clubs. After games, the team usually got together at the Silver Helmut bar, just across from Love Field. She was very pretty and was very social. Most of the guys were married, so they would bring their wives. I decided to bring Colleen to the club. She was a social butterfly, going from table to table, and I was left to sit there at my table until she got back. I think I got to know the wives, Betty Manders, Diane Gaechter, and Gail Edwards, better than I did her. When we got back to her apartment, she was a more laid-back and comfortable to be with. I guess as a singer you have to be on your game when you perform. Our relationship wasn't that serious, but Mom, being a woman, wanted to meet her. So we went out to dinner. She was a big hit with my mother. The game, though, didn't turn out the way we wanted. Fran Tarkenton was their quarterback. He didn't have a strong arm, but he made up for it with his smarts and scrambling skills. He wore out our defensive lineman, chasing him all over the backfield. We lost the game 27–21.

The next week, we went to Washington to play the Redskins. Sonny Jurgensen was their star quarterback. He wasn't as mobile as he used to be. George Andrie got to him on the pass rush and stripped him of the ball. I picked it up and ran twenty-one yards for a touchdown. I would continue to be in the headlines. This usually didn't happen to a rookie. We easily won 44–24.

The next week, we went to Chicago to play the Bears. We won the game 34–3, and they won the brawl. Gale Sayers was out with an injury, so they didn't have much offense. The benches were cleared. Some players got right in the middle of the fight; others lingered on the sidelines. I was somewhere in between, willing to fight if it got out of hand. Football fights never solve anything, and football players usually are lousy fighters. Don Meredith was comfortably on the sideline, watching the show. That was our "Dandy Don."

The next week, we played the Thursday Thanksgiving game. Sonny Jurgensen was hurt, so Washington played Jim Ninowski at quarterback. Our offense started out with a 17–0 lead. After that, they stumbled. Our defense kept making plays. In the fourth quarter,

Washington took the lead 20–19. When Washington got the ball back, Bob Lilly made the play to set up Mike Clark for an easy field goal. We now led 22–20. This was an uneasy lead. The Redskins started their drive on their own five-yard line on the next series. Ninowski went back to pass, and Jethro Pugh and George Andrie got to Ninowski and smothered him with their six-foot-six frames and reach. The ball fluttered. I had a lousy pass rush going and was initially stopped on the line of scrimmage. Because I was late getting to the passer, the ball fluttered and I caught it. Then I nearly walked into the end zone. This was my second touchdown against the same team. What were the odds of that?

We had such an opportunist defense with playmakers causing turnovers—Bob Lilly, George Andrie, LeRoy Jordan, and Chuck Howley, just to name a few. In the NFL, making big plays is a huge intangible in determining who will decide the outcome.

On December 8, we beat the Pittsburg Steelers 28–7.

THE DALLAS COWBOYS COAST TO THEIR ELEVENTH WIN OF THE SEASON 28 - 7 OVER THE PITTSBURGH STEELERS BEFORE 55,000 IN THE COTTON BOWL DECEMBER 8, 1968.

Bob Lilly and Larry Cole.

I remember after the game, I was watching the sports news on one of the local stations. The reporter interviewed Johnny Unitas. After that win, it was determined that the Cowboys would play the Cleveland Browns in the first round. Cleveland didn't have the services of Jim Brown anymore as he had retired, but they did have LeRoy Kelley. He had sat behind Jim Brown for two years, observing how he would run using his balance and toughness. Johnny Unitas predicted that Cleveland would win without any hesitation. What? We were now 11–2, with one game to go. How could he predict that?

The next week, we went to New York City. We stayed downtown. Tom Landry liked this trip because he had played his football career with New York. I went to the Toots Shor bar. This was a famous hangout. Sportswriters were there. Players from both the Giants and Jets hung out there. There was a lot of conversation going on. A number of guys were caught out after curfew. It was easy to forget time in NYC. Even though the focus didn't seem to be there, we won the game. The Giants were no longer in the playoff race, so they didn't play with a lot of passion. We won 28–10. On the trip home, we took off from LaGuardia Airport. It was a wintry day. We had a delay in leaving. We had to deice the wings. We then took off and suddenly started dropping to a couple hundred feet over a neighborhood of homes. I looked out the window and was apprehensive as we were dropping slowly toward the rooftops of the houses. Blaine Nye was my seatmate. He was reading a book and didn't want to be bothered by this event. Dave Manders was turning red in the face with panic. Don Meredith walked down the aisle with a scotch in hand and said, "Well, it's been a goodin'." The ice finally dropped off the wing and we were headed home. We were 12–2 on the way to the playoffs.

Meanwhile, back at the apartment, I hadn't learned how to cook, nor did I want to. I could make sandwiches, but that got old. I ate almost all my meals at IHOP, about a mile down the road. I liked not living in a dorm, but living alone could get boring. At that time, I didn't read much, so I spent most of my time watching television. I remember turning on my record player and listening to Don Ho's album. "Tiny bubbles in the wine make me happy, make me feel fine. Tiny bubbles make me warm all over with a feeling that I'm going to love you until the end of time." I was missing Honolulu. It was such a laid-back place. The people were very friendly and kind. Most spoke with a clear accent. It was hard to understand some of the teachers at times, but they were still very thoughtful teachers.

I also started watching AFL football. At that time, the NFL was considered the superior league by far. They were more physical and could run the ball. The AFL concentrated more on the passing game. I would watch the San Diego Chargers, the Oakland Raiders, the Kansas City Chiefs, and the New York Jets. The Chargers had John Hadl and Lance Alworth. The Raiders had Darryl Lemonica. The Chiefs had Lenny Dawson. And the Jets had Joe Namath. I watched the Heidi Game live. Suddenly, before the game was over, the network switched to the start of the movie *Heidi*. I had to wait until the sports news later to find out who won.

I continued to date Colleen every other week. I told her I would be going back to Minnesota to finish college after the season. We were sort of breaking it off. I invited her to come to Minneapolis to see me after I got settled. She didn't really answer my invitation. I figured I would be out of sight, out of mind.

We were now heading to Cleveland for our first playoff game. The odds were in our favor to win this game. I had watched the Browns play in the early sixties, and Jim Brown was my favorite running back. Cleveland had won the NFL championship in 1964. I expected the facilities to be state of the art. But that wasn't the case. They had a crowded locker room with a baseball field converted in the fall to football. In Cleveland, it rains a lot in the fall. The field conditions were challenging with trying to maintain grass, but instead, the field turned into mud by the end of the season. The game began, and it was close in the first half. The halftime score was 10–10. In the second half, LeRoy Kelley exploded on a couple of long plays and scored fourteen points. Our offense committed four fumbles. They turned it over twice, but on defense Chuck Howley intercepted a pass and took it in for a touchdown. On one of LeRoy Kelly's runs, I missed my assignment on a cutback run. This was a rookie mistake that was burned into my memory. LeRoy took it in for a fifty-three-yard touchdown. He gained eighty-seven yards that game. Don Meredith was relieved by Craig Morton. He didn't do much better. We lost the game 31–20.

Just like that, the season was over. We were in shock. Don Meredith got on a plane to New York and didn't go back with the team. He was done with the Dallas Cowboys. I am sure he was angry about being benched. Tom Landry just couldn't make up his mind on who to start. The fans were split fifty-fifty also.

We got back to Dallas. I packed up my things and headed out for Minnesota. I had this Cinderella season coming in as a sixteenth-round draft choice to an NFL celebrity in three months. I finished the season as the runner-up Defensive Rookie of the Year. Claude Humphrey got seventeen votes, while I got fourteen. Now I needed to concentrate on my studies.

I would be enrolling at the University of Minnesota for the winter and spring quarter. If I had stayed in Dallas or Fort Worth, it would have taken me three off-seasons to graduate because both TCU and SMU were on semesters. One consolation was that I would be able to come home for Christmas, unlike last year, when I was in Honolulu. My older brother and sister were starting to have babies, so I could spend time as Uncle Larry. I had always enjoyed kids. It was a two-day trip to Minnesota, so I stopped at my older sister's house on the way. Then I drove the balance of the trip to Minneapolis. I registered at the university just before Christmas and then prepared to fly to Miami for the playoff bowl. This was the consolation prize at that time. None of us wanted to play this game. I got on a plane with a number of Minnesota Vikings. They had a different take on the game. Bud Grant was their second-year coach. They finished the season with a loss to the Rams. They had a more positive image of the game. They wanted to build off this game in order to propel them to the Super Bowl next year. We arrived at the hotel in Miami and immediately went to the bar to drink until we were drunk and overbloated for three days. The weather was nice, but that was about it. Tom Landry introduced me to Vince Lombardi at the bar. They both coached for the New York Giants together. They had a good-spirited rivalry. Vince liked to get under Tom's skin, but they both respected each other, like a lot of my friends. We lost the game, didn't care, and flew back to Minnesota.

I had the enrollment done. Then I needed to find an apartment near campus. I found a furnished apartment owned by some professor that would be gone that winter and spring. I was getting used to living alone and liked it. On the first day of school, I had to go outside to warm up my car before I could drive it. It had been five years since I experienced a Minnesota winter. The location where I was allowed to park on campus was nine blocks away from my classroom buildings. Some mornings I was so cold I would sit in the first class and forget what was said in the first fifteen minutes while I thawed out. One day, I drove over the Mendota Bridge and encountered some ice. Oops, I forgot all about the ice lower layer and got in a car accident! I needed to take it to the shop, my brand-new Pontiac GTO. In those days, when they fixed them, it was never the same. But I got it fixed anyway and moved on.

I started my first classes and found them interesting. I was getting back into student mode. Football was behind me. I didn't know if my first year was just a fluke or if I would be playing any longer. Either way, I wanted my civil engineering diploma. I applied myself. I liked the teachers, who were so helpful in spending extra time with their students. They encouraged us to study together, unlike in the Air Force Academy. They didn't keep the tests the same, so there was no temptation for anyone to take shortcuts. I was also beginning to take specific civil engineering courses, like soil engineering, hydrology, and sanitary engineering. On a hydrology project, I did my paper on the rivers in Texas. I was beginning to understand the big picture. There was a course in nuclear physics too that was kind of difficult for me. If I couldn't see it, I didn't visualize it. In any event, I was back to getting As and Bs in the other courses.

The first week in January, my buddies at Gustavus Adolphus College in St. Peter, Minnesota, wanted me to come down there, about one hour and fifteen minutes away. Tom (Tork) Thorkelson, my high school best friend, and his wife, Roni, lined me up with Linda Kleinert, the 1966 Aquatennial Queen of the Lakes in Minnesota, on a blind date. Roni knew her from also being in a sorority. I was acquainted with that contest as Pat Wilson from Granite Falls had the title in 1958. This was a blind date. They told Linda that I was a Dallas Cowboys. She thought I was some kind of rodeo guy. She had gone to hockey and basketball games at Minneapolis North High School, but not football. There was a fraternity party in New Ulm that evening. When I went to pick her up, she came down the stairs and it was love at first sight. I hadn't experienced where two people just became bonded in their personalities immediately. I was fickle. I wanted a good-looking woman who didn't have blond hair and blue or hazel eyes like all my relatives. She had dark-brown hair and dark eyes. When I saw her, I just wanted to be with her. We couldn't get enough of getting to know each other. She had experienced celebrity herself as she traveled over fifty thousand miles around the country from Canada to Los Angeles to Tampa Bay and other cities. She took off a year from school to do this. We both didn't want to become phonies. We both were brought up in Christian homes and vowed to stay that way. In the past three years, I hadn't found anyone to share my values with. On top of that, she had charisma and was fun to be around. She had a witty sense of humor, as did Tork. It was a double date. We were in the back seat on the way home. This was the first time I kissed her. I couldn't stop wanting to kiss and hug her. We dropped her off at her dormitory and went back to Tork's house for me to spend the night. The next day was the Super Bowl, with the Baltimore Colts playing the New York Jets. Joe Namath guaranteed they would win, and they did. This was a huge moment for the NFL and its future legitimizing the AFL and the final merger two years later.

I drove back to St. Paul with a good memory of Linda. I wanted to see her again. I was so comfortable with her, and she was genuinely interested in what I had to say. I was looking forward to seeing her again. I got back to my work in school and absorbed myself in homework all week. Mike Rengel, my AFA and Hawaii buddy, was also enrolled at the university for the same degree. We weren't in many of the same classes, but we both decided to play intramural basketball. We were joined by Eddie Brusch. He was one of the good quarterbacks we had in our freshman year at the AFA. He left, after just one year at the academy, to play baseball in the minor leagues. We also had another guy that had played for an NFL team that year. Our team was all about rebounding and playing physical. We had a good team. When it was time for the playoffs, we got blown away by a team that had speed. Our egos were checked.

At the apartment, there were no restaurants nearby, so I tried to cook for myself. I took some raw chicken and tried to burn it in a frying pan. I learned that didn't work at lower temperatures. I also had a corner of the room where I would throw my beer cans until I would gather enough. I would then pick them up to put them into the garbage can. That seemed more efficient. I didn't watch much television because I was studying. There was a bar a few blocks away that I would go to for a beer before bedtime, like I did at the Blue Goose in Honolulu. That was my social life away from Gustavus Adolphus College. There was a concert that weekend featuring Burl Ives. I thought that would be interesting, and it was. We then went to the Flame Bar, the campus hangout. I met some of her guy and girl friends there. They were fun like her. On Sunday, we would go to the park and have a little picnic. By three o'clock in the afternoon, I had to start thinking about heading back for another week of school. I hated to leave and get back to reality. I had homework to do.

The following week, on January 16, the city of Granite Falls was planning a Larry Cole Day. They placed a banner above the train trestle that stated, "Welcome, Larry Cole!" I addressed the student body, and then the Kiwanis Club put on a luncheon at the Crown Dining Room, where they showed some of the highlight clips of the first year. The master of ceremonies was Dr. Odland, whose daughter Cindy was a classmate of mine and was a princess when Linda was queen. I spoke for about twenty minutes and then let them ask questions. It was an all-day affair. I was very honored for what all Granite Falls did for me.

Later in the spring, I agreed to go to the father-son breakfast at the Lutheran church I had attended and to a similar event at my uncle Harold's hometown of New London. I was beginning to sign a lot of autographs. During the season, Bob Lilly asked me if I wanted to join the other front four guys to sign autographs. I said sure. Anything for Bob, as he was my main mentor. He then said I would get $200 to do this. Well, wasn't that nice, getting paid to sign my name!

The next weekend, Linda came to Minneapolis to see her folks. Her dad was a Lutheran minister. I was also Lutheran, so there were no conflicts to work out there. My "damsel in distress" couldn't get into her car, and she called me to help her out. The keyhole was frozen shut, so I got some deice spray and went to where her car was parked. The deicer melted away the ice, and the door opened. She was so impressed. She had a man to take care of her. And I have been taking care of her ever since.

She told me that she was going to have to make a decision on where she would do her interviews and get her first permanent teaching job the coming fall. She asked me what I thought. I told her I didn't want her to do that. Why? she asked. Then I said, "Because I want you to move to Texas." She said she couldn't just go to Texas to work; she would have to get certified in Texas first. That wasn't feasible. Then what? I told her that I wanted to marry her. She got so excited. She had maneuvered me into making a decision. Oh boy! Was I ready for this? Well, actually, I was, but I didn't know it at that time. Most of my teammates were married back in Dallas. I was sick of dating meaningless relationships, and I didn't want to let this one get away and go back to Dallas and start all over again with dating. I was ready to settle down. My siblings were all married, and I wanted to get caught up in having children so the cousins could all be in the same age bracket.

I began preparations to get a diamond ring. After that fiasco in Daytona Beach, Florida, I was more careful on getting quality. She said before she would marry me, I needed to ask her dad for his permission to marry her. He was a very traditional man. I wondered what that would be like. Her parents had moved to Ottumwa, Iowa, where he had a new congregation. They wanted Linda to go to Ottumwa and see their new home. She asked if she could bring a "friend." They said sure. Linda didn't give any details. She drove to their new place in Ottumwa prior to my arriving there. Her dad asked her what her friend's name was. She said his name was Larry. He looked at her a little puzzled. She then told her mom more about me. Her mother was always the gracious host. She was concerned about what she could feed me so that I would like it. Linda told her meat and potatoes. That weekend came. I was nervous about this one. When I got there, we ate first. Her mom was an excellent cook, and the meal was great. I appreciated the effort she went to. It was mostly small talk. It was mostly strained. They wanted to really know what was going on between us. Linda took her mom into the kitchen and told her that I had asked her to marry me. I think I made a good first impression. Now it was time for me to talk to her dad alone. Linda and her mom were waiting anxiously in the kitchen. I then met with him in the living room. I told him I wanted to marry his daughter and I would like his permission. He asked me if I loved her. I said yes. He then asked me if I was a Christian. I said yes. I had been a Christian all my life. He then gave me his approval. The tension was over. Linda was so relieved. Her brother had eloped a couple of years before, so they didn't want that to happen again. I thought on the way back how hard that must have been for him. Now he had put a lot of trust in me, and I vowed to not let him down.

I drove back to my apartment in St. Paul. It was time for another week of school. I got on with my studies. She would graduate in a couple of months. I drove to St. Peter the next weekend and gave her the diamond ring. There were many hills there, but no pretty places where I would give her the ring. I decided to present her with the ring in a cemetery that was surrounded by pine trees. It was the prettiest place on top of the hill in St. Peter. I got ribbed for that by the guys, however. But she was thrilled, and so it all began. The next week, I got a call from Colleen. She was now ready to come see me in St. Paul. I shuddered with this one. I figured she had lost interest in me, so I didn't get my hopes up. I quickly pondered having them compete for me. If that happened, more than likely, I would lose both. I was a big boy and told her the truth. Surprisingly, she wasn't that disappointed. Our relationship never got close enough, anyway, to the relationship I had already made with Linda.

It was now time to take Linda to meet my folks. I told them I was going to marry her, and they weren't so sure about that. They had never met her before. When we arrived in Granite Falls, we walked into the house and Mom had an eight-by-ten photo of Colleen on the tagboard. It was what she signed when she made appearances singing at nightclubs. I didn't realize she had signed one for my mom. Oh crap! That didn't sit too well with Linda. I must have given Mom the wrong impression of how serious I was about marrying Linda. And while Dad liked Linda right away, it took time for Mom to warm up to her. Dad borrowed a snowmobile from one of my cousins, which I drove, and I tipped over Linda onto Mom. I thought, *Oh no!* Instead, that lightened us up. *Welcome to the family!* Oh well, we all laughed about it.

In the meantime, the Cowboys informed me that they would fly me into Dallas to start the off-season training program. Football was out of sight, out of mind. I didn't have time to think too much about that. I enjoyed being an ordinary student. I didn't tell anyone that I was a pro football player. In the engineering department, most students weren't sports fans, anyway. I flew to Dallas and noticed how nice the weather was in March. I was starting to look forward to getting back to Dallas. The coaches reviewed how I graded out for the year and told me what I needed to work on. It was good to see the guys. I told them I was getting married. They weren't that surprised. A lot was going on fast in my life.

It was now time for the ladies to plan the wedding. Linda's mom wanted a formal, candlelight ceremony. Her dad had married off many people, and now he would be able to marry off his daughter. It was decided that my parents would drive to Ottumwa to meet Linda's parents on Easter weekend. I picked up Linda at St. Peter and drove to Ottumwa. They had now moved into their own house instead of the parsonage. We sat through some of the meetings. I dozed off. After a while, it got uncomfortable sitting in with both sets of parents, talking about yourself. We got away for a cup of coffee and later found the only bar in town. It was late when we got home. Of course, her dad thought it would be good to get up for the sunrise service at 6:00 a.m.

We finished out the spring. I finished my second quarter of classes in late May. I had one more quarter left to graduate. I moved in with my brother and his family in Bloomington ahead of the end of the lease. The landlord wanted to move back home earlier than expected. That was fine with me. Being engaged to someone ninety miles away and living alone was kind of boring. Linda was ready to graduate, and her parents and my parents came to see her graduate. She received a degree in elementary education. The next step was the wedding. The wedding was set to be on June 21. My old high school, Air Force Academy, and Hawaii friends wanted to come to the wedding. It was kind of a minireunion. The guys came from Hawaii, Wyoming, California, New York, Illinois, Minnesota, and Iowa. My family, including cousins, came from nearby cities. At the age of twenty-one, everyone was so full of energy. They took over the motel swimming pool and had diving competitions. We found the only bar in town and started having our bachelor party. After rehearsal, Linda's dad invited the guys to come over for punch. Tork snickered at that one. They had other ideas. Linda had the girls over to their house. They decided they wanted to go out for the bride's party. It was supposed to be bad luck for the groom to see the bride the night before the wedding. The girls wanted to party too. They dropped in at where the guys were. It turned out that this was the only bar in town. I tried to avoid seeing Linda. The guys got me lit. We then went back to the motel, where the party continued. No one wanted to go to sleep. We partied until four o'clock in the morning. Mike Rengel was one of my groomsmen. He offered to shine my shoes for me. I thought that was a nice gesture. I gave him the shoes and went to bed.

We needed to get up in the morning for a formal brunch. I had about two hours of sleep. All my family was there with my in-laws, and their children. It was a nice setting. My brother was best man. He spoke for a few minutes, which set up a lot of teasing of me. I was used to it and expected it. The culture we grew up with was a lot of clan, a lot of laughter, and among friends, a lot of teasing. We tested one another.

I went back to the room to rest, but I didn't get much sleep. I was then getting apprehensive about the wedding. Did I really want to do this? This was normal butterflies. The evening started. It was a beautiful, candlelight service with flowers and candles at the end of the aisles. When Linda started walking down the aisle, I was ready to be married. She looked beautiful. My buddies were either grooms-men or ushers. My relatives enjoyed meeting these guys. They were fun and respectful. Linda's dad started the ceremony. When it was time to kneel for communion, the audience saw that at the bottom of my shoes it said "HE" on one shoe and "LP" on the other shoe. I heard a little laughter from the guests but didn't think anything about it. When Linda and I walked down the aisle after saying our vows, she told me to look at the bottom of my shoes. Oh dear! Her dad had said that wouldn't happen at any of his weddings, yet it happened at his own daughter's wedding. Most people were amused by this, though. It was over. Mike did a "Gotcha!" Once the shock was over, it just seemed appropriate with all these guys around. There were at least ten of them. Linda and I went to the reception and cut the cake.

Wedding cake.

After that, they took pictures at the altar. Then the photographer wanted a picture of all the guys together at the church door, forcing me to not back out of getting married.

The guys at the wedding. Notice the bottom of the shoes, with Al
Burchett covering part of the *LP* on my right foot. The guys, from
left to right, are Bruce Haugland, Al Burchett, Charlie Bensley,
Tom Thorkelson, Larry Cole, Ralph Kaspari, Mike Rengel,
Scotty Hughes, Carl Hite, Jim Schultz, and Eli Bebout.

It was then time to drive off. Our tradition was to drag cans
behind the car and use soap to decorate the car. Then everyone
would follow. Since this was a night wedding, most of the guys had
gone back to get into their comfortable clothes. We drove the street
without anyone following us and then headed out to Des Moines. It
would take us about an hour and a half. We got there. Drinks were
in place. The room was cold. We went to bed, fell asleep in fifteen
minutes, and woke up about eight hours later. We then drove to the
airport in Minneapolis–St. Paul. We got on a plane to San Francisco
on our way to our honeymoon in Hawaii. I wanted to show Linda
San Francisco since she hadn't been there. We went to a show and
met Pat Paulsen. He was a very good impressionist. There were sex
clubs too. That wasn't me, but she had been so sheltered I wanted her
to see what was happening in our country.

The next morning, we arrived in Honolulu. We checked into our hotel. It was right on the beach. We got a good price. After a few hours, we realized why we got a good price. They were building a new hotel next door, and they were using a pile driver to install the piles for the foundation. There would be oil droplets on us from the hydraulic pumps when we went to the beach. We decided that was it. We got out of paying for the rest of the week and checked into a new hotel. We then got on with our honeymoon. I showed Linda the campus and where I went to school. We took in all the Honolulu sights, the bird and wildlife sanctuary, and the Don Ho Show. Don was usually "spirited" by the end of the evening. He liked to kiss all the girls. He even French-kissed Linda. It was one of those "oh my!" moments. She was a good sport, though, and didn't ruin the evening. It was a beautiful show. We then flew to Maui and discovered that island. We rented a convertible and sought out to drive around the entire island. On the map, nineteen miles didn't look like much, but with curving single-lane roads, it took a long time. I was burnt red like a lobster. Off the coast was where Amelia Earhart crashed her plane. We then drove to their famous crater and looked down. We weren't campers who walked down to the bottom. The view was enough. And that was quite a sight!

We then moved on to Kauai. That was the most beautiful place I had ever seen. The back part of the island had a valley with clouds below sweeping into the ocean. Hollywood used this site for many movies. You could see the clouds within the steep mountains.

We had a two-story motel on the beach. That was so nice to not be in a high-rise hotel. We could walk out to the beach from our room. We finished the trip, took movies with my Super 8 camera, and preserved the memories. It was time to pack up, go home, and head out for our life together in Dallas.

We rented a U-Haul trailer. Linda had a lot of stuff, as most women do. Our mothers cleaned out their houses for items we would need to set up in our new home. I think they also just wanted to get rid of stuff. We picked up the trailer in Granite Falls and headed for Dallas. Once we got to Oklahoma, we traveled through the hills in the southern portion. The hills were steep for a freeway. As we drove downhill, suddenly the trailer hitch started swinging back and forth. It was getting hard to control the car. I slowed down and was able to stop the car and the trailer without any more damage. A trucker stopped to give us assistance. He said the load was stacked too heavy in the front. We rearranged the weight and got the hitch reconnected. The bumper was damaged, but still functional. We got back on our way with a maximum of caution, but we made it to Dallas. We rented a furnished apartment in the same building I lived at with Eddie Hamel the previous year. I emptied the trailer and turned it in, and we were under the roof of our first home. I was off to training camp at Thousand Oaks, California. Linda bought a plant to sit next to the television set, watched Channel 8 movies at night, and slept on the coach. I was off to Thousand Oaks.

In a little over two years, I had gone from a single twenty-year-old guy fresh out of the military, going from Colorado to Chicago to Houston to Honolulu to Dallas to St. Paul, and back up to Dallas. I was now just one-quarter away from graduation. I could either go to work as an EIT (engineer in training) or play professional football. My mother had stressed to me that football was a means to an end, not the end. A lot had changed for the better. I was blessed in all the good that was happening to me. Prayers were answered.

CHAPTER 6

IN PURSUIT OF A NEW LIFE

I was off to Thousand Oaks, California, for my second training camp. In the off-season, Steve Perkins, a local sportswriter, wrote a book entitled *Next Year's Champions*. That was all we needed. Even more pressure to win the championship. Tex Schramm was quite angry with Steve. What he said in the book was mostly true, in that this team just didn't get focused enough to know how to win in the playoffs.

I was going back as a starter for the Dallas Cowboys. The previous year seemed like some kind of mirage. How could I experience so many good things that happened to me? I then started sorting it out. Willie Townes was back in camp and would be competing against me in order to get his job back. They also drafted Halvor Hagen from Weber State in the third round. When you get drafted that high, you usually get two or three years to make the starting lineup or you are gone. I knew I would need to compete. Willie was a pleasant guy who tended to overeat, so he had to work hard to hold down his weight. He got teased a lot about his weight. He worked hard in the off-season to recover from his injury, and he had lost weight. He played in the preseason. He just couldn't completely straighten his leg, so he wasn't at 100 percent. He also had some calcium buildup in his thigh. He opted to have surgery at the end of training camp so he would be out for the full year.

Players and coaches told me about the sophomore jinx. When you were a rookie, you had so much emotional energy that carried you to keep moving as a rookie. The opposition teams now had you on film and could plan for how to attack your strength and exploit your weaknesses. Now this was a job. I needed to get better at my technique of keeping my shoulders down. I would get blown back at times when I didn't take on the block shoulder to shoulder. I came up too high. One of the strengths most of my coaches recited that I had was that I had a "nose for the ball." I took pride in quick recognition and my natural curiosity of looking to see what was going on for that play. I also needed the discipline to work on my steps. They needed to be shorter and choppier. Bob Lilly demonstrated that to me many times. I also watched George Andrie as he played the same position on the other side. Most teams were right-handed, so the strong side was usually to my side, along with Jethro Pugh and Dave Edwards. Dave was a strong, alert player who could stand up any blocking tight end. He and I had stunts to do. We called it the Tango. If I got blocked by a double team from the tackle and tight end, he would shove the tight end off my block and I would scrape off his block or spin out to make the tackle or drive the runner outside for the free safety to make the tackle. Jethro Pugh had such an unusual tackle build. He had long legs and arms; hence, he could cover so much ground in getting into the backfield and staying strong enough to take blocks head-on. He was a very thoughtful guy who always supported me when I had questions, and together we made lots of play.

He had a teaching degree.

That figures.

I still needed to work on my stance and pass-rushing technique. I watched Deacon Jones of the LA Rams do the head-slap move. He originated it. The key was to be quick off the ball and drive upfield to a point before the offensive tackle got there. While he did that, he would just slap the tackle on the helmet, not hard, just enough to get him to move his hands up. Then he would drive under his arms to make a tight drive to the quarterback. I would later learn a "swim move," where I would try to drive him upfield too far, and then I would push my right arm against him and reverse shoulder from outside to the inside. Ralph Neeley worked with me on this in practice as he was the one who actually lined up against Deacon Jones in games.

I watched Halvor Hagan try to learn the flex defense. It was a lot harder than he expected. Being a starter in my rookie year gave me the experience from playing and observing Bob Lilly, Jethro Pugh, and George Andrie perform the techniques. I started to think back on the previous season. We as a team had fifty-one quarterback sacks and scored off turnovers and recovered fumbles. My teammates were in their prime, and I was just getting started.

One thing we did in practice was running the ropes. It was like hopscotch with ropes. There were about twenty squares of rope openings about eighteen by eighteen inches. We would do them one step in each hole and then cross over, alternating at a diagonal, to test our agility. Bob Lilly was a master at this. It was a drill to get used to a lineman hitting you low, but keep your balance so you don't get knocked off your feet. I eventually got pretty good at this myself.

On the team we would no longer have "Dandy Don" Meredith and Don Perkins. For the past three years, the fans would either boo Don Meredith or Craig Morton. Don was a very charismatic guy. Coach Landry didn't think he took his job serious enough, though, because he was usually in a happy mood. Now it was time for Craig to make his move. He had a great arm and was good at reading defenses. The offense line had a number of people retire because of knee injuries. If Craig could stay healthy, it was his time to shine. Don Perkins was an outstanding running back. He would gain yards on his own. He would get the tough yards. He was undersized and took a beating. He retired after eight years and made the ring of honor in its inaugural year.

We had some new faces. In the off-season, the Cowboys traded for Mike Ditka, who was then at Philadelphia, formerly of the Chicago Bears. He brought a lot of personality to the team and pass-catching ability at the tight end position. Pettis Norman would remain the main tight end blocker, but Mike would be valuable as a pass catcher. Calvin Hill was our number 1 draft choice from Yale. We all said, "Who?" We had never heard of him. In a thirty-two-degree rainy day in August at Kezar Stadium in San Francisco, he made his debut. He rushed for nearly two hundred yards that day. We had our new running back. Walt Garrison would take over the fullback position from Don Perkins. He was tough as a goat. He was a real cowboy who looked and acted the part. His sense of humor kept many of us going now that Don Meredith wasn't around.

In late July, one of the most amazing days of my life happened. We watched the landing on the moon. The coaches canceled the morning meetings so we could witness history. I was so thankful for them to do that. Since I was a science buff it meant a lot to me. Also my favorite President, John Kennedy, had promised in his inaugural speech that we would land a man on the moon by the end of the decade. This was six months before the expiration of that promise. At that time, it was unheard of for anyone to actually land on the moon and beam back pictures of this actually happening. There was a lot of drama with play-by-play description, of the landing. They reported that the landing was successful. We didn't know if we should believe that or not. Then the first picture showed on the screen of the actual landing vehicle. Then Neil Armstrong came out of the vehicle and walked down the steps and took his first step on the moon. We didn't know if his feet would sink into the crust of the moon. They didn't. We all had our mouths wide open. He then said, "This is one step for man. One giant leap for mankind" It sure was. So our country was the first to put a man on the moon. Now, how about getting him back home? Since there was very little gravity on the moon, it didn't take too much power to lift off and rejoin the mother ship that was in orbit around the moon and then take off to get back to Earth orbit. They landed in a capsule with a parachute in the Atlantic Ocean. This was quite a sight to see! We didn't know if they were still alive as communication on re-entry was not possible. They landed and were in excellent shape, but could not walk immediately.

Meanwhile, back at the apartment in Dallas was my new wife. The first couple of weeks were tough with the two-a-days, leaving us not much time to rest and think. I called her to find out how she was doing, but it was not the same as being together. She said she was fine. She didn't complain, though, except that she had burned her legs on the chrome steering wheel. She had never lived in a place where it was over one hundred degrees; most of the days in late July

LIVING THE DREAM ON AMERICA'S TEAM

and early August. Here she was in a city she had never been to. Alone and not knowing anyone. Some of the wives made contact with her, but most of the time it was her, the television, and the plant. She did go to visit my last year's roommate, Eddie Hamel, who lived in the same apartment complex. I arranged to fly her out to California so we could have a little time together. It was great to see her. We could spend late Saturday afternoon and evening together and Sunday during the day. Then it was back to my routine. She went back home and looked forward to me coming home permanently in the next two weeks.

After the San Francisco game we broke training camp with the hope that this would be our year. Now we had another weapon with Calvin Hill's debut.

We broke training camp, and now I had someone to go home to. D. D. Lewis, my rookie teammate would have to report to the Army for four months because of the draft. I was still in the inactive reserves and re-assigned to Denver, Colorado. Thank God for that. We still were in training camp and had meetings morning and afternoon followed by practice. In late August the temperature is still around one hundred degrees so sometimes the afternoon practice was delayed until the evening because of the heat. There wasn't much time to wind down and start the day all over. We rented a furnished apartment. We had a standard size bed. I was not used to sleeping with another person in bed since I was a kid with my brother. When I rolled over, my arm would hit Linda on her forehead. I thought ouch for her! She was such a sound sleeper she didn't feel a thing. She woke up with a bruise on her forehead. We decided to get a king size bed. That did the trick. When I got back from training camp I was contacted by Ben and Marilyn Gunnarson. My mom had given her our phone number. Marilyn was from Granite Falls. Her cousins were friends of all of my siblings. She took Linda under her wing and helped her adjust to the Dallas lifestyle. Linda also got to be friends with Marcy East, Ron's wife, Margaret Lewis, D. D. Lewis's wife and Annabelle Nye, Blaine's wife. Marlene Tubbs, wife of Jerry Tubbs, a former player and current linebacker coach, hosted a wedding shower for her. This is when she got introduced to the wives club that played bridge and did other things. It is quite unique for all these attractive women to take a second seat to their husbands. The fans would usually just ignore them to get to speak or get an autograph from one of the players. Since Linda was a celebrity herself, she understand that some people put you on a pedestal. She was the Aquatennial Queen of the Lakes for the State of Minnesota in 1966. Other wives were homecoming queens. Yes, it's true. Most of us guys married up. She also had a hobby, needle point pottery. She made many creative things.

The second to the last Pre-Season Game was against the World Champion New York Jets. The press asked Joe Namath if he thought our front four were the best in the game. He said no. We weren't that good. That riled up the fans. The veteran guys wanted to show that the Jets winning the Super Bowl was just a fluke. I didn't think it was. The preseason game was a sellout with over seventy-two thousand fans. When the game started Joe Namath came out of the locker room in his dress clothes. He was booed extensively! I actually chuckled at that. He was showing he was quite the entertainer. We were ready to crush him and he didn't give us a chance.

I heard from the University of Minnesota. They said I would have to repeat English Literature because I had passed English with only a D from the AFA.

I decided that I would do this in the fall by correspondence. I could study this at nights. I tried to concentrate on some mythical figures and what their words really meant. Are you kidding me? I am studying to be an engineer, not an English Teacher. I couldn't concentrate with all the things going on in my life. I got a call from Sid Hartman, the legendary sport writer from the MPLS Star & Tribune to discuss the upcoming game against the Vikings. He wanted to know how he could get in touch with a few players. I gave him their phone numbers as he had always publicized me when I was growing up. I then told him about my dilemma. He said he would talk to the university president, Malcolm Moose. He did. He called back and said he got it approved that I wouldn't have to take this class. I was forever grateful to Sid for doing this for me.

The season started. Craig Morton was out for the first game. This was Roger Staubach's debut. He would drop back. He would miss wide open receivers or didn't see them. He would usually just resort to scrambling. He ran all over the field and picked up first downs. Coach Landry didn't like quarterbacks to scramble. Pro quarterbacks were supposed to be pocket passers. Roger wore down the defensive lineman in this hot, humid September afternoon. We beat the St. Louis Cardinals. Craig was back. We won the next three games against the Saints, Falcons and Eagles. The Eagles were coming to town for their second game against us. My Sister, Marlene and family, came to Dallas along with our parents. Marlene & Jim's daughter, Sharon was with them. She was three. Her younger sister, Mary, was also at the game. She was seven weeks old, maybe the youngest fan at the game. I remember cooking steaks on my small second floor patio. Having eight people in that little apartment was quite confining. It was a hot day. We won. I did nothing special, but was plenty sore after the game. My newlywed bride tried to rub my neck to help me relax. She couldn't quite do it hard enough to relax my muscles. My mother said, "Let me do it" She was a nurse and knew more about it. Linda was upset, but didn't say anything. It was her job to take care of me, not my mother. This was one of those mother-in-law moments for my wife. I understand the feelings of both of them. Welcome to married life!

It was nice coming home to someone. I didn't need to go out to eat and I didn't need to go out to have some female companionship. She seemed content enough, but she wanted a dog. She couldn't have one growing up because her brother had severe allergies. I agreed to get the dog. I hadn't had a dog since I was twelve years old. We got a collie/sheltie. We named him the same name as my childhood dog, Snooky. She was a puppy and needed training. That was a big job without a doggy door. Linda was very happy to have a companion when I was not around. There was just one big problem. Our Landlord Lady let us know that pets were not allowed at the apartment. We said we would pay a pet deposit and pay for any damage. That was still not acceptable. She was firm. So we did the smart thing. We bought a new house! Now who does that for a dog. We were looking forward to buying a house. We decided we would do that after I got my diploma. This speeded up the time frame. We found that with my salary we could afford to spend $39,500 for a brand-new house. The interest rate was 9.5 percent. Our payment was $329 per month. We moved in at the end of October. We installed a doggie door. It still took time to keep Snooky from barking all night. She wanted to sleep with us. We finally gave in to let her sleep with us. She then used the doggie door. She was a very smart dog and so loyal to Linda. We rented furniture to have the basics. We then went to Sears to buy things a little at a time. It seemed like we went there every Saturday. The kitchen had a tight carpet floor covering, a really dumb idea, which was catching on. I remember dropping a prime rib on the floor. We could never get that spot out. Linda started putting together the pictures and making our house a home. It was nice to have our place how we wanted it to be. I now had a backyard instead of an upstairs balcony.

Front Four

Meanwhile, back to my job, we played Fran Tarkenton and the New York Giants on October 27. This time we were ready for him. I was beginning to establish myself as more than a lucky rookie. We defensive linemen chased Fran all afternoon, but this time we put him down for big losses. I was credited with two traps. After the game, Fran said he thought this Dallas defense was the best he had seen. We were gelling together. I was catching up with the others, so we were strong at all four positions. To play the flex defense, you had to be smart, make a quick reaction to reading the play, and have the discipline to do your job first before you pursue. Not all players could do that. One player comes to mind. Coy Bacon was a good defensive tackle but just couldn't execute this defense. He was traded to the Rams and had a nice career. We were now 6–0. We were headed back to Cleveland to get revenge for their beating us last year in the playoffs. We were confident. But instead, we got burned again. Bill Nelson, their quarterback, seemed to have his best game against us. We were strong up front on the run and the pass on first and second downs. Then Bill would convert on third down. Our secondary had holes. Cleveland won 42–10. Their coach, Blanton Collier, had our number.

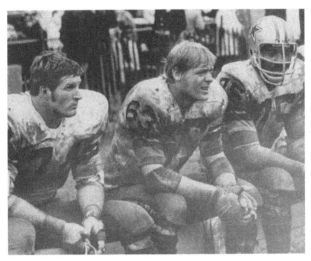

Mud.

The next week, we beat Bill Kilmer and the New Orleans Saints 23–17. They were perennial losers with their new franchise. The next week, we went to Washington to play the Redskins. They had a new coach, Vince Lombardi. They also had a new starting rookie left defensive end, John Hoffman, from the University of Hawaii. We were teammates in 1967 on the team that still holds a bunch of defensive records to this day. We are both proud of that team. The Hawaii football program has made big strides ever since. Also at the game was President Richard Nixon. He wasn't that popular, got enough boos, but he made news by suggesting a play to Vince Lombardi.

During the second quarter, Bob Lilly got to Sonny Jurgenson and Dave Edwards tipped the ball. We had a blitz on. My job was to cover to the flat. When Dave tipped the ball, I was in position to make the interception and returned forty-one yards for a touchdown. Wow, this was my third straight touchdown against the Redskins! What were the odds of that happening? It was also against Vince Lombardi, my favorite childhood coach. We won 41–28. We ran out the clock as they were starting to make a comeback.

The next week, we lost a squeaker to the Rams, 24–23. We still had the lead in the division race, however. On Thanksgiving Day, we played the San Francisco 49ers. The game was close all day. We drove the ball down to the twenty-five-yard line and lined up for a field goal to win the game. I was on the "field goal and extra point" team because I was big. The field goal was blocked because I didn't squeeze down my block. I hadn't played offense since rookie camp. Instead of us winning the game, the game ended in a tie, 24–24. This ruined my whole weekend. Walt Garrison's wife's family had a ranch outside of Lewisville, Texas, where Walt grew up. They threw a nice party, where we got to do skeet shooting of clay pigeons and some live ones. I was lousy, but Linda, who had not shot a gun in her life, won the women's contest. I was dreading film day on Monday, where film would show I didn't do my job. I got reprimanded and replaced on this specialty team. Okay. It was over. I really didn't want the responsibility of doing that job, anyway. I think the coaches decided that putting defense players on the offensive line wasn't such a good idea.

We won our the last three games, against Pittsburg, Baltimore, and Washington. Our record was 11–2–1.This time I was shut out by Washington. It was now time for the playoffs. We would again play Cleveland, but this time it would be at home. We should have a dry field.

Well, the game came on December 28. It was a rainy, cold day in Dallas—in other words, Cleveland Browns weather. We stopped the run most of the day, but we gave up the long play on the pass, as we had done all year long. The fans were mad and booed Craig Morton. Roger Staubach came in late, but there wasn't much time to make a difference. It was a miserable day and perhaps the lowest point for the Dallas Cowboys. Sometimes when things are going so bad, you just have to laugh. Late in the game, we were attempting to kick off. Mike Clark lined to kick the ball, but he slipped and totally missed it. We lost, 38–14. All we wanted to do was just get out of there and get away from football. The next morning, someone threw eggs at our front door. These Dallas people really do take their football seriously. The next day, we packed up and we drove to Minnesota to finish my final quarter at the University of Minnesota and collect my degree. It was nice to get away from all this.

This time we had a dog with us. She traveled well. It was a two-day trip to drive from Dallas to Minneapolis. We usually stopped in Newton, Kansas, to stay overnight with my sister Marlene and her family. Her husband, Jim, was a college professor at Bethel College in North Newton. He was not a football fan, so we never talked about football. When I would talk about politics, he would engage on a deep-thought basis. Now that Blaine Nye, who was from Stanford, was now my regular roommate, I was used to deep conversations. When we got to Minneapolis, I got smarter. We rented an apartment with a parking garage underneath. This way, I didn't have to go outside and warm up the car. I also had Linda drive me to class so I didn't have to walk nine blocks to the building. I thought to myself, *Who does this? Be in Dallas in the heat of August, then go to the cold of Minnesota for the winter. Oh well, just three months to go!*

I started my classes and actually enjoyed them. By this time we were getting closer to actual applications of engineering and not just the basis of the calculations. The course I didn't like so much was a one-hour subject on Algol, the computer language. We would learn to write basic code. We would then go to the key punch machine and prepare the cards for the computer. Then we would line up in this big room to feed the machine the key punch cards. We would watch for the printout to see if we did the cards right. It was neat to actually be able to do this, but if you made a mistake on the cards, the machine would stop, spit it out, and then you needed to go back to the key punch machine and fix your computer codes. Then do it all over again.

We were in this little apartment with a restless dog. We got spoiled living in a house. We decided to get away for a weekend. We went to Spring Green, Wisconsin, where Linda's uncle and grandfather lived. To this point, I didn't know that much about her background. When you marry a preacher's daughter, you are not sure what to expect. Linda and her brother were always onstage to be a perfect example for the others in their congregation. I didn't know her parents well at that time. Pastors can be intimidating. Her dad was quite set in his ways but still had a good heart. Linda's mother, Helen, was the consummate preacher's wife. She was a home economics graduate from the University of Wisconsin in 1936. She was schooled in the formality of dinnerware and the presentation of food.

I wanted to know how my wife grew up. We drove to Spring Green, a town of about 1,500 people. Helen's brother, Harold, lived on the edge of town. He had a large family of eight kids, some by that time having left home already. He raised chickens to produce eggs. In their prime, he would transport a million eggs to Chicago every day. He had eleven chicken barns. I toured those barns and was amazed at the volume of this business. We stayed at her grandfather's house. He had made his way by inventing better quality seed corn grown in Texas. He later became a banker and was chairman of the board of the local bank.

I never had a grandfather because both of my grandfather's died before I was born. He had a bar in his basement, where he served brandy manhattans. That loosened me up to talk to him about my mother- and father-in-law. Linda's dad at that time was total teetotaler. I liked to have drinks, and that was something Linda's dad didn't approve. Linda's grandfather gave me some advice and talked to me about how to handle things. It was like talking to any of my close friends. He was a wise man. He came from the same kind of small-town background I did but had achieved so much. He was an inspiration to me and enjoyable as he shared his experiences.

We headed back to Minneapolis to get on with finishing my classes. I then got a letter from the Cowboys. They were doing a survey. They asked the players to be honest with them about what we, as players, thought about the coaches and the strategy. Was it too complicated? Did we want to change the defense? The Kansas City Chiefs won the Super Bowl against the Minnesota Vikings earlier in the year. All the other teams took note of how they got there. They had initiated weight lifting to bulk up their linemen. The conventional thinking at that time was, weight lifting made you too tight and not fluid enough to be agile. That game sniffed that out. Curly Culp of the Kansas City Chiefs was a national champion wrestler in college. He stuffed many of the offensive linemen he played against. We all answered the questions. We were to remain anonymous. They flew us back to Dallas and told us to bring the surveys with us and we would all put them in a box to protect our privacy. The coaches were willing to listen to us to a point. When I was there, Ernie Stautner told me I graded out well for the year, as if he was also surprised. He also asked if I knew I had twelve traps that season. Well, yeah! I knew that. Ernie was too busy coaching me at that time to stop and evaluate the big picture. He was satisfied with my performance that season. He was a very good position coach.

I graduated on March 17, 1970. My parents and Linda's parents were there. I had fulfilled my promise to my mother to graduate from college, though it took me five and a half years to do it at three schools. This is an accomplishment that no one can take away from me.

We got in our car and headed back home to Dallas. We could then get on with our lives in whatever direction it would go.

While we were gone, Eddie Hamel, my former roommate, lived in the house along with Scotty Hughes, the AFA guy from Queens, New York. They took good care of the place. The neighbor lady said they would go around in their underwear. The grade of their house was higher than ours, and they could see over the café curtains from their kitchen hutch. They were amused; however, they were glad when we returned, so their young children wouldn't have to see this. We proceeded to have the landscaping installed. The area we lived in was a few blocks from the practice field. There were no natural trees in our immediate area. There was a layer of limestone three feet below the surface, so we had to plant a tree that could handle a short root system. They have lasted and have grown in the last fifty years. The soil was black but a very gummy clay. When wet, it would stick to your feet and was easy to track in. That was why the builder suggested that I lay sod instead of seed. I was now a traditional home-owner, mowing my yard and weeding my shrubs. I went to Sears and bought a lawn mower.

I now was ready to look for a job. All pro athletes had to pursue other careers because we didn't make enough money in our play-ing days to pay for after-retirement life. I went to see Jerry Mays, a defensive end for the Kansas City Chiefs. He was a structural engi-neer with one of the major construction companies in Dallas. I told him that I spent most of my studies in soil, sanitary, and hydraulic engineering. He set me up with Southwestern Laboratories. They did soil testing and foundation recommendations. I talked to them and told them my circumstances, that I would be going back to football in the summer. They were okay with that. They hired me. I would be making $875 a month or a yearly salary of $10,500. I immediately started working in their Arlington office. I would be driving to work each day from Dallas. I took the back roads. It took about forty min-utes to get there and back.

I had a lot to learn. The lead engineer, Ronnie Rone, took me under his wing and taught me all about what the company did. First off, there were thirteen different geological formations that outcrop in the DFW area. Each one was different in the amount of rock, sand, and clay, thus the need to test the soil. They would send out a drilling rig to drill usually twenty feet deep and take samples at various layers. They would then test the moisture content and the bearing capacity. Based on all that, they would write a report to the lead engineers for many of the major and minor building projects. It is boring to talk about this at a social event—just ask my wife. But it was very intriguing to me to learn of all the varied solutions. In engineering, you have to be substantially right all the time. That is where engineers design, in a "factor of safety." In other words, they would do the calculations and then double them to cover variances in materials and changes in soil on various sites. Ronnie was a natural salesman and also quite knowledgeable about the details of soil engineering. He was a licensed civil engineer, with a great deal of experience. He grew up in Midland, Texas, and got his degree at Texas Tech. The type of foundation needed for each geological formation varies dramatically. I was a graduate engineer or an EIT (engineer in training). He was the lead engineer, not the manager. He was a deep thinker and great to have a philosophical discussion with. During that season, Texas Stadium was under construction. Texas Stadium was built within a floodplain. They wanted to have it built so they could have a roof. Once they got under construction, they discovered that there was not enough bearing capacity to support a roof. I went out to the site a couple of times and assisted in the testing and inspecting. How many professional football players could say that? About fifty feet below the surface, there was a layer of shale that was strong enough to support a forty-five-degree concrete support system to put up the frame of the roof, which covered the fans, but not the players on the field. The addition of a removable roof never happened. Yes, because the shale wouldn't handle that additional load. Also because, as the saying goes, "God wanted to keep it open so he could watch America's team!"

While I was at work, I would go to Hurst Euless Bedford to do drilling inspections of piers while they were under construction. I also witnessed foundation failures that needed repair. Soil conditioning and soil stabilization were a relatively new concept. When clay gets wet, it can expand up to two times its size. With chemicals added, you could reduce the swelling by about 85 percent. I was taken aback by how many more trees there were in this area than in North Dallas. There was a lot of post oak trees. This area was growing. Highway 183 freeway was widened through the HEB area as the new DFW Airport along Highway 183 in Irving was under construction. A lot of pilots were attracted to this area as it was close to the airport and they got paid enough to afford bigger houses on wooded lots. When the top limit is set, any price under that is in play. I was planting a seed in my mind. Maybe I might want to live in this area sometime. You could get so much more house for the money in this market. I wrote the soil recommendation for these different companies building houses, offices, and retail centers. I included the drilling logs showing what type of soil was encountered at each depth. The lead engineer would review the work and sign off on it. Then the client foundation engineer would use this information and incorporate it in his foundation design.

One day that spring, I got home from work and Linda told me we were going to have a baby. Wow! That was exciting and scary at the same time. I didn't know a damn thing about taking care of babies. We enrolled in a Lamaze class to teach us how to take care of a baby and how to support Linda through her childbirth. They would teach her how to breathe during contractions and how I could assist her. This was all new to me. I worked for about three and a half months and gained some good work experience. It was time to go back to training camp for my third year. Before I left, I received my discharge from the Air Force Reserve. I had fulfilled my six-year commitment to the United States Air Force.

In the summer of 1970, the new rookie class had a number of good draft choices, like Duane Thomas, Charlie Waters, Steve Kiner, Margene Atkins, John Fitzgerald, Pat Toomay, and Mark Washington. There was also a free agent named Cliff Harris. As a result of the player surveys, certain changes were made. Gene Stallings was hired as defensive backfield coach. He was a no-nonsense former Aggie coach who played for Bear Bryant at Alabama. He would communicate with his rookie defensive backs by their number. He said, "If you make the team, I will learn your name." Three of these guys were defensive backs. They would make a difference. On offense, the coaches moved Rayfield Wright to right tackle. He was a backup tight end with a big frame. He gained weight. Ralph Neeley would move to left tackle, playing next to John Niland. He was a good athlete who could move his feet to block the right defensive end, who was usually the fastest lineman on the opposing team. Blaine

Nye, now in his third year, would start at right guard. Dave Manders would remain at center.

After our humiliating loss to Cleveland, we were determined to be more mentally tough and make the plays to put us over the top. We started training camp while there was a strike going on. The players were trying to get more power by forming a players union. Players trickled in one or two at a time. Only the truly committed remained out until the strike was officially over. My roommate was a holdout until the end. I reported about a week before the end of the strike. Blaine gave me hell for reporting early. Oh well, just one more philosophical argument.

The strike eventually ended, so we could play all six exhibition games. Pat Toomay showed himself to be a good contender for a defensive end position. Halvor Hagen was traded to the Patriots. He would settle in as an offensive lineman. Pat was more of a threat to George Andrie than me. George was holding out on contract dispute. Ernie was pissed off that George held out so long. When he reported to camp, Ernie put George on an accelerated workout to get in shape. It was gruesome as I watched on. In the military, they would have called that hazing. George was a tough, strong man, though, and I knew he could take it.

On September 10, the Cowboys finally decided to trade Willie Townes to New Orleans for a third- or fourth-round draft choice. We all wished him well. He could have a new start as he was now healthy enough to play at 100 percent. In the off-season, we traded for Herb Adderly from the Green Bay Packers. He and Mel Renfro would play cornerback. Cornell Green would move to strong safety, and Cliff Harris was the free safety.

We went into training camp with a competition at quarterback between Roger Staubach and Craig Morton. Craig played against Philadelphia in the season-opening game. We won rather unimpressively, 17–7. The next week, Roger Staubach started against the New York Giants. He scrambled all over the place and didn't complete many passes. We were behind 10–0. The offense came to life in the second half after the defensive line got to Tarkenton and forced a number of interceptions that Cliff Harris capitalized on. He got three interceptions and one return for a touchdown. This was his debut game. He was a hard hitter and had the right instincts to read plays. The next week, we went to St. Louis to play the Cardinals. I lined up against Don Dierdorf, their first-round draft choice, at the right tackle. He was a load. They had two running backs that each weighed 230 pounds. It was a physical game, where they jammed those backs down our throat. George Andrie, Dave Edwards, and I got most of the blame. They had a very good offensive line. They were learning how to attack the flex defense. We lost 20–7. The next week of practice was more physical punishment. Ernie finally got over it by Thursday of that week. The next week, we played the Atlanta Falcons at the Cotton Bowl. It rained continually all game with sheets of water. If you could make a tackle, you would slide another three yards. I felt like a kid at play. Thank God we won, because it was hardly a regular football game. We won 13–0. We didn't have to watch the game films as there wasn't much there to coach. We were 2–1 going into Minnesota to play the Vikings. They were coming off their appearance at Super Bowl IV, where they lost to the Kansas City Chiefs.

I would be going home to the site of where I had my debut against the Vikings two years earlier. This day would be different. We couldn't do anything that day. Craig Morton started the game, completed four of ten passes, then hurt his knee, and Roger came into the game. He didn't do much better. We lost, 54–13, the worst loss in the eleven-year history of the Cowboys. The press was turning on us, and things would get worse before it got better. We felt we were snakebit.

We licked our wounds and went home to get ready for the next week. We would be playing the world champion Kansas City Chiefs. We went to Kansas City. Duane Thomas was making his debut. He was a different kind of runner than Calvin Hill. He was such a smooth runner who could change direction and time his hitting the hole. On defense, our line dominated their offensive lineman and chased Len Dawson around all day. They had never played against a flex defense. They didn't quite know how to play it. Their offensive splits were wide, and we took advantage of that. We won 27–16. Now we weren't sure what kind of team we had. How could we have been so terrible in Minnesota? We got home and played Philadelphia again and won 21–17. I had never lost to Philadelphia.

The next week, we would be going to New York to play the Giants. We were now 4–2. St. Louis was a game ahead of us in the division. We had so dominated the Giants in the past couple of years. During the week, as we were preparing for the game in practice, I got a call from Kitsy Lilly, Bob's wife, at the end of the practice. She said that Linda had her water break at Clint Murchinson's house and that she would be in labor. I was directed to go home and wait for further instructions. Since Kitsy already had two children of her own, she knew what she was talking about. It turned out that when Linda had her water break, she searched for a bathroom in that large mansion. She was leaking onto their tile floor, and Kitsy noticed. Kitsy took Linda to the hospital. I got home and waited and waited. I walked in circles from the kitchen to the living room to the den to the kitchen and on and on. Finally, after a half-hour, I got the call and drove to the hospital. Linda was checked in and sitting in the bed. She was a little apprehensive but excited to get this over with. Because her water broke, they gave her a shot to initiate labor. This was about seven thirty at night. They said it would take about two to three hours. We sat there and tried to make her comfortable. The nurse told me that if Linda wanted to get up to go to the bathroom, I was not to let her do it. She listened to me the first few times, then she got hysterical and cussed me out for not letting her do it. I caved and said fine. She went to the bathroom without any negative consequences. Geez, I didn't need this! Since her contractions were coming more often, we knew we were getting there. It wasn't until after midnight that they took her to the delivery room, however. I got on my robe and gloves and entered the delivery room also. I got there and observed what was going on. Soon my baby boy was born! He let out a roar, and I knew all was fine and he was healthy. He was three weeks early but looked normal. I was relieved, as was Linda. This was no easy birth for her. They took the baby, wrapped him up, and put him into his mother's hands. She was smiling and happy! This is one of the most exciting moments in life, the miracle of birth.

It was now November 3. I went home exhausted and went to sleep. I woke up with a smile on my face. I wanted a boy first because in my family the girls came first for my brother and me. We sure hoped the next baby would be a girl. We talked about how many kids we wanted. She wanted two, like her family. I wanted four, like my family. We agreed to compromise at three.

The next day, I went back to the hospital and the nurse put my baby in my hands. I experienced a feeling that I had never had before. The bonding was such a good feeling. I was now a parent. I was looking forward to this new responsibility. It just seemed to come naturally to me because I felt loved by my family and my wife. I went back to practice the next day. I passed out the cigars, a tradition at that time. I had a hard time concentrating, but my job was to fly to New York and play the game. We had beaten New York quite convincingly in the last couple of years. This year, they had a new coach with a little different approach. They disguised some of their plays where our keys weren't as obvious, as they were for standard play. I remember a couple of times, I didn't read the play right and their running backs, McArthur Lane and Sid Edwards, were able to go up the middle for a couple of fifteen-yard runs. I wasn't sharp because I was too excited about being a new father and was not concentrating on execution. We lost 23–20.

I got home and took Linda and Mike back to his new home. I had to be shown how to hold a baby with support of the neck. How to make sure the bottle was the right temperature. Linda didn't have much experience with taking care of little kids either, but she was a quick learner. Being a mother came naturally to her too.

We were now 5–3. St. Louis had a one-game lead ahead of us and had beaten us in head-to-head competition. If they could beat us a second time, they would be in the driver's seat to win the division. Ernie was not happy that week. He felt we weren't physical enough. He played for the Pittsburg Steelers. Up to that time, that was all they knew. We had a drill where Ron East would block me and I would need to use my forearm better to neutralize the block. Ernie wanted it harder. I then just decked Ron East on his helmet. He swung back at me. I don't blame him. He was a former Marine.

My arm hurt. Ernie said, "Go inside and tape it up and come back." They put a doughnut (foam rubber with a hole in it) on where the pain was on my arm. I went back out there, hit Ron again, and this time the pain was twice as bad. I had broken the small bone in my arm in half, as it turned out. I was sent to the doctor to get a cast on it. Crap! A lot was happening in my life.

Now the team would have to replace me for the St. Louis game. They figured they would start the game with Bob Lilly at left defensive end, where he played earlier in his career, and Ron East replaced him at tackle. The game was nationally televised on *Monday Night Football* with Frank Gifford, Dandy Don Meredith, and Howard Cosell. Since I wouldn't be playing, Ermal Allen, the backfield coach, took me up to the box so I could see the game from that perspective. The game started, and St. Louis was running the ball.

Bob Lilly was missing some keys, and Ron East wasn't making the plays Bob usually did. By the end of the first half, they put Bob back at his tackle spot and Pat Toomay at left defensive end. That seemed to work better, but not enough to make a difference We lost 38–0. This was the low point of the franchise. The sports reporter started writing that Craig Morton was too much an individualist to be a good leader. Roger Staubach got too confused when trying to read the defenses. Don Meredith said there were forty players playing their own game, but not enough confidence to win. We were now 5–4, with St. Louis taking a two-game lead, with five games left to play. It looked like there was no way we could get to the playoffs.

With my broken arm, I could just stay home instead of going to practice. I was able to help Linda with the baby. I would rock Mike and give him his bottle. I then was instructed how to change diapers. I had no idea how to do that. In those days, we needed a diaper service to pick up old cotton diapers, wash them, and return them. There were no Huggies. I then needed to be shown how to put in a diaper pin, since I could accidentally poke a hole in the baby's skin if I did it wrong. I then put my fingers under the side of his bottom before bringing the flap up and over to attach. Now, Linda had a new job for me: get up in the middle of the night to change his diaper. Uffdahh! That was when he had his smelliest diaper. I changed him, gave him the bottle, and got him back to sleep. I was told that he would probably cry when I put him down, but if he didn't cry more than ten minutes, it was okay. That was what happened.

The following weekend, I watched the Cowboys–Redskins game on television. They were playing loose. Craig was completing passes. Calvin Hill and Duane Thomas were gaining yards. Pat Toomay was doing a good job filling in for me. We won 45–21. There was still a chance we could make the playoffs, it seemed. I was told that at practice the coaches just let the players play touch football at the end to try to relieve the tension and play relaxed. The next week, we played Green Bay and won 16–3. Then we blew away Washington again, 34–0. Now it was time to play Cleveland, our nemesis, again in a regular-season game.

I had healed up enough to be activated for that game. The defense hadn't given up a touchdown for thirteen quarters. The attitude of the team was, "Just keep them out of the zone." Our offense was so unpredictable that we went into each game with attitude; if we don't give up more than three points, we should be able to win, even if we had to score on defense. We were a lot more serious going into this game with quiet confidence, not confidence based on standings. We were determined to not let the playing condition affect our play. Coach Landry had us fly out a day early so we could have a team practice on their field. We needed to make sure our shoes had the right traction. The equipment guys replaced the front two spikes of our shoes with longer ones so they would dig in better. That was mostly for linemen. In pro football, you look for any edge you can because the talent is very competitive. The saying going at that time was, "On any given Sunday, any team can beat anybody." We were now 8–4 and still in contention for the playoffs.

The Cardinals were 8–3–1.

The game started with the usual muddy field. This time, we didn't let the game get away from us; we focused on the details. *Everybody, just do your job.* Dave Edwards came back from a knee cartilage injury. I came back after being out four weeks with a broken arm. I played with a soft plastic cast. We were able to get pressure on the quarterback and stop their passing game this time. Dave got an interception early that led to a score. Cleveland got a safety earlier in the game. By the fourth quarter, the game was coming down to a defensive stop for us to win the game. We were leading 3–2, but Cleveland was driving and getting first downs on third or fourth downs. When they were threatening at around the twenty-five-yard line, in the back of our minds we were saying, *Oh no! Here we go again.* We talked to one another in the huddle about not blowing an assignment. On a short pass to sideline, Dave Edwards stepped in and made the interception. What a relief! The offense moved down the field, added a field goal, and as they say, the rest is history. We won 6–2. We overcame the jinx. Once we got on the plane, we heard St. Louis lost their game. That put them at 8–4–1. We were 9–4. We had just won the division! This was the biggest turning point in Cowboys history.

We returned to Dallas and finished out the last game of the season with all the confidence we needed. We played the Houston Oilers with Jerry Rhome, a former teammate, at quarterback. He was a smart player, but short for a quarterback. I remember I blocked one of his passes with my broken arm. It hurt real bad. I thought, *Oh no! Not again.* Well, it immediately started feeling better. I was told it knocked off some calcium buildup. We won the game 52–10. We gave up a touchdown, but who cared? We were division champions! And we did it the hard way. We had a different mentality. The press wrote that we probably had the best defense yet. The reason for that was, the defensive backfield got settled. Mel Renfro was our best player there, followed by Cornell Green. Bringing in Herb Adderly from Green Bay made a huge difference. He brought a lot of confidence with him from all the championships he had won in Green Bay. By putting him at cornerback, his natural position, Mel Renfro could go back to the other corner and Cornell Green could play his natural position, strong safety, even though he had played cornerback up to the that time. During the season, Cliff Harris established himself as a solid player, but during the season, he got called up to the National Guard. They would let him out on Sundays to play in the game on specialty teams. In the meantime, Charlie Waters filled in for him. He also played well. He was a smart player, a student of the game. We didn't miss a beat. Cliff and Charlie were best friends. Eventually, they would both be on the field at the same time. We appreciated the press article, but we knew the fans were skeptical and frustrated. This time we wouldn't get ahead of our emotions. We all dedicated to focus only on football for the playoffs.

The first game in the playoffs would be against the Detroit Lions. They had gotten a whole lot better when we beat them bad two years earlier in the 1968 opener. They had Mel Farr from UCLA. He was coming into his own and was a threat every time he got the ball. Greg Landry, their quarterback, had a good year. They were also 10–4. The game was a defensive battle. I hadn't won a playoff game in my three-year career. We were mentally ready. It was another one of those slugfest days. Mel Farr was a tough player, as I knew when I played against him twice in college. He had a sore shoulder, but he would play for his team. He was mostly a decoy. On defense we mostly wanted to keep them out of field goal range. Their running game was starting to work. Late in the second quarter of a 0–0 game, I hit running back Altie Taylor and caused him to fumble. Charlie Waters picked up the fumble and ran it twenty years to get them out of scoring range. Earlier in the first quarter, we scored on a field goal. Duane Thomas had a good game as he ran 135 yards.

Craig Morton cut his right hand during the Cleveland game and just couldn't throw like he had all year. During the second half, we exchanged turnovers. I recovered one of those fumbles. In the fourth quarter, we were driving for a touchdown. We got the ball to the two-yard line. On fourth down, we went for it. The play was wide open as Duane Thomas cut to the outside and tripped over John Niland's block. Detroit would get the ball back on their two. On defense, we were so determined to get some breathing room. When Greg Landry dropped back to pass, George Andrie came in from the right. I came in from the left, Bob Lilly up the middle, and we all got to Landry at the same time. We would drop him for a safety. That gave us some breathing room. We were ahead 5–0. Detroit would get the ball back. They replaced their quarterback with veteran Bill Munson. On the final drive, Detroit was on their own thirty-two yard. On fourth down, Bill Munson hit Earl McCollouch for a fifty-one-yard gain to the twenty-nine-yard line. The stage was set. For all the veterans except me, the pain of losing in the final minute to Green Bay in 1966 and 1967 must have come to mind. Detroit was in position to score a touchdown and would take the lead 6–5. On third down, Munson threw to McCollouch on a down and out. Mel Renfro stepped in, read the play, and made the interception. Game over! We did it. There was a picture of Tex Schramm and me hugging with huge grins on our faces. Those were relief-exhilaration smiles. That picture would run fifty years later as a piece of NFL history in *USA Today*.

We now were headed to San Francisco to play the 49ers for the NFC championship. The winner would go to the Super Bowl. Dick Nolan took the San Francisco head coaching job in 1968. He was a player with Tom Landry with the Giants and had coached the defensive backfield in Dallas. He decided to install the flex defense just like we had. We looked at film and saw that he had some good athletes on the defensive line but they really didn't execute the defense as good as we did. They didn't have the discipline on their steps. We tried to help the offensive linemen understand some of the details so they would know how to block them. Before the game, Ernie Stautner told me he talked to Dick Nolan during the week before the game. Since they were both on the same coaching staff on defense, they had developed a pretty good friendship. He asked Ernie what he was going to do about the left end position, because Willie Townes was no longer with the team. He was the left end for two years when he was on the Dallas staff. Ernie told me what Dick Nolan said. That really pissed me off. I had played three years up to this point and was having a good year. Ernie knew I would be pissed off. No respect. That was why he told me. He knew how competitive I was and was pulling my strings. I'm glad he did.

The game began at Kezar Stadium in San Francisco, the same place where, while I was a player for Hawaii, the coaches took us to a 49er game. At that time, I had no idea that, three years later, I would be playing for the NFC championship game there. It was a sunny, beautiful day. John Brodie was San Francisco's legendary quarterback. He had a very good arm. The game was mostly a ground game struggle. Walt Garrison played hurt with a torn cartilage in his knee all season and had a chipped bone in his shoulder. During the game, he sprained his ankle. Walt was a real-life cowboy in the off-season. He exemplified the mental toughness our team felt. During the game, he would get a sprained ankle too. Duane Thomas ran up 135 yards. He had such a unique glide to his running. He could feel the seam to cutback and gain yards up the middle.

During the first half, John Brodie drove his team down to the ten-yard line. We had a blitz called on that play. My job was to cover the running back out in the flat. The blitz got to Brodie. He threw the ball in the flat to the running back on a perfect pass. Instead of catching the pass, he couldn't see the ball as the bright sun was in his eyes, so he wasn't able to follow in the catch. I was totally out of position and was not in a position to make the tackle because I didn't see him coming out of the backfield with the sun in my eyes. *Thank you, Lord!* On games like this, you wouldn't want to be the one who cost the team the game. They had to settle for a field goal. We went in at halftime, tied 3–3.

Early in the second half, San Francisco had the ball on their twenty-one-yard line. We had a blitz called. Dave Edwards got to Brodie and dropped him for a seven-yard loss. That put them at the fourteen-yard line. Brodie decided to pass again. This time, I got to him and deflected the pass. LeRoy Jordan got the interception and took the ball down to the seven-yard line. From there, the offense took it in to score. We would take the lead 10–3.

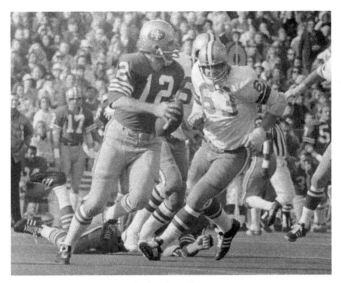

John Brodie.

Later, we would take the lead 17–3. Brodie put together a drive later in the game to make it 17–10. We won the game on the strength of our defense and the strength of our running game. The turning point of the game was that tipped pass and LeRoy's interception. *Take that, Dick Nolan!* Sorry for being self-absorbent for a moment. I was and remain part of the Dallas Cowboys history for doing my part to win. That is the greatest satisfaction, being part of the team and making a difference. We were headed to the Super Bowl for the first time in Dallas Cowboys history!

We left for Miami on Sunday, January 10. We would spend the next week at the Ocean Gault Hotel on the beach. We were there to win a game, not frolic on the beach. They would let us out early in the week to get over the excitement of being there. One place we went to was Bachelor's Three, Joe Namath's bar. He was there. We found him to be very personable. He bought all our drinks. We had been there the two previous years, where we licked our wounds from losing to Cleveland two years in a row. We lost first to Minnesota, then to the LA Rams the next year. The Vikings used the game as a bridge to them going to the Super Bowl the next year. The Rams were just as frustrated with themselves as we were. We then spent time in the bars with them. We lost the game 31–0. Boy, had we come a long way in just one year! All the changes that were made by the coaching staff provided dividends. We had two good running backs, Calvin Hill and Duane Thomas; a much better offensive line with Rayfield Wright and Blaine Nye; and a better secondary with Herb Adderly, Mel Renfro, Cornell Green, Cliff Harris, and Charlie Waters. Craig Morton was recovering from his injuries and doing better. Roger Staubach was mostly on the sidelines but learning the offense. In December, about fifteen of us caught a virus that was a throat infection. We had a doctor that prescribed a drug called Keflex. At first, it was to take one thrice a day, then two thrice a day, then three thrice a day. Nobody was getting any better, maybe worse with our weakened immune system. On the week before we had to leave for the Super Bowl, Craig Morton couldn't speak, so he stayed home all week. He would be all right by the end of the week.

We were confident going into this game. We would be playing Johnny Unitas and the Baltimore Colts. Never in my wildest childhood dreams did I think I would line up against Johnny Unitas in a Super Bowl. We stayed close to business during the week. Our wives came in for the weekend. Now that we had a baby, we had Ben and Marilyn Gunnarson take care of our son, Mike. Our parents lived in Minnesota, so that was too far to take him. Linda flew to Florida on Friday. The first night she was there, she stayed with Iree Niland, John's wife. Then after the game, she could move into our room. When the wives started to come in, we started to feel the excitement. We were confident that we were a better team than they were.

On the Saturday before the game, I got a telegram from over 250 people from Granite Falls, Minnesota, my hometown. That was so nice. Granite Falls has a special place in my heart. It is a womb-to-tomb place, where my parents lived their entire lives in this part of Minnesota. People take care of one another. They have a whole lot of empathy for others and a strong dose of common sense.

Larry Cole #63
Super Bowl V

The game was now at hand. It wasn't quite the spectacle it is now, but after Joe Namath put the Super Bowl on the map, it was getting to be a big television event. Tickets were $15 each. I didn't know what to expect the first year. We had representatives from the city of Fort Lauderdale and the Super Bowl committee meet us. There was a picture of a woman in a bikini giving Craig Morton a kiss on the cheek. We had finally earned a spot to play the big game and earned the respect we so desired. The game started out as a slugfest. Yards were hard to get on both sides. Johnny Unitas threw three interceptions and fumbled the ball, scrambling. George Andrie had a great game. All of us were getting a good pass rush. He knocked Unitas out of the game. Earl Morrell came into the game. He changed the tempo. He was able to move the ball better but also threw an interception to Chuck Howley in the end zone. We went in at halftime leading, 13–7. Early in the third quarter, the offense marched down the field with Duane Thomas carrying the ball. He fumbled with the ball on their two-yard line. We could have taken control of the game, 20–6. Dave Manders recovered the fumble; however, the refs said that Jim Duncan recovered the ball. Bubba Smith showed his potential as an actor as he pointed the other way to sell it to the refs that Baltimore recovered. There was no instant replay in those days, so we had to live with the call. We stopped their running game and shut down their passing game until a fluke play happened where Morrell threw the pass to Ed Hinton. The ball deflected off one of his players, but the refs said it bounced off Mel Renfro. The ball sailed downfield, where John Mackey caught it and went in for the score. That tied up the game at 13–13. The ball moved back and forth. With one minute remaining in the game, we still had a chance to win the game. We were driving down the field to get in field goal range. Craig threw a pass to Dan Reeves that was a little high, and Mike Curtis intercepted and took it into field range. The Colts had a rookie kicker, Jim O'Brien, who had missed other attempts, lined up, and with time running out, hit a thirty-two-yard field goal to win the game. We were devastated. Bob Lilly threw his helmet. I shrugged in rage and dropped my head. Jim O'Brien leaped in the air and became part of Super Bowl history forever. We lost. The game would later be known as the Blooper Bowl. There were eleven turnovers by both teams. This was one of the most physical games I had ever played. Our linebacker Chuck Howley got two interceptions and was voted the game's Most Valuable Player, the only time in history that the MVP was on the losing team. This loss was a huge disappointment. We got dressed, went back to the hotel, and had our Super Bowl dinner and party. All we wanted to do was be with one another so we could have group therapy. After a couple of hours, our outlook started to lean toward the positives. We resolved to get back to the Super Bowl next year and make sure this didn't happen again and finally claim the Super Bowl trophy. The season was over.

When we got to Dallas, there were ten thousand people that met us at the airport. What a difference a year made! I went back home and was so run-down physically and emotionally that I lost my voice for a week, just like Craig Morton did before the week of the Super Bowl. I recovered in about a week and went back to work at Southwestern Laboratories.

Ronnie Rone of Southwestern Labs invited us out to Bedford in October, where he was planning to buy a house that was not finished. He wanted me to take a look at it and give my opinion on whether he should buy it or not. The builder went broke, and Ronnie picked it up for a good price. It was facing a creek in a wooded area of Bedford. This area was so much different from where we lived in Dallas. Both Linda and I had lived in smaller towns most of our lives. We stopped at the local builder's sales office, Lenco Builders. He drew his own plans, and his partner and his cigar did the building. He was getting ready to start a house at 1104 Edgecliff Drive. He had started to clear the lot. He wanted to know if we wanted to customize it for ourselves. We would think about it for a couple of months.

After the season was over, we decided to build a new house on that lot in Bedford, for the following reasons. We felt Dallas was too congested as we had to stand in line most everywhere we went. Since the Cowboys were building a new stadium in Irving, we assumed that they would practice there too. That didn't happen until after I retired and they built that facility at Valley Ranch in Irving. I was working in Arlington, so living in Bedford would be a shorter trip to work in the off-season. Also, we liked the idea of custom-building to get specifically what we wanted. We signed the contract in February and moved in by June, a month before training camp. I had a lot of common labor to do as I installed the sodding myself. The lot was over a half-acre and needed a lot of maintenance. By the time I was to go to training camp, I was ready to do something other than yard work.

We met friends of Ronnie and Roberta Rone, Bud and Mary Forman. Mary belonged to a sorority group that got together for bridge. She invited Linda to get involved, and Linda felt comfortable with that group. Most of the people that moved to this area went to TCU or Texas Tech. The local restaurant owner, C. A. Sanford, was an SMU graduate. He owned the only sit-down café in Hurst. He also was the mayor of Hurst. He was a colorful guy and good friend with Don Dodson, the mayor of Bedford. It turned out that he would be our neighbor around the corner. The people in the neighborhood were very friendly. We met Stan and Mary Ann Wied, who lived two doors up the street. He was a pilot for Braniff Airlines. It turned out that he would be the pilot for the team on many occasions. They had three daughters. The older two were babysitters for us. How convenient! This was already becoming home to us. We were glad we made the move, even if I had to drive to Dallas for practice. That would take forty-five minutes to get there. When there was traffic between 9:00 a.m. and 10:00 a.m., I would cut it close. I was fined a few times, and sometimes I just quietly waited until we broke up into offense and defense to go to their respective rooms. The guys knew I was late and just kept it to themselves. I was fined a couple of times each year, but it was worth it to live where we wanted. Bedford quickly became our home.

I left for training camp. It was July 1971. The Cowboys' number 1 draft choice was Tody Smith, Bubba Smith's brother. They also drafted Bill Gregory in the third round as a defensive tackle. Pat Toomay established himself to get more playing time this season. He backed up George Andrie. Bill Gregory would back up both Jethro and Bob. Tody was penciled in as the person who would replace me. He missed most of training camp with contract negotiations. The first time we saw him was at an exhibition game at the Cotton Bowl. He was very athletic. He was a little undersize for an NFL defensive end, certainly a lot smaller than his brother Bubba, who was about six foot six and 275 pounds. The Cowboys signed Forrest Gregg from the Green Bay Packers as an offensive tackle backup. He was in his sixteenth year. He was a good addition. He was an SMU graduate, so he was home. He talked to us about how, if we just won the Super Bowl like they did, opportunities would open for all of us. Getting the $25,000 in total playoff money could make a big difference. He talked about how Willie Davis got a car dealership in Los Angeles. Having his confidence around was good for all of us because he and his teammate Herb Adderly had both won championships and Super Bowls. Now they were both with the Cowboys. Going into this season, Coach Landry announced that Roger Staubach and Craig Morton would both compete for the starting job. During training camp, they both did well. When the season started, they would alternate starting. Craig would start the first week against Buffalo. Roger would start the following week against Philadelphia. He got hurt early with a concussion and didn't return. Craig played well and seemed to be getting the edge on Roger. We played Buffalo in the mud and gave up more points on defense than we expected. We still won with a big performance by Calvin Hill. We won 49–37. The following week, we crushed Philadelphia again, 42–7. Mostly all of us on defense sacked or pressured the quarterback, Pete Liske, caused fumbles, and had some interception returns. It was a quarterback's nightmare game.

The following week, we played the Washington Redskins. They would be different this year. George Allen was fired by the Rams, and he took over this team, which hadn't done much in the last few years. He didn't like draft choices. He would trade draft choices for seasoned vets. He hated mistakes. He signed a number of players that weren't getting their chance with other teams. One of them was John Wilbur, from the Cowboys, who lost his starting job to Blaine Nye. They signed Billy Kilmer from New Orleans as Archie Manning was now taking over the Saints. On defense, they picked up Diron Talbert. He was one of those native Texan guys who liked to taunt quarterbacks. He liked to get in Roger Staubach's head. George Allen liked the psychological games himself. There was a motel located in the back of our practice field. He rented a room to set up cameras to film our practices, to see what our game plans were.

We sent over equipment guys to see if this was true. By the time they got there, they had abandoned the room. They came back the next day. Because of this, Coach Landry moved the practice to the Cotton Bowl. There were rumors they were there too, but no one could see them. This was a distraction from our normal routine. We looked at their roster and felt that they weren't a match for us. We would be wrong. They played disciplined ball, made few mistakes, stopped our offense, and got enough points to win. We lost 20–16. The press loved the story of Coach Landry and Roger Staubach having Diron Talbert and George Allen get under their skin.

The next week, we had an uninspiring win over the Giants, 20–13. We were a much better team but didn't play consistently. The following game, we played the New Orleans Saints with their new number 1 draft choice, Archie Manning. Craig Morton would start this game. We started the game with just chasing down Archie Manning in the backfield. He got pummeled many times. He didn't get much blocking. On defense, we thought he would throw a key interception. He didn't. We saw what a good arm he had, as he threw the ball down the field. Since the offense wasn't moving the ball, we were back on the field many times. New Orleans blocked a kick and ran it for a touchdown. Then there was the fumbled-punt catch by Charlie Waters, where the ball was taken out of his hands and intercepted to take the ball down to the fifteen-yard line. As Coach Landry told us, you let a young team hang around too long, they would get confidence and it would be too late to come back. Then Archie Manning showed his running skills and ran the ball up the middle for a touchdown. They were leading 17–0 at halftime. Craig went 9–22 without much pass protection. Roger came into the game in the second half. He moved the ball in the second half to get a couple of touchdowns. We still lost 24–14. What was wrong with us?

In the meantime, the Cowboys traded Pettis Norman, Ron East, and Tony Liscio to San Diego for Lance Alworth. Tony didn't go, so when Ralph Neeley got hurt riding a motorcycle, Tony stepped back in. We also picked up Billy Truax, a six-foot-seven veteran tight end from the LA Rams. We needed someone to take the pressure off Bob Hayes. Lance Alworth was an established AFL star. He would make a difference. The next week, October 24, 1971, we played the Patriots in our new Texas Stadium in Irving. Roger would start this game. We played a near-perfect game. Duane Thomas was running all over the field. Bob Hayes had a great game. We were leading 34–7 at halftime. We finished the game winning, 44–21. Maybe we were on track. Coach Landry was getting pressure from the press to just have Roger take over. The next week, we played Chicago. Because Coach Landry wasn't able to make a choice at quarterback, he decided to play both Roger and Craig in alternating plays. What! Yes, Roger would come in with his play, run it, and then Craig would come in with his play. They ran up over four hundred yards, but it only produced nineteen points. On defense, we chased Bobby Douglas, the 225-pound quarterback, all over the place. Unlike Fran Tarkenton, this guy was tough to tackle. He seldom completed a pass but would get first downs with his running. We lost the game, 23–19. We were now 4–3, with Washington taking the lead in the division race.

Coach Landry finally made the decision to play Roger the rest of the year. We couldn't afford to lose another game. I think Coach Landry finally understood that leadership and the confidence the team has in its quarterback are extremely important. The next week, we went to St. Louis to play the Cardinals. We knew how motivated they would be after we knocked them out of the playoffs the previous year. The game was tied at 13–13 and would be settled with a last-minute field goal. The offense got some tough first downs and got in place for the last second field goal. Tony Fritch knocked it through the center with no problem. We won a close one. That was significant to get our groove back from last year. We beat Philadelphia again the next week and were ready for the showdown with the Washington Redskins to take the division lead. This time we respected them more. We stuffed their running game this time. Their best player was running back Larry Brown. This was a game of decoy as Bob Hayes and Lane Alworth tried to get open, but in the end, the running of Roger Staubach into the end zone made all the difference. We won 13–0 and were glad that the game was over. We won the rest of our season games and were now 11–3. We would be taking on the Minnesota Vikings in Bloomington. The weather forecast was "Viking friendly." Bud Grant said weather is just a state of mind. I grew up in Minnesota. That was true to a point. This was their big home field advantage. Two years earlier, the LA Rams spent the week practicing in the nine-degree weather, to no avail. Practicing at nine degrees and playing a game at nine degrees are two different things. The extra physical movement in a game and the adrenaline keep you moving.

Coach Landry figured out that it was best to just practice at home and get the game plan in and just get there the night before and wake up to whatever the conditions were. Since the 1967 Cowboys played in the Ice Bowl, the press wanted to write about it.

In the meantime, Christmas was on Saturday before the game on Sunday. The *Minneapolis Star Tribune* loved this story that I would be home for Christmas. We would have our traditional Norwegian Christmas dinner, lutefisk and lefse. I had dinner with my brother, Roger, and his wife, Suzie, and their children, Cindy and Steve. My mom and dad drove in from Granite Falls, about two hours away. My wife and our one-year-old son would stay back in Bedford. We would celebrate Christmas when I got home Sunday night.

The newspaper took a picture of the family. It was on the front page of the sports section the following morning. I'm sure some of the Viking players said, "Really?" We got up the next morning. The temperature was in the low twenties, much better than single digits. The game started. I hit Dave Obsborne and caused a fumble in the first quarter. Jethro Pugh recovered, and we had the ball on their thirty-six-yard line. The offense moved the ball to the twenty-sixth and got stalled. We made a field goal to get the first score. Ron Widby kicked a short punt. Minnesota took the ball to the twenty-seven-yard line and scored their first field goal. It was 3–3. Later in the second half, Chuck Howley made an interception and got the ball to the forty-seven-yard line. The offense picked up a few yards. Mike Clark kicked a forty-four-yard field goal to take the lead, 6–3, at halftime. Early in the third quarter, Bob Lee, the Viking quarterback, pumped a fake throw to Bob Grim and then Bob took off deep. Cliff Harris stepped in and got the interception and took the ball to the Vikings' thirteen-yard line. On the next play, Roger faked a pitch to Calvin Hill and then handed the ball to Duane Thomas for the score. It was now 13–3. On the next possession, Charlie Waters had a twenty-four-yard return to get the ball to midfield. Then, on a three and fifteen, Roger hit a thirty-yard pass to Lance Alworth as he circled back to the sideline instead of going deep. Then, Calvin Hill ran a screen pass for a ten-yard gain to the fifteen-yard line. Then on third and ninth, Roger Staubach rolled out to the right, looking for Bob Hayes. I think everyone was expecting Roger to run it in, but Bob Hayes reversed his pass pattern and got himself open. Roger threw a dart and scored. We now led, 20–3. On the next possession, Alan Page trapped Roger Staubach for a safety. Thereafter, Gary Cuozzo came into the game and drove the ball down the field but was intercepted by LeRoy Jordan. Cuozzu would later add a touchdown to Stu Voight, but it was too little too late. We would now go back to Dallas. This time we would play San Francisco at home for the NFC championship. We were one game away from our goal of getting back to the Super Bowl and to win it this time.

We would be playing San Francisco again for the NFC championship game. John Brodie had a good year. They edged out the LA Rams for their division title. They were a better team than the year before. We were too. Our running game of Calvin Hill, Duane Thomas, and Walt Garrison was better this year. Adding Lance Alworth gave us two all-star receivers. The game began as a defensive chess game until my compadre at the other defensive end, George Andrie, then a ten-year-savvy veteran, read a screen pass thrown by John Brodie and intercepted the ball on the eight-yard line and ran it to the third. From there Calvin Hill punched it in to take a 7–0 lead in the first quarter. The rest of the game was a defensive struggle. But the object was to just win to get us into the position so we could atone for the previous year's devastating loss to the Baltimore Colts. We won the game 14–3 as we shut out Brodie. The game was over. We were relieved. We didn't celebrate like we did the year before.

The next day, we had a team meeting, and the energy and anticipation of going back to the Super Bowl were beginning to build. Unlike all the previous weeks and previous Super Bowl games, we had two weeks to prepare for the big game. The coaches would meet on our day off and prepare a game plan. Because of all the distractions of Super Bowl week, we would have the entire game plan developed and tweaked the week before. We would be playing the Miami Dolphins.

On defensive, we knew we had to stop their strong running game of Larry Csonka and Jim Kiick. Don Shula was their coach. Like Vince Lombardi, he liked to perfect running plays so that by repetition and execution, they basically said, "Here we come. Go ahead and see if you can stop us." The Dolphins had acquired Paul Warfield from the Cleveland Browns in the off-season. He was an all-pro and was one of the most talented wide receivers in the League. We would put our all-pro cornerback Mel Renfro on him whichever side of the field he went.

Our offense designed a game plan to enhance our running game. The coaches noticed how Nick Buoniconti, the middle linebacker, was so quick to pursue the outside running game. Our coaches developed a plan whereby the lineman stayed with their blocks a little longer, and Duane Thomas, our star running back, would cut back "against the grain" and turn a three-yard run into seven yards or more. That was the plan. By the end of the week, we had our plan for the game. Now it was time to plan for the event.

As players, we all got the right to buy twenty tickets at $15 apiece. I decided to sell ten of the tickets for $100. That left ten tickets for the family. With that money, I bought plane tickets for my parents to come to their first Super Bowl, and my wife, Linda, her second Super Bowl. My parents were accompanied by my godparents, Uncle Harold, Dad's brother, and Aunt Phyliss. Also my cousin Arlys and her husband, Don, were at the game. Arlys was an only child. We spent most of the holidays with her family. I was like a brother to her. The other three tickets, I sold to friends at the ticket price. My good friend Mike Rengel lived in the New Orleans area. He was a big help taking around my family during the week before the game. The Super Bowl was in New Orleans that year. The restaurants in New Orleans were fabulous, and Bourbon Street was where all the action was. After we arrived at the airport, we found we were staying at an average suburban motel. Not quite the expectation for the Super Bowl! The coaches didn't want us to be distracted during the week. Of course, we were anyway. All it meant was that the cab ride from downtown just went farther to our motel in the suburbs. When you arrive at a Super Bowl, it is very exciting, so early in the week, young guys like to go out to see the nightlife, have a few drinks, listen to the music, and interact with the fans, for or against. By the end of the week, the curfew is enforced and the family is starting to come in. You start to feel the pressure with the totality of your life. I'm a cousin, son, nephew, husband, and father. All of us want to share this moment with family, but you need to have enough discipline to not lose your focus and still enjoy your family.

The day after we arrived was press day. We had a light workout in our "shells" (not shoulder pads). After that workout, the media and press come in from all over the country. We practiced at the New Orleans Saints facility. The practice field was filled with reporters, television cameras, newspaper photographers, and beat writers. I remember an incident where one of our rookies, Margene Atkins, challenged Bob Hayes to a jumping contest. The competition was to dunk the ball over the goalpost. Margene and Bob were both about five foot nine. During the season, Margene would race Bob, now in his eighth year, to a sprint. Bob Hayes had won the Olympics earlier in the sixties and was known as the world's fastest man. Margene beat Bob at that, and the press noticed. Later, Margene landed a career with the New Orleans Saints. All our stars were being interviewed and posed for pictures. Even specialty team guys were talking to the press. Most went to them to get noticed. In the meantime, Blaine Nye, Pat Toomay, and I were sitting on the bench with no one around. Nobody was interested in talking to us. We took the attitude as, "Well, we don't want to talk to you either." So thence the Zero Club was formed. Proclamation number 1: "Thou shall not seek publicity. If we save the energy of having to talk to the press, our lives will be simpler and we will live longer."

Later that year, when we were at training camp in Thousand Oaks, California, Pat came down to our room at around six thirty and visited with us. Blaine was my roommate for eight years. It was a Saturday night, and we were just lying in our single dormitory beds. We talked about going out to get something to eat, but that would require getting a cab, and that was more trouble than it was worth. We decided to order pizza. We got that, and at seven thirty, the dormitory was totally empty. Everyone had gone out to a restaurant or a bar, and we just didn't want to spend the energy to do something. Then by eight thirty, we decided we had to do something but were sure we wouldn't have a good time. We saw a rookie come out of the building. He offered to give us a ride. I think we were too embarrassed to turn him down, so we went to go out to a bar. Once there, we enjoyed ourselves. This led to my first Zero Club proclamation: "We are going to have a good time, even if it kills us!"

The night before the Super Bowl, my family went out to dinner at a very nice restaurant. After a week of meat and chicken, I decided I wanted to try something new, quail. They hunt quail in Texas. It is a small bird native to Texas. It takes a lot of skill to hit that small target. At that time, I didn't really know how big they were or what portions they served. My plate came out with two pieces of quail that couldn't be more than one and a half inches wide and two and a half inches long, and some vegetables. It tasted fairly good, but that was it. I ate a dessert, but I was still hungry. Here I was, going into the biggest game of my life, and I would need my energy for that game. To satisfy that need, we stopped into McDonald's on the way back to the motel to get me a burger and some fries. God, that tasted good!

I went back to my room. The team decided it was best we did not spend the night before the game with our wives. I got back to my room, where Blaine Nye was there. I introduced Blaine to my parents. He then told them I was his "surrogate wife." Blaine was a Stanford grad. He loved intellectual conversations, and he had a wry sense of humor that I enjoyed. When you are a football player, you have a lot of downtime. You can read only so much before getting extremely bored. Curfew came at 11:00 p.m., and now it was time to sleep. We both could feel the tension for what was coming up and the big moment to rise up to have a different outcome for this Super Bowl from the one the previous year with the devastating loss to Baltimore. We stayed with our normal routine and disciplined ourselves to get a good night's sleep.

We woke up the next day and went down to breakfast. It was a beautiful, sunny day. The low was in the thirties, and the temperature at game time was around sixty degrees. In my estimation, perfect for football. The Super Bowl game started in late afternoon, so it was a long wait before we got on the bus and went to the game. On top of it all, halftime was usually about thirty minutes rather than the usual ten minutes. We would have to pace our emotions. Before we got on the bus, Ronnie Rone, my mentor at my off-season job, came to the room.

Ronnie gave me a pep talk in a quiet, deliberate way to prepare myself for the right mental attitude and discipline to take into the game. Early afternoon, we got on the bus and went to the game. The locker room was fairly quiet. We were well aware that the Dallas Cowboys had not won the "big one." Since we were leading the entire Super Bowl until the last sixteen seconds last year, we were not going to take anything for granted. We warmed up and were now ready to play the game. For the first time, they did a flyover with Air Force fighter jets called the Thunderbirds. They cracked a sonic boom just above the stadium, and the crowd erupted in excitement. That pumped me up as I had witnessed that so many times at home games for the Air Force Academy. We were ready for kickoff.

The game began slowly, with each side having three or six plays in and out. Late in the first quarter, Bob Griese dropped back to pass. Both Bob Lilly and I escaped our blocks. Bob first took a shot of running him down, but he suddenly turned to his left and I adjusted my rush to turn him back to the middle for the opposite side of the field. Then Bob took a second shot at him and took him down for a twenty-nine-yard loss. This is still a playoff record. The game moved on. Our defense stopped their running game cold. We played the flex defense perfectly. Larry Csonka had a great year. He was so big and strong and hard to stop, but with a little more passion, as it was a Super Bowl, we were able to shut him down. The offense started out a little sluggish. They were getting gains, but they were for three or four yards. The passing game was off as Miami's defense was able to make Roger Staubach scramble and not find his targets after they pressured him. Later, game film showed how open Lance Alworth was on many plays. Nevertheless, Bob Hayes caught some passes and Mike Ditka caught a pass in the end zone to get the halftime score to 10–3. We went in at halftime with a lead but were still concerned that if the momentum changed, they would do what they had done all year, a heavy dose of Larry Csonka, a little bit of Jim Kiick, and a whole lot of Paul Warfield.

While we were in the locker room, the Grambling marching band made their debut on the nig-time stage. They performed perfectly to the awe of the crowd. Most had never seen such precision. When we started the third quarter, the offense made some adjustments and the running game started working better, like the game plan had designed with the cutback against the grain-running attack. Duane Thomas was such a glider as the holes opened more and those six-yard gains turned into ten- to fifteen-yard gains. Duane took a break, and Calvin Hill gave a changeup with his style of running.

We scored a touchdown, and now the game was 17–3. While we felt good about the status of the game, we were still worried that Miami would get untracked. They gained enough yards for a few first downs and got down to the forty-yard line. Then Paul Warfield got open on the five-yard line for the first time. Mel Renfro had shut him down all game. Griese threw the ball to a wide-open Paul Warfield. What happened on the play was that Cornell Green, our strong safety, backed up when he recognized the play and deflected the pass. The drive was over. They had to punt. Cornell was a college basketball player from the University of Utah. He had not played any college football. He was one of the many guys that Gil Brandt found out there in the country. Our offense stalled on the next drive. We punted, and Miami got the ball back. Then, Chuck Howley, our weak side linebacker, jumped the drop-off pass, and intercepted the ball. He ran about twenty yards before his legs failed him. Our offense got the ball and drove to the three-yard line. Then, Calvin Hill fumbled with the ball, and Miami hoped this would be a momentum change. They marched down the field and got to our thirty-five-yard line. Then Larry Csonka fumbled with the ball on the handoff. He hadn't fumbled all year. The ball trickled my way, and I recovered it. The offense set a Super Bowl record for the rushing record at that time of over two hundred yards.

SB VI Csonka Fumble Recovery

After the clock reached zero, Rayfield Wright and I lifted Tom Landry on our shoulders. Tom had one of those ear-to-ear grins. He finally got the monkey off our back! Craig Morton shook Tom Landry's hand and said, "Congratulations!" He was such a class act.

In the locker room, there were a lot of grins and cigars. My high school idol, Jim Brown, entered the room and spoke for Duane Thomas. Duane chose not to speak during the year as his way of protesting his contract. Tom Brookshire, television analyst, interviewed Duane and Jim Brown. Tom asked him, "Was this the ultimate game for you?"

Duane asked, "If it's the ultimate game, why do they keep playing each year?"

To which Tom had no answer.

We had a nice party after the game. Our luggage was moved into our wives' room so we could spend the night with our wives. The next morning, we flew back to Dallas. We got home, and our neighbors had made a banner on our front entrance, saying, "Super Bowl Champions!"

We had talked to the Rones about going to Las Vegas. We recently bought a Mercury Marquis. We decided to drive to Las Vegas. We left a few days later. During that trip, Ronnie was complaining about the direction of the Arlington office as he was passed over after the current divisional manager decided to leave the company. I told him to quit his bitching and form his own company. When we got to Las Vegas, I got a call from the Cowboys' public relations department. They asked me if I wanted to do a commercial for the Dep hair cream. They would fly me and my wife to Los Angeles, set us up at a hotel in Hollywood, and I would be paid $500. We talked to the Rones and asked if they would drive our car back to Texas. They said they would. During that trip, they decided to start their own business. Well, he launched Rone Engineering Inc. He successfully ran the company for thirty-plus years and sold out when he retired about ten years ago. Yesterday, I saw one of the trucks with "Rone Engineering Inc.," but with a different logo. His legacy lives on.

We were off to Hollywood. We took in the sights, went to the clubs, and had a nice time. I went to do the pose for the commercial.

Dep was a setting hair gel. When they did my hair, it didn't stay in place, so they added something else to plaster it down. The ad ran about two months in *Esquire* magazine. My modeling career had started and ended there, as it should be with a member of the Zero Club. It was time to get back home and get on with the next stage of our lives.

CHAPTER 7

THE MIDDLE YEARS

When I finished my work at Southwestern Labs in the summer of 1971, it became clear to me that I wouldn't possibly advance in this profession by just working six months of the year. It didn't work that way. Clients needed continuity with the engineers they worked with as jobs came in and new ones got started. One of Southwestern Laboratories' clients was the Vantage Companies, a company owned by John Eulich. He and Trammel Crow were friends and competitors in the newly lucrative office, office showroom, and warehouse market. Major companies were relocating to Dallas now that we had a major regional airport opening in 1974. Love Field in Dallas couldn't handle all the traffic.

I visited with Jerry Ridnour, who was the manager of the Arlington office. He said he couldn't offer a paying job but he could give me a $500-a-month stipend for my expenses. I would be a leasing agent and help solicit occupants for the office showroom they were building. My friends thought I was insane for working for next to nothing. It was the best decision I had made up to that point. I went to work and spent a lot of time understanding what they were doing at that time. They were building speculative office and warehouse space. You could build tilt-wall construction panels for the walls at a very inexpensive price. Warehouses didn't need windows for most of the building. They would drill piers for support of the panels, tilt them up, weld them together, and finish the front with windows and doors. John would get investor friends, such as doctors, to put up capital to buy the warehouse as an investment. They would then get a loan from the bank to build the building, with investors providing the equity. He would figure in a fee for putting that together. Then the construction company got a fee for building the structure. Then the leasing agents charged a fee for finding end users of the building. This now became tax-sheltered income property. They would hold the building for five to ten years, then deduct the interest, taxes, and depreciation of the building. He would then have his Realtors sell the building for another fee. The investment was set up as Vantage Companies as the general partner, with usually 51 percent controlling interest, and the investors as the limited partners at 49 percent. When the building was sold, all the investors and general partner would all pay the capital gains tax, keep the profit, and move on to the next building. I learned more in that four months about business that I knew from any college course. They were a very fun-loving company who worked hard and played hard. They took us to Austin, to a resort community, for a summer retreat. It was a pleasure to be part of that company for that spring and early summer.

After we got back from Las Vegas, we got back into the routine of living in Bedford. Most of the people moving in were our age or a few years older. It was exciting to be part of this new community. We got involved with all kinds of community activities. We hosted a party at our new house. Instead of a living/dining room and a den, we just had one big sunken den with a wet bar and a dining room above the length of the den. We could entertain about twenty people. I remember, at the party, listening to Chris Kristofferson singing, "The Silver Tongued Devil and I." "I took myself down, to the Tally Ho Tavern / To buy me a bottle of beer / And I sat me down by a tender young maiden / Whose eyes were as dark as her hair." It was a great sing-along song. The party would last until 1:00 or 2:00 p.m. We had a big-enough yard to spend time outside in the back. We also had a bathroom with a little-boy spout where the water came out for the tub. My niece was so intrigued by that when they came to visit. We had a bumper pool table in the basement. It wasn't big enough for a pool table.

That spring, I met a builder named David Barfield. He was building a new town house community he named Chateau Valee in Bedford, located on Pipeline Road, across from an established community named Morrisdale Estates in Euless. He asked if I wanted to invest in the project. It would take $15,000 to become a fifty-fifty partnership. I had just received my check of $15,000 for winning the Super Bowl. I had earlier received payment for the two playoff games we won, so I had a little cushion. Since I had always been interested in construction, I decided to go ahead and make the investment. His brother John Barfield "JB" Sandlin and Herman Smith were the main builders and developers in the area. There were not any larger outside tract builders at that time, so these guys were able to set the market. Houses were selling left and right. David was a very creative guy, unlike his brother, who was more of a nuts-and-bolts guy. He had acquired lots in a small new neighborhood where he built all kinds of totally different kinds of houses.

On one house he built a sports court in a basement on the side of the hill for a guy from his church. The ceiling was twelve feet instead of the usual eight feet. He had a lot next to it and asked if I wanted to build a house from scratch using his subs. He would not charge a fee. He had an idea of having a castle look with motes to operate as a fireplace. There would be a regular basement on the side of the hill. In Minnesota, you had to have a basement because the freeze line was about eight feet below the surface. I liked the idea of having a basement. We had only lived in our new house for a year, and now I was considering building another house so soon. Why would I do that?

I finished my time at the Vantage Companies in July. In the meantime, that spring and early summer, I was keeping an eye on the Chateau Valee investment. I would go by there at the end of the day and check in with the on-site sales agent. This community consisted of six acres of land with one narrow U-shaped drive. There were two fourplexes and four sixplexes. They was a clubhouse with a pool in the middle, along with a shortened tennis court.

Sales were going okay; however, the cost of a couple of the buildings was over budget. David gave such attention to detail on the outside look that the sales price couldn't quite keep up with the cost. There was only so much people would pay for a smaller town house. They liked the idea of not having a yard to take care of, but the area was quite cramped and had very little parking for guests. By the end of the summer, this investment didn't look like it would make any money. David wasn't much on the management side of the business; he was a cheerful guy who expected things to work out. I was concerned. I didn't have any liability for the debt, but my investment appeared to have been wasted. The bank had covered many overdrafts because of his brother's strong financial statement. I got a call from the bank to let me know that the account had been over-drafted for a long period. What David would do was write a check for the subs on Friday and leave it in his office for the sub to pick up. On Monday, he would check to see how much he could draw on the loan and make the deposit. Sometimes it came up short, so the account was overdrafted for another week. I got a call from the bank loan officer. He called me in and asked if I would straighten this out. He was getting pressure from the bank examiner to stop covering overdrafts. I got the account straightened out, and because of that, he would later give me a loan to build out the rest of the project. I would buy the land site as needed. David continued with his custom-building business. I took over selling and building the town houses that fall. I decided to go ahead and build that house with the basement so I could learn the business. David would schedule most of the subs. They all knew what they were doing, so I had to learn from them how building a house really works. I always liked construction. I figured I needed to get involved in building if I wanted to save my investment. I realized after work at Southwestern Labs and Vantage Companies that no one would take me seriously in business unless I was the one signing the checks. The house would be built while I was playing football that fall and in early 1973.

I went back to training camp in July 1972. We were the defending world champions. Before camp started, we heard from Goodyear. They wanted to do a commercial using the front four. We left home a couple of days early to do this. This would be a commercial played live on network television. So Bob Lilly, George Andrie, Jethro Pugh, and I went out there. What they had set up was for the four of us to block the blocking sled with Goodyear tires on them and drive them into four silver metal spears. The producer kept trying to tweak the film to look the most impressive of what beating the tire could take. He was always positive. We hit the sled over and over. "Great stuff, puss. Do it again." I think *puss* was the cameraman. There was a lot of downtime when filming scenes. We thought this would take about an hour, but we would end up being there all day. It was also tiring. We got paid about $1,000, and then we would get royalties when it ran on television. The season came. They ran the ad twice for ten seconds on *Monday Night Football*, and that was it.

I was returning to camp for my fifth season. We were the reigning Super Bowl champs, and everyone would be gunning for us. Before the season started, Tom Landry had had enough of Duane Thomas and traded him to the Patriots, but he didn't pass their physical, so they backed out. The San Diego Chargers stepped up and took him. Our number 1 draft choice was Bill Thomas. He got injured easily and didn't last long. We picked up Robert Newhouse, a running back from the University of Houston, and Jean Fugett, a tight end from Harvard. They would be productive.

We played seven exhibition games because at that time, they had an opening game for the reigning Super Bowl champions against the top college stars. It was a meaningless game, which later was canceled. On August 12, Roger Staubach decided he could take on linebacker Marlin McKeever when he scrambled to the sidelines at a preseason game against the LA Rams and separated his shoulder on his throwing arm. He would be out for most of the rest of the season.

Tody Smith would be back for his second year. He had set out all training camp in his rookie year to negotiate his contract. He was the number 1 draft choice. He had shown what a good athlete he was in his limited playing time. He would be given every opportunity to take over the left defensive position. Before training camp, he hurt his knee playing pickup basketball at his alma mater, USC. He was limited preseason in his playing time. George Andrie was developing severe back problems. He had hurt himself lifting weights that off-season. Pat Toomay would back him up and played most of the time. We won most of the preseasons games. Craig Morton picked up admirably and was off to having a good year. We won the first two games against the Philadelphia Eagles and the New York

Giants. We then played the Green Bay Packers. They won in a slug-fest, 16–13. The next week, we played the Pittsburg Steelers. They had a young quarterback who had a great arm but couldn't get the ball to the receivers with throwing interceptions or fumbling. His name was Terry Bradshaw. Late in the first quarter, I got tangled up on a running play. Their center, Mike Webster, came after me and hit the area right below the knee while the offensive tackle hit me high at an angle and something had to give. I was down with pain. The trainers came out to the field and tried to diagnose the condition of my knee. As they walked me to the sidelines on their shoulders, my right leg suddenly went forward. I had hyperextended my knee. That meant that my knee went forward instead of backward. They took me to the sidelines and put ice on my knee and left me there. Tody Smith came into the game and filled in good enough as he blocked a couple of Bradshaw passes. At halftime, the players and coaches left for the locker room. They forgot about me. I had to holler to them to come back and help me into the locker room. This only added to my image as a forgotten teammate from the Zero Club.

This was the first major injury I had ever had. I didn't break any cartilage, so they concentrated on the torn exterior cruciate liga-ment. I would ice my leg, then put my foot into a hot whirlpool tub, then repeat. I would be out for seven games. I was bored to death! I finally read some books. One was *I'm OK–You're OK*, then the *Peter Principle*. The other one was on astronomy. I was a Scorpio, as was my wife. I would ask my teammates when their birthday was and see if the book was close to their actual personality. I was finding their personalities were very close to what the book said as to what their "sun sign" was. I'm sure I was grasping for straws to try to make my life relevant at that moment. It was weird watching the Dallas Cowboys on television without my being there. It was like watching your career fade away. I got off crutches after two weeks and started to walk, then run, and after six weeks, I could return to practice. That was great, just getting back to work. On the Friday before the game, I asked the doctor when I could suit up. He said it would be in another week. Ten minutes later, Tom Landry walked into the training room and said, "You are suiting up this Sunday, okay?" I said okay.

During this time off, Linda told me she was pregnant. We were happy about this in that it would put the ages of our children no more than two and a half years apart. In those days, we didn't know the sex of the baby. Actually, we really didn't want to know. She would be expecting the baby to be born in March of 1973. Either a boy or a girl would be fine as we had agreed to have three children.

Back to football, we were playing the St. Louis Cardinals in St. Louis on December 3. When I ran, I could feel the stiffness in my knee. I wasn't 100 percent, but as a veteran, I could make up for a lot of movement by going to the right places. I would have to burn off the rust of lack of live football activity. On one play, I was trailing in pursuit and got hit on my knee. It was painful. I recovered a fumble. Then the pain subsided and I got full movement of my leg. I must have done okay, as I got a game ball for my performance, mostly for coming back during the season. In the meantime, Tody Smith got mononucleosis and would be out for most of the rest of the season.

We were now 9–3, with two games left. We needed to beat the Redskins to get in the playoffs. We got a break. Larry Brown, their star running back, would be sidelined for this game. We went on to win the game, 34–24. We played the New York Giants the next week. We couldn't win the division by beating them, so we played the game without a lot of commitment. We lost, but it didn't matter in the playoff race. We would finish the season 10–4. The Washington Redskins would win the division. We would be the wild card team. We would then play San Francisco yet again, the third time in three years. They had beaten us on Thanksgiving Day quite convincingly.

We flew out to San Francisco for the game. We were confident but realized we were a little battered up. Playing hurt is part of the game, but we knew we weren't as good as the previous year but still felt we could beat them.

They took a 21–13 lead at the end of the first half. Then in the third quarter, they extended their lead to 28–13. They were feeling good and started taunting us. "How does it feel to lose, you motherf——ers?" Tom Landry then put Roger Staubach in the game with about five minutes on the clock. He drove the ball down the field far enough to get a twenty-seven-yard Toni Fritsch field goal with three minutes, thirteen seconds to go to make it 28–16. We then got the ball back for the offense on a third and out. Roger then hit Billy Parks in the end zone for a twenty-yard touchdown. It was now 27–23. Time was running out. All we could do was execute an onside kick. Our kicker, Toni Fritsch, made an onside kick to the opposite side with his back foot. No one was expecting the ball to go to that side. Mel Renfro recovered the ball. Now all we had to do was score a touchdown. Roger found Ron Sellers in the end zone for a ten-yard pass and the go ahead and score. We won 30–28. That was unbelievable!

I had not ever experienced that kind of comeback. I was used to so many moral victories in college and with the Cowboys. I didn't know what to do with myself. I rolled on the ground in celebration as I wanted to let out my emotions. Lance Alworth joined me. NFL Films got a clip of that, and it is in the archives forever. My most memorable performance in the NFL was rolling on the sidelines.

In football, the coach always wants you to play hard no matter what the score is. Usually, you do it if you want to keep your job. As a pragmatist, I felt like telling the coach, "Hey, Coach, what are the odds of a comeback like this? Come on, be realistic." Well, this come-from-behind victory became a reality. This would be the first of many Roger Staubach comebacks in the future. And I would be there for all of them. Roger made us believers.

Now we would be playing in the NFC championship for the third straight year. We would travel to Washington, DC, for the championship. There had been a long drought since the last time Washington was playing for a championship. The city went crazy! I always loved playing at the RFK Stadium. The fans would stomp their feet, and the noise would drown out the quarterback calling the plays. When the starting lineups were introduced, we got the biggest boos there, more than any other place.

The game turned out to be a disaster for us. Charlie Waters played injured and then broke his leg during the game. Larry Brown had one of his finest games of the year. Their off-tackle play worked over and over. Roger Staubach would start this game instead of Craig. He wouldn't do much. He was chased all over the backfield. We lost,

26–3. We went home, licked our wounds, and forgot about football until the following year.

I now could set my own hours of work. The house was in the finishing stage by January 1973. I now had the time to work full-time on my business. David turned over most of it to me. I was learning a lot along the way. I learned the whole procedure with inspections and what came before each task and what could be done at the same time. The new house was two blocks away from our current home. Chateau Valee, the town house project, was just down the road from the new house. I didn't need to drive from Dallas to go work or drive to Arlington, where the Southwestern Labs and Vantage Companies offices were. I just got immersed in my new business. I opened an office in an eight-story building in Bedford on Central Drive in March. I hired a builder's daughter, Cathy McGeehee, to be my secretary. She was acquainted with all the terminologies. I remember buying this new electronic device called a calculator. It would cost me $125. It did all the adding, subtracting, dividing, and multiplying with digital results. It also had a tape to check your work. Now that calculator costs about $25. The first floor was occupied by First State Bank. This was the bank that provided the initial construction loan for Chateau Valee. I had taken over the bank account for the company. The bank president, Blaise Tibbets, also named me to the HEB hospital board, to replace an existing member. The three connected cities, Bedford, Euless, and Hurst, each appointed three members to the board. We were building a new hospital to serve this area. I served on that board for approximately ten years. I enjoyed getting to know the other men, all older than me and learning from them. I enjoyed getting the perspective of different points of view. I also joined the chamber of commerce. Linda became involved in charity events, raising money for cystic fibrosis, a disease the child of one of our friends had. We were living life in a hurry.

We needed to sell our house on Edgecliff Drive before we moved into our new home. It sold in early January. We then had to move to an apartment until our house was complete. We had to take a second-story, two-bedroom apartment. Linda was eight months pregnant, with a two-year-old boy. After living in two houses, we got claustrophobia living in an apartment. Linda had to drag the clothes down the stairs to do the laundry. I just would go for a two-hour drive on Sundays just to get out of the apartment. Finally, the house at 837 Chaparral Court was ready to move into. We wanted to get in before our new baby was born. We moved in the first week of March. We brought over our stored furniture. It was so nice to get settled.

On a Saturday night on March 17, we went to a party at Sotogrande. It was an apartment complex where some of our friends lived. Linda started to have contractions at around eight o'clock that evening. The ladies there helped Linda count the time between contractions. When it was time, we stopped at the house, picked up Linda's suitcase, already packed, and headed for St. Paul Hospital in Dallas. We drove down Forest Lane Road, which was bumpy with a lot of patches at that time. Linda felt every one of those. The rest of the way was freeway. We checked into the hospital. Linda was in her room. Thirty minutes later, they took her to the delivery room and told me to get dressed in my gown. I could come in when I was ready. I walked in, and the baby was already coming out. It was a girl! Linda didn't have to go through much pain. This birth couldn't have been better. She was so alert and cute! This was another exciting day in my life. Becoming a parent is like no other feeling.

My mother flew to Dallas and helped out for a week with taking care of Mike and settling into our new house. We named our new baby Christina Marie Cole, not after anyone in particular. We wanted our kids to have middle names that were easy to pronounce. After about a month of taking care of two kids and the fact that we now had a boy and a girl, we decided that two children were enough. I would get a vasectomy. Christy was such a good baby. She would sleep the whole night so I didn't have to get up and feed her too early. Once she could stand up in the crib, she would rock it back and forth, so we started to call her Bamm-Bamm, the cartoon character in *The Flintstones*, a television show. She was strong and eventually busted her crib. I was proud of that. She was my baby girl!

The house we built was a unique and one-of-a-kind dwelling. We had a ten-foot-diameter turret at the left side of the house. Our basement and garage were accessed on the side of this cul-de-sac street. All the bricks were removed old bricks from warehouses they were demolishing in Chicago to rebuild new buildings. Some builders bought Mexican brick for a broader color selection, but that brick wouldn't stand up to the colder weather north of Mexico. The brick would flake off. Most of the brick in this area came from Oklahoma or Arkansas. It was hard clay-fired brick. That is the standard for this area now. The Chicago brick had withstood Midwest winters for many years. We lived on Chaparral Court, just two blocks from the Edgecliff house. We could maintain our friendships with the people in that neighborhood. There were five other families on Chaparral Court. We got to know them all. Across from us lived Ben and Billie Loflin. Ben was a loan officer in Dallas. Billie was a legal secretary in Fort Worth. Her boss was Walter Cook. He was a longtime Fort Worth resident who knew all the movers and shakers in Fort Worth. I told her I had an opportunity to purchase nine acres in the back of where they lived and I needed an attorney who practiced real estate law to help me put this deal together. She introduced me to him, and he and I hit it off. He told me what I needed to do before buying the property. This would be put on the back burner until the next off-season.

In early April, I got involved in local politics. I got talked into running for city council. I would run as a slate with Gaylen Mayfield, one of the incumbent city councilmen, and Larry Manire, a bank loan officer. I had this political consultant who set up coffee to go to certain supporter homes and discuss the issues. Her name was Anisa Larson. She was disappointed in my candidacy. I didn't meet her expectations. She thought I should go knock on doors in all the neighborhoods. Well, I was busy running my company. I ran against an incumbent city councilman. He was an airline pilot. The election was the first Saturday of May. The incumbent got a little over 1,000 votes. I got about 950 votes. Larry Manire and I lost. Gaylen Mayfield, the incumbent, got re-elected. Actually, I was relieved. How could I find time for that, especially during the football season? Later in the fall, the pilot got transferred to another city. I was then offered the job to finish out his term. I turned it down. I just didn't have the time. The fact that I ran for office made the back of one of my football cards that year. My political career was started and ended. Thank God!

At the end of the spring, I hired a construction superintendent, Larry Elliot, to take over the construction superintendent's job during the season. He worked for the Joe Howard lumberyard in Fort Worth, where I bought all my lumber. I also moved my office out of the bank building to a single office and reception with direct access to the outside. On Fridays, subs would come in to get their paychecks. This was the standard way to operate a building business. I had so much to learn and was motivated to learn it all. I wouldn't recommend this way to anyone. Having a college degree in engineering doesn't prepare you for running a business. What other choice did I have? I could wait until I was done playing football to start my business, or I would just do both. I was inspired by Chuck Howley, who did the same thing with his commercial cleaning business. I noticed that as soon as practice was over, he would be the first one in the shower and out the door. He was going to his office to catch up on what happened during the day. You couldn't take calls during football meetings and practices. That spring, I took a night school course at UTA in Arlington. It was a great course taught by a good professor. He had put together a booklet outlining how to run a construction business. It covered estimating, purchasing, bookkeeping, accounting, marketing, sales, construction techniques, and subcontractor management, complete with standard one-page contract forms. I had taken law in college, and if I learned anything, it was that what was a written document always superseded any oral agreements. I would refer to that book many years to come. I also got my real estate license at another evening course in Dallas. My mind was thirsting for knowledge. I found my passion was to develop unique neighborhoods and build houses. I wanted to do it all, including building offices and office showroom, just like they did at Vantage Companies.

In April, the off-season weight lifting and training began. With such a disappointing ending to the last season, we all wanted to be in shape when we got back to camp and get our edge back. I worked to strengthen my right leg and my upper body strength. I did a lot of leg extenders, squats, and dead lifts and got on my stomach and used the weight to strengthen my hamstrings. I actually made that recovering leg stronger than the other one. I then worked on my quickness by using my ankles to move quickly. At the end of last season, after I sprained my ankle, I just couldn't get the jump on the offensive tackle like I did in the past. I drove to Dallas at around 3:00 p.m. during the week and would get back home at around 7:30 p.m. We would eat later. This would be my sixth year. I felt I was in my prime at twenty-six years old and was ready for camp.

After all that went on the first part of 1973, I was ready to go back to camp. It was a break from my family responsibilities, my business, and my civic duties. I had a full load. It was time to check the draft picks and see who would replace me this year. Harvey Martin was drafted in the third round at defensive end. Tody Smith and Billy Parks were traded to the Houston Oilers for draft picks. I am not sure why, but I suspect Ernie Stautner felt he just couldn't teach Tody anything or keep him on the field because of nagging injuries and attitude problems. He was a private kind of guy. I think there was a lot of pressure on him to be as good as his brother. That would be hard to do. He had the celebrity part down as he loved to wear mink fur coats. He loved fashion, being from LA. I went to camp. A number of older players had retired. Chuck Howley, George Andrie, Lance Alworth, Dan Reeves, and Herb Adderley were retired. They were all outstanding players. Mike Ditka and Dan Reeves became full-time assistant coaches. They added a lot to team communication between players and staff.

This was a good year in the draft. It brought us Billy Jo Duprie, Golden Richards, Harvey Martin, Bruce Walton, Rodrigo Barnes, Jim Arneson, and last but not the least, Drew Pearson. He was a free agent signing from Tulsa University. He had gone to the same high school as Joe Theismann, in South River, New Jersey, and was one of his receivers. Then when Joe went to Notre Dame, Drew succeeded him as quarterback. As soon as Drew was drafted, he came to Dallas and asked Roger Staubach if he could work with him in the off-season catching passes. Roger said sure. Drew took advantage of this opportunity. He was ready to compete on day 1. Roger Staubach would be ready to go. He still had to compete against Craig Morton. If either wasn't playing, the other wanted to be traded.

During training camp, my roommate, Blaine Nye, was always obsessed with contract negotiations. Since we had been to the conference championship three times and the Super Bowl twice, I didn't think too much about the money. After my second year, the Cowboys offered me a $1,000 raise from what I was supposed to receive for my third year, from $17,000 to $18,000, but I had to add a year to the contract. I said okay and moved on. Then we won the Super Bowl and I had a good year, and they did it again. Now I went from $19,000 to $20,000. I started to talk to Blaine about what his contract was. He had made the Pro-Bowl after the 1971 season. He was telling me that players from other teams were making a lot more than we were. He loved this kind of negotiation. He would spend time negotiating his contract. The Cowboys considered that he and I should be in the same salary category. I didn't like negotiating contracts. I had to deal with Al Ward. Blaine mostly negotiated with Gil Brandt. I quit the contract extension trick and just let my contract expire in a year rather than three years. When Blaine was done negotiating, I would tell Al Ward to just give me what Blaine was getting and I would be okay with that. Blaine grunted that he did all the work.

I said, "Yes, you did. Thank you!"

We had a very open relationship, where we could let each other know our feelings and keep them confidential. Blaine was a big guy with a booming voice and was not shy about taking on issues, but he was also a very smart, kind, and likable person. He was also a good confidant. He was a Stanford graduate, got a master's degree in physics from the University of Washington in the off-season, and then worked on a doctorate back at Stanford. He bought a house in Menlo Park near Stanford and has been there ever since. He completed his contract negotiation. I was able to move my contract up to $28,000 for my sixth year, $32,000 for my seventh year, and $35,000 for my eighth year.

We started the season against the Chicago Bears. Our offense sputtered, but on defense we created five turnovers. Dave Edwards got two key fumble recoveries. I caused one. Later in the game, I recovered a fumble caused by LeRoy Jordan. We won 20–17. Then we took on the New Orleans Saints and blew them away 40–3. Those two teams had beaten us in the 1971 season before we went on a ten-game winning streak. We then beat the St. Louis Cardinals. Our offense was starting to click. We were 3–0. Then reality set in. We lost to the Washington Redskins, 14–7. They always seemed to start strong. We wanted to avenge the previous year's NFC championship game loss to Washington. But it was not to be. Then we played the revamped LA Rams. John Hadl, quarterback, came over from San Diego and led this young team to a win over us 37–31. Then, the next week we would play Norm Snead and the New York Giants. I had a good game. I was beginning to get back my quickness. We were leading, 10–7, when I stripped Norm Snead of his pass and I picked up the ball and ran it forty-seven yards. The offense took it in to take a seventeen-point lead into halftime. We went on to win, 45–28.

The next week, we played at Philadelphia and lost 30–16. This was the first time, as I can recall, we lost to Philadelphia. We were playing inconsistently and just didn't respect them enough to be ready to win. As the line goes, "On any given Sunday, any NFL team can beat the other."

We had a team meeting called by LeRoy Jordan to get our heads right for the next game. The Cincinnati Bengals were coming to town, and they had a new, impressive quarterback, Kenny Anderson. They were coached by the legendary Paul Brown. This was the only game I saw two head coaches with coat and ties and also fedora hats. Paul Brown was one of the coaches Tom Landry looked up to. Coach Brown brought in a lot of WWII veterans to make up his team and coaching staff when he was coaching the Browns. He wanted to upgrade the image of pro football and make it into a more thinking-man's game and change the image from a bunch of dumb football players. His coaching tree is impressive, with Bud Grant, Chuck Noll, Bill Walsh, and others. LeRoy Jordan had a great game. He made three interceptions and was named NFL Defensive Player of the Week. Tom Landry commented on my play also. I had two quarterback traps, and many quarterback pressures, one that caused an interception. We won 38–10. I was feeling at the top of my game. That was what I set out to do before the season started. I wanted to be the one to change the outcome of a game. We then had a rematch with the Philadelphia Eagles. Roman Gabriel came over from the Rams and was their quarterback. He got hit by Pat Toomay and Jethro Pugh. His elbow was bruised, and he was taken out of the game. John Reaves came in and was ineffective. Our offense was gaining momentum and getting better at consistency. We won, 31–10. Unfortunately, I sprained my right ankle and got rolled up on. The next week would be the rematch with the Miami Dolphins, the reigning Super Bowl champs, on Thanksgiving Day. The game was only four days away. I had little time to heal. My ankle was swollen up the next day. I went in for treatment on Monday, and I was treated with hot and cold treatments twice daily to try to get me ready for the big game on Thursday. What a lousy week to get hurt without a full week to recover! This was a sellout game. I couldn't think of a worse team for me to play against with a sprained ankle. I had suffered against Larry Csonka in the Hula Bowl and knew what I was up against. My foot was not healed by Thursday but was improving. They taped me up, and I started the game. They ran Csonka right at me. I was on the injury report. I just couldn't plant my feet strong enough to get off the block and tackle Larry Csonka. My injury was costing the team. This was the first and only time I went to Ernie and told him to take me out of the game because I was hurting the team. He put in Bill Gregory. He did a better job than what I was doing, but we still lost the game.

We went to Denver the next week. I was pretty much recovered from the ankle sprain. It was a pretty basic game. We won, 22–10. Bob Lilly and I jumped on a fumble at the same time. Bob got to the ball before I did; however, he tore his right knee and was hobbled the rest of the season. That would be costly. The next week, we hosted the Washington Redskins. We wanted our revenge and got it. We won, 27–7. It was a decisive victory. The George Allen era was being challenged. He played all these older vets. Our theory was that he wore them out early in the year that by the time it was the end of the season, they had run out of emotion to play above their talent. We beat St. Louis the next week and finished the season with a 10–4 record. Roger Staubach won the NFL passing competition. We would be playing the LA Rams in the first playoff game. We had lost to them earlier in the season. We would be ready for them this time. It started as a defensive battle when Roger Staubach found Drew Person on a pass over the middle. Drew took it in for an eighty-three-yard touchdown. This would be the first of many big Staubach to Pearson completions. We won, 27–16.

The next week, we would host the Minnesota Vikings. The Vikings would be different this year. They signed Fran Tarkenton to be their new quarterback. We knew all about him as we played him twice a year when he was with the New York Giants. He would make a big impact on this team. They also added a very good running back, Chuck Foreman. They both would add some offensive muscle to their always-strong defense.

Fran Tarkenton had a new wrinkle in this game. He was a clever guy. He would throw on first down and run on second and third downs. They turned over the ball four times in the second half, but we couldn't convert on any of them. That was unusual for a playoff game. Roger Staubach threw four interceptions, uncommon for him. I recovered a Chuck Foreman fumble early in the fourth quarter. Roger Staubach threw a pass intended for Bob Hayes. Bobby Bryant of the Vikings stepped in front of the ball and took it sixty-three yards into the end zone. It was a missed opportunity for us to score. Instead, it went the other way. The game was put away by a Tarkenton to John Gilliam, fifty-four-yard touchdown pass. Minnesota would be going to the Super Bowl for a second time. This time they would take on the Miami Dolphins.

I went back home and got on with my business. When you own a business, you take it everywhere with you, but being on the job is much more effective. The town house project was going well. We were about 60 percent sold out. I then started the last building of the project's forty town house units. This was a new lifestyle for this area. It was for people who didn't want the burden of taking care of a yard and enjoyed having the swimming pool and clubhouse for community events.

The previous year, I had dabbled in politics because it is important for real estate developers and builders to get their development plans approved by them with the size of lot they wanted. In order to develop land, you had to get the zoning approval of the planning and zoning commission and the city council. There were nine acres of commercial property on the northwest corner of Forest Ridge and Pipeline Road in Bedford. This land had a broad C-1 zoning, allowing for a wide variety of commercial use. The neighbors were concerned about this being so close to their house. Most asked why this property was zoned that way. Well, I later found out that this used to be a pig farm years ago. In order to get rid of the pigs, the owner agreed to take the pigs off the property in return for granting C-1 zoning for this property. This had happened about ten years earlier.

I had met an investment broker, Tom Hodge. He represented a number of commercial lending companies that would invest money to finance income-producing properties. I was planning to develop four commercial lots. The balance of the land, I would change the zoning from commercial to residential. He could provide me the money to finance the two-acre project, one building at a time. I would get a residential loan to develop seven acres of the land from one of Walter Cook's clients, Equitable Savings, a local savings and loan company. Their banking restrictions for cash reserve were less severe than those of conventional banks, so I needed less cash for equity. There were about eight houses in two neighborhoods that backed up to the commercial property. They were concerned that a big shopping center might be in their backyard.

It took about three to five months to get a final vote to approve a zoning case. I would go to the city council meeting and see that J. B. Sandlin and John Barfield would be on the agenda to rezone different tracts of land. They were long-established local developers. They would argue their case. In growing cities, there are always two factions, the pro-growth and no-growth factions. The no-growth people don't want the city to change. By favoring only large lots, they are for having fewer citizens. The pro-growth people point to the benefits of more residential tax dollars' income, creating more retail demand from city sales tax revenue. I would listen to JB and John make their presentation and then answer questions. They were applying logic in making their case. I would see how angry they would get at times trying to communicate with councilmen who had their minds closed. As long as they could get three out of five councilman votes, it would pass. If you are rezoning agricultural property, it provides an immediate value in the land. Then once the water, sewer, and streets are installed, you can sell lots with a markup to builders or buyers and make it more valuable.

Since I was giving the adjacent neighborhood a benefit to downzone from commercial to residential, the case would be easier. Because of the topography of the land, I didn't really think this was a retail shopping center site myself, so to limit the commercial to office space was no big deal to me.

I got support from some of the neighbors and got some to speak to the city council who would voice their support for the zoning. The zoning passed. I would develop seven acres of residential lots and two acres of offices.

When I presented the case, I needed a civil engineer to prepare the documents to first present a conceptual plan of the lot layout. I chose David Farrington from Fort Worth. He was a smart, patient engineer that was good with councilmen when he presented his part of the case. Now, I would need detailed plans to design this project. It first started with a soil test from one of the testing labs like I formerly worked at. Then we would need a new survey. Also, they would need to make the engineering calculations to determine the grades needed for the water and sewer infrastructure to connect to the existing city lines. Then they would need to design the streets and provide for storm drains to collect the water into the city's storm drain system. Having a background in engineering was very helpful to me to understand what the engineer was presenting and being able to make changes if necessary. Once the plans were completed, they would be presented to the city's planning and zoning commission. These people were appointed by the city council to provide oversight in evaluating the development of construction plans. The city would have their own city engineer, who would provide his comments to the commission. They would hold their meetings bimonthly. My engineer and I had to be there to do a presentation and answer questions. Then they would take a vote to recommend, table, or not recommend the plans to the city council. The council would go through the same process. Their vote was the one that counted. Once that was approved, the project was ready for construction. We would put the plans out for bid to three or four contractors in three categories, excavation and grading, utility (water, sanitary sewer, and storm sewer), and paving. Then I would prepare the final budget and present it to the loan company. They would fund money in progress payments during the course of construction. I got with Walter Cook to prepare the loan documents. I signed them and got them back to the lender. I could now get the project underway.

I didn't plan to build any more town houses. They were a hard sell, with a very limited market in that area for them. I decided to expand my custom home-building business instead. The local market was very hot for local small builders. These builders were able to build and sell spec houses. The houses would get started, and some would sell before completion, and the builder would let the customer make the final selections. If the house didn't sell on completion, he would list it with a Realtor and sell the house, then start another one. About 10 percent of the market would completely custom-design their house and would sign the "build to suit" contract.

JB Sandlin had developed a new development in Colleyville named Woodbriar, just adjacent to Bedford and in the same school district. He offered to sell me some lots, but I needed to buy three. I agreed to that and had a residential designer, Richard Dick, find plans that would fit on these lots. He had a number of base plans he said were successful over the years to choose from. He would then alter it with my input to make it different. As a builder, you wanted a spec house plan that had successfully sold in other neighborhoods. I then got two houses underway. This would keep my job superintendent busy enough while I went back to football for the 1974 season.

There was labor unrest at the beginning of training camp. The players were dead determined to make their point rather than just cave in to the owners. The coaches wanted us all to come in or all stay away. Of course, that didn't happen. Calvin Hill was our player rep. He was a Yale grad and was well-connected in Washington. All the contracts required each player to take a 10 percent discount the year after their contract expired. Then they could be a free agent and sign with any team. In the meantime, the World Football League was opening that fall with no big-name players. Since this would delay training camp for me, that was just fine. I could use the extra time for my business. Pat Toomay kept me informed. Roger Staubach and Cornell Green were the first to report to camp. Craig Morton was still around, so Roger wanted to keep his edge. This year, the number 1 draft choice was Ed "Too Tall" Jones. He reported with the other rookies. Normally, rookies got about ten days by themselves before the veterans reported. Bob Lilly reported early to camp because he wanted to rehab his major injury from the year before against Denver. Ed was a good student and spent time after practice with Bob Lilly and Ernie Stautner to teach him how to play the flex defense. You had to be able to learn the technique by practice and more practice. It would take about two years. Harvey Martin came in passing situations on both sides his rookie year. Like all of us, he didn't know how to use his hands. The guys on defense watched a film clip of Harvey playing against those always-huge LA Rams in the early days of the previous year. That tackle just swallowed him up by holding him inside. The guys teased Harvey that he was Dino Ho, opposite of Houdini. He took it with a good sense of humor. He was a determined guy, but not very tough yet. He did come in and got some traps. His run defense wasn't very good. Coach Landry wanted to put a rush job on getting Ed Jones on the field as soon as possible.

As the strike continued, various players reported to camp. Pat was getting antsy. We wanted to keep solidarity, but Pat felt he needed to get in. He decided to play out his option this year and start negotiating for 1975. He decided to hire Marvin Demoff of Steinberg & Demoff as his sports agent. He talked me into going to

Los Angeles for both of us to see him. He had impressive offices and was well-connected. This was the last year of my contract, so I would be negotiating for the next year. I signed an agreement that he would get 10 percent for negotiating my next contract with the Cowboys. I had zero interest in playing for anyone else. Pat was willing to play in the WFL or any other NFL team.

We then reported to camp. Ed would back up Pat, and Harvey would back me up. Then, at the end of July, Coach Landry announced that Pat and I would play the run and Harvey and Ed would come in on passing situations. Oh, great, whoopie! Eventually, the strike was over. Blaine, my roommate, reported to camp. He grumbled that I should have held out longer. It was about a week. Oh well, time for us to reattach. We were like the odd couple. He was a big brother. I was a little brother. So we assumed our roles. That summer, the Richard Nixon hearings were on television all day long. We watched a lot of the hearings because nothing else on television was interesting. We just wanted to rest in our room. We just wanted training camp over with. This only added to our Zero Club reputation. Pat Toomay would join us at times.

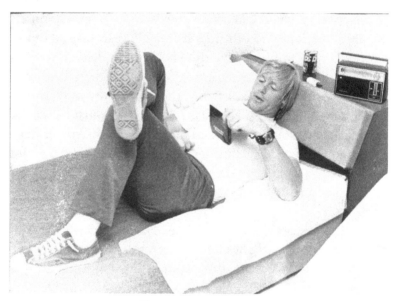

Training camp room.

The season got underway. Craig Morton had enough and finally got himself released to go to the New York Giants. We got off to a rousing start with blowing away Atlanta, 24–0. Then we lost four in a row. We weren't the team we used to be. We had a lot of young guys that hadn't reached their prime yet. We were used to slow starts at the beginning of the season. We were 1–4. I had not experienced that in my career. We then won the next four games. One of them was against the New Giants, with Craig Morton as quarterback. The game was at Yale Stadium because the Giants and Jets' new stadium at the Meadowlands was not complete yet. There were about twenty thousand people there. It was like a college game with a half-empty stadium. It was weird playing against him. Now 5–4, the same record we had in 1970 before the Super Bowl run. We split the next two games, and it was time for the Thanksgiving game against the Washington. Roger Staubach got injured and taken out of the game. Clint Longley came in and started throwing pass completions right and left. He had a good arm. He hit Drew Pearson in the end zone with a come-from-behind win, 24–23. The fans went nuts! My roommate, Blaine Nye, called it "a triumph of the uncluttered mind."

We beat Cleveland the next week, but to have a chance to get in the playoffs, we needed to beat the Oakland Raiders. It was an away game. It was mostly a passing game for Oakland, so Harvey Martin and Ed Jones played most of the game. Kenny Stabler was coming into his own as a strong-armed quarterback. We lost, 27–23. The season would end on December 14, 1974. This was the first time I did not make the playoffs. This was a very disappointing season. I just wanted to get away from it all for two weeks. We decided to take our new family of four on our first semivacation. We drove to Minneapolis, where Linda's parents lived and stayed during the week before Christmas Eve. Then we spent Christmas Day at my parents' house in Granite Falls, two hours away. We were living like normal people. We then drove to Fort Collins, Colorado, to visit Linda's brother Gary with his wife, Leigh, and their two children, Chris and Courtney. They would be able to get to know their cousins on the other side of the family at an early age.

Young Cole family.

We got back to Bedford and went back to work. I joined the home builders' association. This organization promoted this industry on a national and local level. Getting to know other fellow builders was not only fun but also let me learn about other markets. They talked about how hot the Arlington market was. I was working the HEB (Hurst, Euless, Bedford) market only. I decided to buy a few lots in the Tiffany Park neighborhood in Arlington, where a couple of Texas Rangers baseball players lived. This was for the $90,000 market. I also bought five lots in the neighborhood named Oak Ridge for the $50,000-plus market. I would start a couple of speculative houses and a couple of build-to-suit houses. Then I would sell them and buy more. Once a neighborhood has been established, it is easier to sell because the risk of a failed neighborhood is less.

At the same time, Fox and Jacobs, a Dallas production home builder, came to Bedford to take advantage of the hot market that only local builders were feeding. They wanted a piece of the action. At the end of 1974, the country was in a recession, with interest rates going up. They had developed seventy-five lots in the east end of Bedford with choice eight-hundred-square-foot wooded lots. They decided they would sell off two-thirds of the lots they developed as they got off to a slow start. Tommy Riney, a fellow builder, offered me a chance to buy twenty lots. He would build out on twenty lots himself. I wanted to get houses at an affordable price for more home buyers. I took him up on his offer. This turned out to be a good move. The houses started at $45,000. We built standard plans, but we would let the customer customize their house after the house was Sheetrocked. My wife, Linda, began working full-time. She did the bookkeeping and was the office manager when I was away at football practice. She also did the interior decorating. She worked with the supplier reps and our job superintendents to finalize the light fixtures, paint, wallpaper, carpet, tile, bathroom fixtures, etc. We wanted to establish our niche as the builder who went further and let the customer customize spec houses with their own decorating decisions. We seldom moved walls, but we would take out carpet if need be and add it to the price. We now had a full building company with houses in two different markets and in five different neighborhoods.

We got the housing development at Forest Ridge Drive underway. As a developer, I was able to pick the name of the street, provided the name didn't conflict with one already picked. There was only one street, so I just needed one name. I decided to name the street Linderhof Circle, after my wife, Linda. One of our close friends, Ben Gunnarson, gave her that name. It was a castle in Germany that had all kinds of gold decorating it. That was what the ladies wore in those days. How many guys can do that for their wife? The project was underway by spring. We decided to build a thirty-by-thirty office/sales building on the first lot in on the right. We wanted to build it before the development was complete, so that when the streets were complete, we could market from day 1 when it was completed. We had our boat full with expanding our building operation. I was a little stressed but enjoying it all immensely. I loved the creativity of it all and the satisfaction of building developments and buildings that would last for a long time.

In early spring, Bob Lilly announced his retirement. I was then told that with Bob Lilly retiring, Bill Gregory and I would be competing for the right tackle spot. I would start preparing for this change during off-season workouts. The Cowboys hired a new strength coach, Bob Ward. His approach was totally different from those of the strength coaches we had before. He had a doctorate in physiology. He wanted to test us in water, out of the water. He wanted to know our percentage of body fat. He wanted a base file. I felt like this was none of his business, but he eventually won us over because his techniques worked and he was such a patient and persistent teacher. He had a target range for different positions with offensive linemen allowed to have lean body weight 20 percent or more. Most of the players, he wanted at 12 percent or less. I got to 16 percent. That was the best I could do (or was willing to do). I was now at an age when it was easy to put on weight in the off-season, so I had to train to remove it before training camp. He also taught us how to train running. He demonstrated how your hands and legs should move to be aerodynamically efficient. I had learned how to use my hands in hand-to-hand combat classes at the Air Force Academy. He embraced that and introduced a lot of martial arts techniques. The younger rookies really took to it. What astounded me was, he had us run "buildups." We would take off on the whistle and drive gradually to full speed, and by the time we got to the opposite thirty-yard line, we would then slow down. Then turn around and walk back one hundred yards in a three-minute time limit. Then do it three or four more times. In the past we would have to run one hundred yards, gasp, then turn around, and then return in about a minute. These were called gassers by the players because it seemed like the coaches wouldn't stop until the big guys would bend over and show their fatigue. My roommate, Blaine Nye, the offensive guard from Stanford, was very good at acting, so the coaches would end the drill when enough linemen were gasping. What I found with Bob Ward's technique was, we were conditioned better with less pain. I liked that. He showed it was more important to recover because football is a game of short bursts of energy for the length of one play. Training like this gave us endurance.

As I prepared for playing tackle, I knew I needed to get more upper-body strength. I worked the bench presses more, dead lift, squats, and lift and thrust the weight above my head. I worked on my legs to strengthen them to be ready for more short choppy steps and getting hit more below the knee. I learned to shift my weight from one foot to the other when I got hit on that foot. It would prevent me from having that foot vulnerable to getting my foot trapped. I would collapse the pressure on that foot. I also worked on different escape techniques we needed as an interior tackle. I would thrust one of my hands forward to get the offensive guard to raise his hands up. Then I would rotate my other hand, like a circular chop move, then drive my other hand under close to his body so I would be able to take the shortest distance to the quarterback. I would need to get back to training camp with a fresh attitude. I would have to learn the loop technique that Bob Lilly and Jethro Pugh had done so masterfully for so many years.

I left for training camp in late July. Linda would be in charge. She had a full schedule. Besides doing the decorating and bookkeeping, she was also involved with a group called the Oakcrest Women's Club and the dilettantes. Both did community charity work. She would head up the fundraising effort for those organizations. She also worked with the Miss HEB Pageant. The winner would complete for Miss Texas. Linda had an elementary school degree and believed in early education for the children. They went to various day-care centers but also Montessori school. We all lived busy lives in our home. I tried to manage the company from training camp, but that was just not possible. I had to focus on my main job, playing football first.

When I went to camp, there were a lot of new faces. Bob Hayes, John Niland, Walt Garrison, Dave Manders, and Cornell Green had retired. Cornell would move to the scouting department after retiring. Calvin Hill signed a contract with the Hawaii of the WFL. He got a big contract with money up front. Pat Toomay did not show up for training camp. He demanded to be traded. The Cowboys finally agreed to trade him to the Buffalo Bills.

This year was the best year's draft ever. There were twelve rookies that made the team. Randy White was the number 1 draft choice, followed by Thomas Henderson. They were both drafted to be linebackers. They both had a lot of talent and would play other roles with the team. The other players were Burton Lawless, Bob Breunig, Pat Donovan, Randy Hughes, Kyle Davis, Mike Hegman, Mitch Hoopes, Herb Scott, Scott Laidlaw, and free agent Percy Howard. Before the season started, Tom Landry decided to bring back the "shotgun formation." It had been used at times in the sixties by Coach Red Hickey for the San Francisco 49ers. Coach Landry felt that this would help Roger Staubach have more time to read the pass coverages before he took off and ran. He had a handful of plays that worked masterfully. Coach Landry would devise a trap play where the defensive end would close in on what appeared to be a pass and Roger would throw a "shovel pass" to the running back, who would come underneath the defensive end. He would be going one way, and the defensive end would pass on by. The defensive end would be helpless to stop this play by himself. The Cowboys signed Preston Pearson to beef up the offensive attack. He came over from the Pittsburg Steelers. He was a disciplined, smart player who played passing situations, ran this play perfectly, and caught many third down possession passes when Roger threw the ball.

The coaching staff decided to move Ed Jones to left end instead of right end. Also, they moved Harvey Martin from left end to right end. It made a lot of sense. Most team members were right-handed and had their power running to our left side. Also, with a right-handed quarterback, his blind side was on our right side. If the right defensive end could get a good start off the ball, he might get to the quarterback before he could even see him. This was starting a new era of defensive lineman that could run to the forty-yard dash in the 4.7 to 4.9 range. In my defensive-end era, Pat Toomay and I could run it in the 5.0 to 5.2 range in our best years. Ed and Harvey, and later Randy White, could all run in that 4.7 to 4.8 range. Randy was drafted to eventually replace LeRoy Jordan. Tom Landry thought he had another Dick Butkus. Randy was a tough, strong, and quick product of blue-collar Pennsylvania. He went to the University of Maryland, but he was Pennsylvania tough. Tom Henderson was a different type of athlete. He was as strong as any linebacker and as quick as a defensive back. They would use him on kickoff returns. He was a confident player with a lot of hubris. All the others would become eventual starters. They were learning the positions after watching the veterans who had won a Super Bowl, who knew what it took to win a championship.

I worked at practicing to learn the loop technique. Since I am very left-handed, playing the defensive right tackle was a lot harder for me. Playing the right defensive tackle requires an explosive move off the ball. Most teams had their power plays to their right and would pull the offside guard, who would pick off the other side linebacker. If you got off the ball quick enough, you had a chance to be there at that time the quarterback handed off the ball. You might cause a turnover or make the tackle. I worked on it all training camp and could do it the best I could, but not even close to what Bob Lilly and Jethro Pugh did.

Both Bill Gregory and I played the preseason games. We both had some injuries. Neither of us played stronger than the other, so Coach Landry decided that we would both play. I would start the first series of the game, and Bill would come in for the next series and rotate every other series after the first two possessions. We both hated this arrangement. We thought that after the Craig Morton and Roger Staubach debacle in 1971, he wouldn't repeat it. Just when we got warmed up to get in the rhythm of the game, we would have to come out. Bill was a patient guy and a solid player. We both realized that we were competing against ourselves. We just accepted it as the decision wasn't in our hands.

The season began against the LA Rams. I started the game and played the position well enough and made several plays. The Rams were a predicable team that believed in the execution of the tried-and-true plays. The flex defensive was designed to stop that. Both Harvey and Ed played well and provided a lot of edge pressure. Jethro was his usual consistent self. Harvey was beginning to develop that mean streak that our coach Ernie was trying to bring out. The next week, we played the St. Louis Cardinals. I started that game. I sprained my ankle and would be out for the next week against Detroit. The next week, we played the New York Giants. Bill Gregory had a good game. He had an interception, a quarterback sack, and a fumble recovery. On October 25, the day before we played the Green Bay Packers, Bill Gregory was named the starter. His long wait was finally over. Larry Cole was the reigning starter by default, and now Tom Landry said he would be the starter. He wouldn't commit to it being that way the rest of the season. We were 4–0. We then lost to Green Bay, beat the Eagles, and lost to the Redskins in overtime.

We then went to play the Patriots. I lined up against Joe DeLamalier. He was the strongest player I had ever played against. He didn't hold excessively. I still managed to make a number of plays, but at the end of the day, I was worn-out and sore. He would go on to the Hall of Fame. Coach Landry acknowledged that I had a good game and decided to just rotate Bill and me the rest of the season. We won the next four out of five games. By the last week of the season, we were headed for the playoffs. We then played in the coldest game of the year. It was against the New York Jets at Shea Stadium. The temperature was five degrees, but with the wind coming in from the Atlantic, the chill factor was twenty-five below.

Joe Namath was the quarterback. He was always an engaging guy. He would talk to us during the game. He said, "Let's get this game over and go in where it is warm." They ran their rookie running back, John Riggins. He would gain about four or five yards a carry. When it is really cold, it is hard to take down a physical runner. When we stopped him to put them into a passing situation, he would throw the ball and pick up a first down. Then when he started to pass on first down and miss, we said, "Wait a minute, you are stopping the clock." He then agreed to run the ball more so the clock would run faster. They were out of the playoffs, so when teams played their final game, the last thing they wanted to do was get hurt, so by the time the second half came along, the passion for winning had subsided. We won the game and got out of the cold weather. We achieved our two goals. We were back headed to the playoffs.

Our first game would be against the Minnesota Vikings. We were the underdog by a lot. We were a confident young team. We knew we had the talent, but did we have enough experience to know how to win? The game was played at Metropolitan Stadium in Bloomington, Minnesota. It was a defensive battle. At the end of the first half, the score was 7–0, in favor or the Vikings. Early in the third quarter, we jumped on a fumbled-punt return on their fourteen-yard line and Doug Denison took it in for a touchdown. We then tied the game, 7–7. Later, we added a Toni Fritsch field goal. We were ahead 10–7. Then, Fran Tarkenton engineered a long drive, with Chuck Foreman and Brent McClanahan carrying the ball down the field.

Chuck Foreman took it in for the touchdown and the lead, 14–10. There was a minute and fifty-one seconds left in the game, and we were on the fifteen-yard line, eighty-five yards away from the end zone. Roger hit Drew Pearson for a couple of short passes. Then John Fitzgerald hiked the ball low and we lost six yards. It was now fourth and sixteenth. Roger then hit Drew for a twenty-five-yard completion on the sideline. After an incompletion, with twenty-five seconds left in the game and us on the fifty-yard line, Roger Staubach called a play that Drew Pearson had suggested to Roger early in the game. He said he could beat Nate Wright deep. Roger pump-faked the pass and then heaved it up with all he had. The ball was a little short. Drew adjusted to the ball. Nate didn't see the ball in time, so Drew came back for the ball, with Nate Wright dropping to the ground. Drew then just strode in the end zone for the touchdown to take the lead, 17–14. A new word was added, a new term to our vocabulary, the *Hail Mary pass*. Roger, a devout Catholic, said he just said a prayer after he heaved it up.

The Vikings thought Drew pushed off to free himself from Nate Wright; however, the way we saw it was, it was a close call and Drew was just clearing his catch. Finally, the close call went in our favor. The saddest part of the whole day was that Fran Tarkenton's father suffered a heart attack and died. I felt so sorry for Fran.

We got on the plane back to Dallas. When we arrived, the fans were welcoming us home. We had an exciting team, and the fans appreciated what we had accomplished. Our next opponent would be the Los Angeles Rams. We would play them in LA at the Coliseum. For us it was like a home game, because during preseason, we played preseason games there every year. They were the favorite to win. Most sportswriters considered the win over the Vikings just a fluke. We knew better. We executed our game plan perfectly. The shotgun formation was performed perfectly with runs, passes, and Staubach scrambles. Preston Pearson had a big day with three touchdowns. Fred Dryer and Jack Youngblood, their defensive ends, were guessing the plays, and most times they were wrong. Coach Landry opened up the whole playbook. We led 21–0 at halftime and went on to win, 37–7. We were going back to the Super Bowl.

The Super Bowl was in Miami. We would be playing the Pittsburg Steelers. They were the all-out favorite. Their defense was so stout they were called the Steel Curtain. On offense, they had Terry Bradshaw, who was starting to come into his own, and receivers Lynn Swan and John Stallworth, a tandem that was formidable. They also had a formidable running game with Franco Harris and Rocky Bleier. Tom Landry had put together an aggressive game plan. He called a reverse on the kickoff return, and Tom Henderson took the ball down to the Pittsburg's twenty-nine-yard line. Then Drew Pearson caught a twenty-nine-yard pass and took it into the end zone. We took the early lead. Then Bradshaw took the ball down the field with the running of Franco Harris in short doses and short passes. They got on the clock by the end of the first quarter, and the game was tied. We sparred back and forth with punishing defense on both sides. Later in the second quarter, Toni Fritsch added a thirty-six-yard field goal. We led at halftime, 10–7. No one expected that. In the third quarter, the game was getting even more physical. The referees weren't calling the game close. Jack Lambert was hitting our receivers after the play and getting away with it. Their linebackers were like a pack of dogs. They were hitting very hard. We started to do the same. There was no scoring in the third quarter.

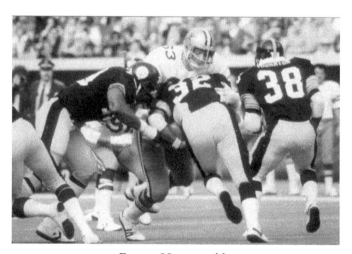

Franco Harris tackle

Early in the fourth quarter, the dam started to bust. Pittsburg blocked a Mitch Hoopes punt, and they scored a safety. Our lead was now down to 10–9. We got the ball back but didn't move it into a scoring position. They got the ball back, and on a third and long, Lynn Swan caught an unbelievable pass over Mark Washington. He was in perfect position to defend the pass, and Lynn Swan reached out the entire length of his arms and legs horizontally and caught the ball. They would later go down to score a field goal and took the go-ahead lead of 12–10. Another field goal added to their lead of 15–10. We were still in range to beat them. We had a lot of young players who had never experienced a Super Bowl. They gave it all they had. They had a lot of energy. In the middle of the fourth quarter, we had a safety blitz called. The defensive tackles would engage their blocker and let the safety pass through before continuing on to the quarterback. Cliff Harris got there, but we he was tripped up to hit Bradshaw low. I came in and hit Bradshaw on his helmet. I was determined to do what I could to win the game. Terry got off the pass to Lynn Swan with a perfectly thrown pass to the end zone. I was a split second too late to affect the pass. Lynn Swan scored a sixty-four-yard touchdown, and the game was seemingly put away. After the play, Terry Bradshaw was down and eventually walked to the sideline. On the sideline, they determined that he had a concussion and would not re-enter the game.

They missed the extra point, so the game was now 21–10. Terry Hanratty came into the game to replace Bradshaw. He had hardly played all year. If Lynn Swan had not caught the pass, we would have a real good chance of winning the game. Now it would be harder. The offense got the ball and went down the field and scored on a thirty-four-yard touchdown pass to Percy Howard. It was now 21–17. We stopped Hanratty again, and Pittsburg had to punt. Roger drove the team down the field to give it one final shot. With time running out, Roger drove the ball to the fifteen-yard line. He threw another pass in the end zone to Percy Howard again. They ball bounced off his fingertips. We thought there was pass interference on the play by Jack Lambert, but the refs weren't calling the game that close. The next play turned out to be an interception, and the game was over. We lost, 21–17. As history would record, this was the first and only pass Percy Howard would catch in the NFL. Injuries plagued him the next couple of years. We walked off the field disappointed but proud how tough we played against the Pittsburg Steelers.

We licked our wounds and went to our Super Bowl Party. After a couple of hours, we lightened up because we liked our team and knew we would be back to the Super Bowl. The next morning, we found out that Terry Bradshaw stayed overnight in the hospital. The play happened so fast. I remember hitting him, but I didn't remember hitting him in the helmet. The next morning, the papers said it was Cliff Harris who hit him. When the video came out, it showed I hit him in the helmet. With today's rules, I would have been ejected from the game. I was glad that Terry made a full recovery. I didn't mean to hurt him. I later spoke at a fundraising roast of Terry Bradshaw. I said that the helmet hit was the reason Terry was so goofy. He was a gregarious guy who took it all in stride. In my opinion, 1975 was Tom Landry's greatest coaching year of his life. He was innovative, he showed patience with the younger players, and his coaches did a great job of teaching technique. Certainly, we had a lot to build on for the next year.

It was now time to get back to my business. It was January 1976. International Village was almost complete. We would have our grand opening on February 21. Roger Staubach was gracious enough to come to Bedford and help promote this event. We combined this event with a fundraiser for the March of Dimes with poster child Robbie Harville. The local McDonald's would donate twenty-five cents out of every purchase that day to the March of Dimes. Roger picked up Robbie and bonded with him right away. Robbie was about five years old and had to use crutches. We had the ribbon cutting at the project, with all three local mayors present, and then went on to McDonald's. There was a big turnout. The local community really appreciated getting to meet Roger Staubach.

I had big plans this year. For us to increase sale of houses, I would need my own sales team. I ran across a man named Harold Holland. He was an unconventional guy who was a natural salesman. He was high energy and had a vision to be one of the biggest home builders in the area. He came up with a logo in the shape of a red football with "Larry Cole Homes" on it. He would run ads every weekend in the local papers, the *Mid-Cities Daily News* and *The Grapevine Sun*. He also found a local TV magazine that was a free advertising catalog located in front of grocery stores with houses for sale in the area. It had my ad on the front page. On weekends, he would place directional signs all over town. You could put them up on Friday and take them down by Monday morning. He must have put out about seventy-five signs in the HEB area, Grapevine, and Arlington. You would think I was the biggest builder in the area! I had to pay him a base salary, but all his help was strictly on commission so we could get a lot of leverage with the money spent. At one time, he had six sales agents. Our sales were doing well in the $49,000-plus range in Bedford. We were getting sold out, so we picked up some existing lots in Timberview Estates, where the houses were in the $59,000-plus range, and soon we would be under construction in the $79,000-plus range. In Arlington, we were selling houses in Tiffany Park from $79,000-plus range and would agree to buy five lots in the third and final phase. In the Oakridge neighborhood in Arlington, we built five houses in the $55,000-plus range. We had long-term plans to be able to get lots for about five years. There were ninety lots under development, twenty of which we expected to be able to buy. We chose to have our houses a little more decorated and customized. We sold the first couple of houses. We then got word the developer was going to sell all the ninety lots to a tract builder. This would undercut our prices. We had to sell the last three houses at a discount just to get out of that market, because we couldn't compete with their bulk pricing. Arlington was an excessively pricey, competitive market. The market was big, and there were a lot of builders there to serve that larger market.

As time went on, we could sell the houses, but we needed to build them faster. My job superintendent, Larry Elliot, was not experienced in building a lot of homes at a time. So I decided to hire someone who had the experience building in Arlington, where the market was so fierce. Larry Elliot resigned because he didn't want to work under him. Bobby knew the business. He was the type of guy who could push the subs to get houses built faster. He was getting the job done. We were moving along with him quite nicely. Harold did the selling along with his salesmen. Linda did the decorating of the spec houses and the presold houses, and Bobby was getting the houses built. I had a full plate. Now I was in the people management business. I had a secretary named Jodie, who wanted to control the people who could come see me. Harold had found her. Our office was at 868 Chateau Valee Circle. We had our office in one of the only one-story town houses. Bobby hired Gene Lemoine to do the "punch work." It was his job to finish out the house and tend to warranty work after the customer moved in. He operated out of the utility room without any complaint. He was a very congenial and loyal guy. Harold would pop in the office but never had one of his own.

By the end of the spring, International Village had four houses under construction. The thirty-by-thirty office we built from scratch was now complete, so we could man the building with salespeople on the weekend and then Linda and the job superintendent during the week. They were able to get some presales, so we got those under construction along with some spec houses. My vision was to build all the houses with different styles for colonial, Old English, Spanish, and a New Orleans style with a balcony. I wanted the neighborhood to be unique.

On May 1, I participated in one of the most fun events I had ever participated in. There was a demolition derby at Texas Stadium. Roger Staubach and Dan Pastorini of the Houston Oilers headlined the event. They had the usual stunt shows, but a special event was pitting some of the Dallas Cowboys players and some of the Houston Oilers against one another. Golden Richards participated in the event; however, his car didn't start. Mike Ditka, Forrest Gregg, and I drove the cars we selected. The object of the competition was to see who could last the longest without getting their radiator knocked out and eventually stopping the car. We would mostly drive in reverse, then go forward and do it again, and then back into the others' cars. It was like playing football with a car. When you took out another driver, it was very exhilarating. It got down to the three or four drivers. Roger made it pretty long but got knocked out. I got knocked off next. Then Mike Ditka lasted until Dan Pastorini took him out. He would win the competition. He had done this before. We hadn't. When the press asked Tom Landry if he knew Roger had driven in a demolition derby before, he said, "What?" Then he said, "I thought he had better judgment than that!" Then in his tongue-in-cheek style, he said, "That is why he calls it 'Roger's plays.'"

July came around, and it was time to get back to training camp. I ended the season with Bill Gregory and me sharing equal time at right tackle. We both didn't like it, but we didn't hold it against each other. We had an enthusiastic team to return to. Ed Jones and Harvey Martin had established themselves as starters. Cliff Harris and Charlie Waters were fan favorites as they made big plays and big hits. Mel Renfro was still around as the old pro. Benny Barnes and Mark Washington showed their skills.

On offense, Golden Richards was establishing himself as a reliable wide receiver along with Drew Pearson. Doug Dennison and Scott Laidlaw ran the ball by committee with Robert Newhouse, the workhorse. The offensive line was stout, with John Fitzgerald establishing himself as the center, Herb Scott and Burton Lawless sharing time at left tackle next to Ralph Neely, and the power side of Blaine Nye and Rayfield Wright were all-pros. Roger was coming off a good year and was ready to take this team to the next level. We had new draft choices of Aaron Kyle, Butch Johnson, and Tom Rafferty. They would be making their mark later. Danny White was drafted by the Cowboys in 1974 but wouldn't join the Cowboys until 1976. He played in Canada. He was a very versatile guy. He would join the team as the punter and backup quarterback.

During that summer, the Clint Longley incident happened. Clint was developing as a quarterback. He wanted to complete for the job with Roger Staubach. That summer, Danny White joined the team. He would also compete for the backup quarterback job. Instead of taking out his frustrations on Danny White, he took them out on Roger. He felt Roger was ignoring him now that Danny was around. There was an episode when Clint shoved Roger and Roger punched back at him on their walk back to the locker room after practice. I was in the locker room and saw the sucker punch, where he hit Roger in the back. The guys pulled Roger and Clint apart. The coaches took over. Since Clint was in my dorm wing, the coaches asked me to locate Clint's pistol in his room. He liked to shoot rattlesnakes with it. They were concerned he might use it because he was in a rage. I did that and got it to the coaches. Then I was charged with escorting him back to his room because he would immediately be removed from campus. The drivers picked him up. We would never see him again. He keeps a low profile and lives in rural West Texas, where he grew up. What a waste of talent!

We got on with completing training camp. The coaches were satisfied with most of the players' output. Landry started referring to us as the Front Five. Between Bill and me, we were productive at the right defensive tackle position. He said he would spell Jethro a little more this year with Bill and me as he was the eldest defensive lineman. We lost the first three preseason games. Just before the fourth game, we played in Memphis against the Detroit Lions, I finally called out Al Ward. The season would start in three weeks, and I wasn't under contract. My agent, Marvin Demoff, did next to nothing to get me a new contract. He could get me a contract with Hawaii, of the WFL, or I could just play out my option year and we could negotiate with other NFL teams next year. I would have to take a pay cut. I decided to take control of the situation. I called Demoff and asked them to release their contract for $6,000.

He agreed to. Never again would I use an agent. For me, my choices were to play or not to play. I didn't want to go to any other team. I had a business to run. I would have to retire. I had a meeting at the hotel. The Cowboys were starting to get concerned about the WFL. Calvin Hill had left. Jethro Pugh and D. D. Lewis had signed contracts with Birmingham to play the following year. I think they were concerned about being left hanging. They didn't want to lose both Jethro and me. I was able to bring my salary up from $35,000 to $60,000. Finally, I was getting paid as much as comparable players in the NFL.

We won that preseason game and the next. The last game was against the Houston Oilers. It went into overtime. Nothing like a meaningless game that we had to play overtime. I was motivated to get off the field. I hit John Hadl, now with the Houston Oilers, separating him from the ball. The offense got on the field, and Scott Laidlaw ran into the end zone to end the game.

We were now back to regular-season schedule. My weekly routine started on Sunday. I would get up in the morning and make myself breakfast of bacon or sausage and eggs. I would drive to the stadium about two hours before the game. I hated waiting around the locker room for the game. The smaller guys liked to go on the field before the warm-ups to get into the magic of the moment. I was an old veteran. I wanted to preserve my emotional and physical energy. Most linemen were the same way. I would go to the locker room, get my ankles taped, and then lie in my locker bench and just chill. My mind was programmed for the game. I was reviewing in my mind my assignments. As the game got closer, I drank two cups of coffee to get alert. Playing the game was a series of quick decisions, and some not so quick. You had to figure out the guy you were playing against. You might have beaten him the last time you lined up against him, but that could change this time as he was blocking differently. We got warmed up. Then we went back in the locker room until the referee told us it was time for kickoff. On the sidelines, Jethro Pugh and I had our routine of slapping my hands on both his shoulders and then tapping his helmet twice with both hands, and he would do the same to me. I also developed my own ritual. I would walk and tuck my back foot and hit the back of the other foot, and then vice versa. I was trying to simulate getting hit below the knees and keeping my balance to stay on my feet. When you fall down, you seldom ever become part of stopping a play. As I went on the field, I would say to myself and the other guys, "It's time to go to work."

After the game, I needed to wind down. I would get back home and spend time with the kids. The next morning, I would wake up sore. I would go to the office at about ten o'clock and see what sales were like over the weekend. I would drive to Dallas at noon. Sometimes I would go to the title company to sign lot closing papers the next morning. They marveled that yesterday they saw me in New York and today I was there. Then at the practice facility, we watched the film of the previous game and then did a light workout before we went home. We would be off Tuesday. Besides me, the coaches didn't have a day off. They immediately started next week's game plan Monday afternoon. For me, I stopped by the office again and then went home for dinner. The next day was a full workday for me. I used my time to get myself into my builder/developer mode. I could meet directly with my sales and construction people. I couldn't make any major decisions, but it was helpful to know exactly what was happening. On Wednesday, we would have our meeting at 10:00 a.m. I would leave at 9:00–9:15 a.m. It would take fifty-five minutes to get there. On Wednesday, we had our meeting, where we put in the game plan for next week. At 3:00 p.m., we went on the field. The offense would run their game plan in full pads on Wednesday, and we were the scout team, then on Thursday we would do the reverse. Friday was the same meeting schedule, and on the field we didn't do any hitting and mostly adjusted the game plans from the previous days on field practice. I would go home on Friday.

Piano Family

Friday night was Linda's night. She had as busy a week as I did. Instead of playing tennis, she wanted to get out and dance to get her exercise. We would get a babysitter and go out to dinner. Then we would stop by the Beach Street Ramada Inn to dance when the live group started playing at 10:00 p.m. Saturday was the kids' day. They let us bring our kids to practice. It was one of the favorite memories of our kids. While we were in meetings for about forty-five minutes, the kids would go out on the field and throw the football around. Our equipment manager, Buck Buchanan, loved kids, so he was happy to supervise. He would hand out doughnuts. They just loved this. My son did this many times, and my daughter too. He also brought along his friends for his birthday party. One of them was Tommy Maddox, who played for UCLA, the Denver Broncos, and the Pittsburg Steelers. Grant Hill, the famous basketball player, was also there with his dad, Calvin. My son, Mike, played college football for the University of Illinois, and his friend, Brent Koontz, played football for the University of Oklahoma.

Late afternoon on Saturdays, we would take our kids to Chuck E. Cheese to play and have pizza. Then we got home and I chilled the rest of the evening, hoping to get a good night's sleep before the game. On away games, we would get on the plane Saturday after-noon and arrive late afternoon. We would either be served at our hotel or go out to dinner at some of the finer restaurants in town. I enjoyed that a lot. I enjoyed all the different personalities of each of the cities.

We started the season 5–0. We were on a roll. Then we met up with St. Louis at their place. Don Coryell was their new coach. Things were changing. He was an innovator. He had Jim Hart, now a seasoned veteran with a strong-arm quick release, at quarterback. He had Terry Metcalf at running back, and Mel Gray at wide receiver. They beat us 21–17. We would meet them again at home. The game came down to the wire. This was when Harvey Martin started becom-ing a playmaker. When it was third down, Jim Hart would just barely get off the pass and pick up the first down. He was marching down the field. They were down 19–14. With a touchdown, they would win. When we needed it the most, we dialed up Harvey Martin on fourth down and he got the key sack to close out the game. This would be repeated many times. He would make the all-pro team, as well as Cliff Harris and Charlie Waters.

We ended the season with an 11–3 record. We were confident going into the playoffs. We would play the Rams at home in the first playoff game. We blew them away with a different quarterback, Ron Jaworski, last year in the playoffs, 37–7. Pat Haden would be their new quarterback, the former USC hometown quarterback. He threw three interceptions in the first half, but Roger also threw three interceptions. We got an Efren Herrera field goal in the first quarter. In the second quarter, Pat Haden scored a running touchdown and our Scott Laidlaw ran in a touchdown. The score was 10–7 at halftime. Pat Haden threw three interceptions, but so did Roger Staubach. Lawrence McCutcheon would score a touchdown in the fourth quarter, giving the Rams a 14–10 lead. Then our specialty team scored a two-point safety, edging the game closer to 14–12. All we needed was a field goal. It wasn't to be. We just couldn't get it together. This was a big disappointment. The season was over without us advancing in the playoffs.

In early January of 1977, Harold Holland made me aware that there was a family he knew that was interested in selling their 130-acre farm in Colleyville, just across the street from Bedford. They were the Sparger family. There were four siblings, two boys and two girls. The schools were in HEB ISD, at that time a big advantage. Colleyville had some small neighborhoods with 1/2-acre or larger lots. I had seen many planned unit developments in California when I was in training camp each year. I wanted to do something different in Colleyville. They had a PUD zoning classification where you could have 1/3-acre lots, provided you had some open space. There was an area in the floodplain that couldn't be built on of about 9 acres. They wanted a park there and wanted it to be named Sparger Park. I had no problem with that. In those days, land was being sold with land sale contracts. You would put down 10 or 20 percent, and then the seller would carry a five-year loan secured by the land at a prescribed interest rate. Interest would be due quarterly. There would be a release clause in the note. The buyer would pay about 120 percent times the per-acre price to release that portion of each phase of development. If the quarterly interest was not paid, the land would revert back to the seller. The land sale was contingent upon receiving a positive zoning decision. I was able to negotiate the contract prepared for me by Walter Cook with the Spargers.

I got the contract signed, and I proceeded to get the zoning case prepared by David Farrington. He came up with a loop street inside the land with cul-de-sacs branching off the spine road. It was perfect. Cheek Sparger Road was designed to be connected so five acres were across the street. I would request that to be an office / retail shopping center. The area designated for Sparger Park would be accessible from Bedford Road and a pedestrian trail surrounding the property at the rear end of the lots. The path would be about one mile long. I loved the plan and had the engineer prepare the preliminary conceptual site plan. We submitted the plan to the city of Colleyville in late February. The reception was mixed. The no-growth people came to write letters and show their resistance. It was our job to present the other side and point out the advantages of a nice neighborhood where you could get out of your house and go for a walk or to the adjacent park without getting in your car. The main opposition was that Colleyville didn't have the water pressure to support this development. I had an answer for that. The water would be supplied by the Trinity River Authority extending their lines into Colleyville from Bedford. They got their water from Joe Poole Lake, south of Grand Prairie, Texas. Water infrastructure had already been advanced to Cheek Sparger Road. We just needed to advance it into Colleyville. It would actually help the current water situation, as Colleyville would no longer have to rely on their well system only. Also, some opposed it because it would add burden to the Grapevine/Colleyville ISD. I then informed them that this land was in the HEB ISD. They were happy about that. Finally, they wanted me to reduce the density and increase the lot size. I reduced the density from 215 lots to 201 lots. I provided three house-size categories: 75 lots would have a minimum house of 2,300 square feet, 60 lots would have a minimum house size of 2,800 square feet, and 66 lots would have a minimum house size of 3,200 square feet. With these changes, the zoning was passed by a unanimous vote by the city council and mayor. I was quoted in the paper as saying, "I will do everything I can do to make this a development Colleyville can be proud of."

I got up the next day with a bounce in my step. I had secured my future if I could sell the lots. I knew I could, because this was a beautiful piece of property and there was a market for the lots. I went off to training camp knowing that I had the plan in place to seamlessly retire on my own terms.

At training camp, my roommate, Blaine Nye, didn't show up. He was getting his PhD in microeconomics at Stanford. He wanted to negotiate his salary with Tex Schramm. These were two proud men, so getting either to budge would be hard. Tex was holding the cards, and Blaine had to fold. That was the end of his career. It's a shame it came to that. He was a very good player. Tom Rafferty took over for him and did a good job. Also, Pat Donovan proved he could play either right of left tackle on offensive. Both Ralph Neeley and Rayfield Wright had injuries, so his filling in competently was immensely valuable. It seemed like any lineman that played for Penn State was schooled in the fundamentals. Dave Edwards and LeRoy Jordan also retired. Both would be missed. LeRoy was such a good leader. He knew when to and when not to buck the coaches. He had my back a couple of times in getting me back on the field after injuries. Dave played next to me for seven years. He was the consummate pro who did his job, made big plays, and never complained. I modeled myself after him.

My roommate would now be D. D. Lewis. He was a rookie the same year as I was in 1968. The only thing he and Blaine had in common was, they were both tobacco dippers. I hated the spittoon always being around. My dad was a dipper for fifty years. When he spit out the window, it would land in my face in the back seat. I adapted and lived with it. DD was into country music. He loved Willie Nelson, Waylon Jennings, and Jerry Jeff Walker. He also liked Roger Williams. Eventually, I learned to like the relaxation of listening to some of their songs. Unlike Blaine, DD liked to go out all the time. I went along with him many times and broke my Zero Club behavior. I was trying to have some fun during training camp. We would go to Malibu and Calabasas plus the local restaurants.

This year's rookie class would be headlined by Tony Dorsett, the Heisman Trophy winner from Pittsburg. That was a big deal! We out maneuvered the Seattle Seahawks to get this pick. We finally had a breakaway running back to take the ball the length of the field. He was tutored by Dan Reeves and Preston Pearson, bringing him along with as much as he could handle. The other draft picks were Glenn Carano, quarterback; Tony Hill, wide receiver; Guy Brown, line-backer; Jim Cooper and Andy Frederick, offensive tackles; and David Stalls, defensive tackle. This was also a good draft class. Bill Gregory beefed up with weights in the off-season, determined to finally win the job of right defensive tackle that he so patiently was waiting for. We both complemented each other as we both had minor injuries when we couldn't go full speed the previous two years. By this time, I had learned that every year was a new team. We were all hopeful for this year, but we still had to go out there and win it.

We got through preseason with a lackluster 3–3 record, but we were playing a lot of people. Randy White was not getting the job done at linebacker. In one of the meetings, he came up to me and said, "Bubber, they are going to cut me." I said, "Yeah right, they are going to cut you and keep me. I don't think so." About a week later, after the team meeting, after the last preseason game, Ernie Stautner came up to me and said they were moving Randy White to right tackle and he would be the starter. Uhhh, *okay*? That was stunning. Well, my logical mind knew they needed to get Randy White on the field. They first tried to make Randy the middle linebacker replacement for LeRoy Jordan. Then they tried him at outside line-backer with limited success. At that time, I wasn't thinking of how Bill Gregory took the news. I bet he was infuriated but probably was told he would spell Jethro Pugh a lot.

This was reality. My career was coming to an end. I had not been a starter since I was a freshman in high school. This was new. In the first game of the season, we played Minnesota at their place. I stood on the sidelines with nothing to do. I didn't want to give the coaches the satisfaction that I would just accept this demotion and ask to be put in. I avoided Ernie the whole game. It was a boring game with little offense. Late in the fourth quarter, he saw me on the sideline with my uniform perfectly clean. He asked if I had been in the game. I said no. He then said, "Get in there!" I played seven plays. I got one tackle, one trap, and one sack for a ten-yard loss in overtime. Minnesota shanked the ball, and we got the ball on the forty-seven-yard line. Roger hit Golden Richards and Drew Pearson, and they marched down the field. Roger hit Preston Pearson with a perfect pass just over the end zone.

We won, 16–10, in overtime.

On film day, Coach called out kudos to me for making plays off the bench. That helped ease the pain a little. I was happy for Randy White. He and I had always had a good relationship. He had played a down-edge lineman in college, and they tried to make a Butkus out of him. His ideal position would be the outside linebacker on a 3–4 defense. The next best place was the right defensive tackle, usually the weak side, where his speed could be used to run down plays in pursuit. He adapted to the flex defense. He was quick. He could recover fast enough even if he didn't take his steps properly. We went on to win the first eight games, many of them blowouts. One of those games was against the St. Louis Cardinals at their place. The right offensive guard was Conrad Dobler. He had the reputation of being a dirty player who would do anything to get the advantage. He would punch defensive linemen in their throat. He would leg-whip the defensive linemen. That would later be banned in the NFL. I also saw him take a bite on Jethro Pugh's calf muscle. Jethro wasn't having much success against him, so Ernie put me in the game against him. He tried to do that stuff against me. I had watched Merlin Olsen of the LA Rams kicked out of the game when he fought back against him earlier in the year. Merlin was a mild-mannered guy like myself. I took my time just hitting him straight on and punching him in the gut like a boxer does. I got him to back down and drop his holding hands off me. Randy White, our physical player nicknamed Manster (half-man, half-monster), approved of my play. He hadn't seen that side of me. When I got really pissed off, I fought. He didn't know that side of me. Later in retirement, I would meet Conrad Dobler at a Players Association meeting in Dallas. He was an outgoing, bombastic guy with a good sense of humor. Off the field, he wasn't such a bad guy. Even Randy White agreed.

We won the next four games. We then got a reality check from St. Louis in week 9, when they played in Dallas. Don Coryell had figured out how to design influence plays that would give false reads on the defensive line. The next week, we lost to the Pittsburg Steelers. They were always up to beat us. We ran the table the rest of the way, and we finished the season with a 12–2 record, the best since 1968, my rookie year. Tony Dorsett emerged gaining over 1,000 yards, with a 4.8-yard average. Roger had a good year. We were a very diverse offense. On defense, we were overpowering. Moving Randy White to defensive tackle was good for two reasons, his talent and the fact that it freed up Bob Bruenig to take over as middle linebacker. He was a smart player and student of the game. Charlie Waters took over the leadership of the defense before Bob emerged as the leader. Our other linebackers were D. D. Lewis, who was a solid veteran in the mold of Dave Edwards, and then Thomas Henderson and Mike Hegman, both great players with their own set of skills. This year it was our team in the NFC that dominated the league, and the Denver Broncos were the dominant team in the AFC, with the "orange crush" defense led by Lyle Alzado, the tough nose tackle. On offense, they were led by Craig Morton. He was more or less his own offensive coordinator. He was masterful in running the naked bootleg, where, on a power play, he would not tell anyone if he was going to pull the ball back and run the other way. He was able to do that without being injured because he ran for the sidelines with the ball. He had taken many hits in his career.

By December, the mold had been set. It looked like my career was coming to an end as I didn't get much playing time. I settled in and gave it my best when I did get a chance to play. I had a good run, and now it was time for somebody else. We were so strong on the left side with Ed Jones and Jethro Pugh. Their size alone just snuffed plays. On the right side, Harvey and Randy were so quick and did stunts. They could get to the quarterback. We were confident going into the playoffs. We beat Denver 14–6 in the last game of the season. Craig didn't play. We got a preview of how strong their defense was.

We started the playoffs with a blowout of the Chicago Bears, 37–7. Then we took on the Minnesota Vikings and outlasted them, 23–12. We were back in the Super Bowl. This time we were going to win it. It was a good thing we played Denver in December, since we now had film on them. Part of the Landry genius was that he was a master at designing plays against different teams. There were turnovers on offense, but we were gambling that our defense would prevail. Butch Johnson caught an unbelievable pass in the end zone, stretching out beyond his normal reach. We took a 13–0 lead. A lot of games came down to matchups. The Denver offensive line was no match for our defense. Craig Morton was smothered by all our linemen, especially Randy and Harvey. Ed and Jethro shut down the running play with abandon. By the second half, Craig Morton was pulled for a more mobile quarterback to run for his life. That was when I came into the game. It was kind of a mercy thing. Both Bill Gregory and I were in at the same time. I was very conscious of not letting the momentum change, so we did a lot of chasing of the quarterbacks. We didn't want to have them stage a comeback to turn around the momentum. When the offense performed a trick play with Robert Newhouse throwing a perfect pass to Golden Richards, the game was sealed. We won our second Super Bowl. Randy White and Harvey Martin would be named co-MVPs of the Super Bowl. The 1970–1971 team was the best team I had ever played on. This 1977 was the most talented team I ever played for. I walked out of the locker room across the Superdome field thinking this could have been my last game. The press asked the question: Was I retiring? I told them I would wait until July to make a final decision. The season was over. I needed to get back to work, with a full plate of decisions to make.

CHAPTER 8

THE FINALE

I had a lot to do this off-season. It was January 1978. The development construction plans for Tara Plantation were being finalized. I needed to name the streets. I had Linda research names from that era of Georgia's past. We had Butler Court, Scarlet Circle, and Plantation Drive, just to name a few. In late January, we drove to Houston for the National Association of Builders Convention. While we were there, we drove to one of the northern suburbs where we saw the community named River Plantation. They had a covered bridge at the entrance. I liked that idea because we had to cross a bridge to enter the community. We designed a covered bridge with one word on the face of it, Tara. This would prove to be a great marketing symbol. A lot of people just came by to see it. There was nothing like that in any comparable neighborhood in Tarrant County. In February, the development of phase 1 was under construction. We would break the neighborhood into four phases. It is always exciting to do the initial excavation to see your vision come to life. I knew this would be a winner. One perk of being a developer was that I would be able to choose the lot I wanted to build my house on. I chose a one-and-a-half-acre lot backing up to the park. It had a gorgeous view. I started drawing conceptual plans of the house, but actual building wouldn't take place until we received enough profit from sale of the first-phase lots.

We liked our house on Chaparral Court, but our future would be in Colleyville, not Bedford. That spring, we took a bus trip with a number of friends to Shreveport for the horse races. We had a nice time. Our kids were on a trip to Disneyworld with their grandparents and cousins. When we got home, our house had been broken into. They stole my Super Bowl VI ring and two of my NFC championship rings for 1970 and 1975. They also took some of Linda's grandmother's rings she had given her. It was a horrible feeling. It was like you just got spit on. They didn't take any of the televisions or anything else of value. We called the police, and they did their report.

Later on that fall, the Euless police solved the case. This was a crime ring where guys were told where to go and just complete the job. One of the burglars was a Cowboys fan and felt bad he was doing this to me; however, he had no choice. He had to finish the job for the crime ring or face consequences. They found that some of Linda's rings didn't have any value other than sentimental, so they threw them in the Trinity River. The rest, they melted down along with my NFC rings. They did recover my Super Bowl VI ring, minus the diamonds, and a little of the melted metal of the two NFC rings, which I threw away. I was happy to get the Super VI championship ring back. I had a local jeweler friend of mine install new diamonds in the ring so it looked close to new. We had suffered so hard to get that first championship that this battered ring to me was symbolic. This kind of changed how we looked at that home. It was a block away from the heavily traveled Pipeline Road that we felt the house would be a target for more vandalism. We decided to sell the house and move to one of the spec houses in International Village that hadn't sold. It was a New Orleans style home. We listed the house with Gladys Vance of Stimmel Realtors. She had done a good job selling our Edgecliff house a few years ago. She got the house sold by the fall, so we moved over to the other house in International Village. It was the New Orleans-style house. The design seemed like a good idea at that time; however, you would have to walk up the steps to get to the main floor, where the kitchen, living room, and bedrooms were located. Downstairs was just a game room and garage. Our kids loved the downstairs room, where they were away from their mother's watch. I played my favorite songs on the record player and then taped them for future use. They loved to sing along.

By late spring, I got the first of four office buildings under construction. The first building was 10,250 square feet. We would occupy about 3,000 feet, and the balance would be leased out to four other tenants. This was a partnership with Tom Hodge. Tom furnished the financing as he was a real estate investment broker. This new building would be ready to move in to during the spring of 1979. I would move my offices there from the town house office. We were down to the last lots in International Village. I would move that thirty-by-thirty sales office to Tara Plantation once the streets had been completed. It would be used to sell lots and houses. It had worked out well enough at International Village.

By this time I had eight employees. I had a payroll to cover. It took a lot of houses to feed that beast. I completed the houses in Tiffany Park in Arlington and decided that I would only focus on building in the HEB area and Colleyville.

There was a lot of friction between Harold Holland and Bobby Taylor. When Bobby would get with the customer, they would tell him that he or his sales agents agreed to include items not found in the contract. At the same time, Gladys Vance told me that Harold's reputation with other Realtors was not good. He had cut out a number of Realtors of getting their commissions. I am sure there were two sides to that story. I called Gladys, my real estate mother. She was like a big sister looking out for me and my reputation.

Since I was moving into being primarily a real estate developer, I decided to end the in-house sales team and let Bobby Taylor go. I needed to cut the overhead. I hated to fire or lay off people, but at times you have to do what you have to do. There are always two sides to the story, but I just wanted to simplify my life. I decided to let them all go and keep Gene Lemoine. He would work with Linda on doing mostly build-to-suit houses, where the house was sold before we started construction. When spec houses don't sell within four months, you usually lose money or break even before paying salaries.

I thought about retiring, but I just wasn't ready to retire. I felt good physically. When I arrived at training camp, I didn't know what to expect. This would be my tenth year. I didn't like alternating with Bill Gregory, and neither did he, but it was easier on my body. I might have extended my longevity. Jethro Pugh was in his fourteenth year, so there still could be room for me. I looked at the draft list. Who was going to replace me this year?

The number 1 draft choice was Larry Bethea, a defensive lineman from Michigan State. The second round choice was Todd Christenson, a tight end. Then in the eleventh round, they chose Dennis Thurman, defensive back. The number of draft choices was reduced from seventeen to twelve this year. This wasn't a very good draft class. Todd Christiansen was a very good tight end. He would have a good career at Oakland. Billy Joe Dupree and Jay Saldi were too good to beat out. Dennis Thurman was one of those smart players who would get himself into position to make interceptions. Mel Renfro retired. He was one of the greats in NFL history. He would go on to induction in the Hall of Fame. Also, Ralph Neely retired after thirteen seasons. He was such a good fixture for the team. He played both right and left tackle with skill. He helped me learn how to pass-rush.

I saw Larry Bethea at practice. What a physical specimen! Of all the guys they brought in, I thought the way he moved his body was so natural with strength and quickness. I kept thinking what I could do with my experience and use his body. As any rookie, he was not ready to step in right away. He was a happy-go-lucky guy who was friendly to everyone. He wasn't too mature at that time.

After I got back to camp for a week, I was glad to be back. I liked playing with these guys. I was the old pro. Most of my life, I was the little brother in my family and the earlier Cowboys teams I had played on. D. D. Lewis and I went to a LA Dodger Baseball game. DD knew one of the Dodger players. We met him a couple of hours before the game. He took us into the clubhouse and introduced us to Tommy LaSorta. He was every bit like his sports image, a very engaging and considerate man. During the game, they displayed on the scoreboard, "Welcome, D. D. Lewis and Larry Cole, 1977 Dallas Cowboys, Super Bowl Champions."

We started the preseason. The number of preseason games was reduced to four, and the number of regular-season games moved from fourteen to sixteen games.

After the third preseason game, Bill Gregory was traded to Seattle. I'm sure they knew that if they traded me, I would retire and they would get nothing. I couldn't afford to play football in another city and run my business at the same time. Bill had already left the premises. I couldn't say goodbye and wish him well. He was such a class guy. Jethro Pugh would be entering his fourteenth year. I would be coming in on passing situations. I liked that. I settled in at left defensive tackle. That was where I was the most comfortable. I am left-handed, and I would be able to move quicker to the left than the right. We got the season started. We blew away Baltimore, 38–0. Then we beat the Giants, 32–24. The following week, we lost to the LA Rams. It seemed like with Minnesota, Washington, and LA, we traded off each year who would win. They were great rivalries. The following week, we took care of the Cardinals, 21–12. The Washington Redskins had a new quarterback, Joe Theismann. He had sat on the bench his rookie year, and now it was time to get him on the field. He was known as kind of a "hot dog" at that time. Our offense couldn't get anything going. We had held them to nine points, but we only scored five points on offense. At the end of the game, Washington got the ball on their own five-yard line. Joe Theismann took the ball back into the end zone and was dancing around until the clock expired. I started running off the field on the way to the locker room. I went up to him and took a cheap shot with my forearm to his shoulders and took him down. The ball came out and traveled outside the end zone. I kept running to the locker room to make sure his teammates wouldn't get to me to retaliate. The game was over. We lost. I thought to myself, *I shouldn't have done that. I am more professional than that.* On film day, I was ready for Tom Landry to lay into me in front of the whole team. He complained that the team had lost its fight to play hard until the game was over. He then complimented me on knowing that if I could separate him from the ball, I might have been able to recover a touchdown in the end zone to win. I thought, *Yeah, that's what I was thinking.* I had taken the blame for many things I wasn't responsible for. I chuckled and moved on.

We beat the Giants 24–3 the next week. Then we played the Cardinals. Then we had one of those finishes. This one went into overtime. Harvey was able to make the key sack on Jim Hart, and we won by a field goal. We then lost two of the next three games to Minnesota and Miami. We were now 6–4. There was a lot of talk that we had lost our edge. It is hard to defend a Super Bowl. When you come to town as the defending champions, this may be the biggest game of the year for them.

The next week, we played the Green Bay Packers. They had gotten off to a good start with Bart Starr as their head coach. David Whitehurst was their starting quarterback. Randy White and I had a stunt that we called a "cha-cha." We both looped around the other. We both met at the quarterback at the same time below the knees. It tore up his knee. We didn't intend to do this, but it happened. I love tough, hard competition, but these are things that can happen on the field. He was out for the season. We went on to win 42–14. The next week, we played the Saints. I got an interception and tried to run the ball. I saw fifty yards to the end zone. Ed Jones was in my way. I think he wanted me to hand it to him, but that would be a forward lateral. I was only able to run the ball thirteen yards into a crowd. We joked about it later. The offense scored and put the game away. I was starting to get my groove back. Jethro's knee was bothering him a lot, and by December, I was playing the whole game with some relief when Larry Bethea came into the game. I had learned over the years to turn up my game a notch at the end of the season. We won the rest of the games and were 12–4 going into the playoffs. I was beginning to be rediscovered by the press. They thought it was a great comeback story. I told them I hadn't gone anywhere. I loved playing next to Randy White. When we ran a stunt, I would disguise my initial move into the center, where I would trap them into making the double team on me. This would free Randy to get to the quarterback one-on-one and clobber them. I loved outfoxing them. Playing next to Ed Jones wasn't bad either. When I did a stunt with him, he was so big that I could hide behind him before I drove to the quarterback, not giving the center time to see me and pick me up.

We hosted the first playoff game against Atlanta. Steve Bartkowski was the quarterback. He had a good arm but wasn't that mobile. During the game, Roger Staubach went down with the back of his head bouncing off the turf. He suffered a concussion. He would be out the rest of the game. We didn't want that to cause us to be eliminated this early in the playoffs. The defense had to step up.

We were behind 20–13 at halftime. We had to claw back. I was able to get two traps and get the ball back to the offense. Danny White came into the game and was up for the task. We tied the game at the end of the third quarter. We then shut them out the rest of the way. They didn't score a point in the second half. We were able to win 27–20 with a sigh of relief. Roger would be back the next week. This year, the Rams had a better record and had beaten us during the season. We would have to go there to play the NFC championship game. We had a lot of Cowboys fans there, so there wasn't much of a home field advantage. The Rams had a good running attack with John Cappelletti. This was a very physical game. On the second play, I hit Cappelleti and caused him to fumble. As the game developed, it looked to me that they were trying to single me out with influence plays by not blocking me at all when I was reading the offense. I had to have the discipline to stay put when either Cappalletti showed up or Pat Haden took off on a run up the field. I was able to get a number of tackles of both guys. We just flat shut them down. Pat Haden was pressured all game. Charlie Waters was able to get two interceptions. We dominated the entire game. I felt this was one of the best games I ever played. I sacked him, tackled him on a scramble to make it short of a first down, and then the kicker missed the field. I also had a quarterback pressure where Randy Hughes picked off an interception. Pat Haden was knocked out of the game on a hit by Randy White. He hurt his shoulder. Randy also broke a bone in his finger. He would have to wear a cast the rest of the way. We won the game 28–0. We would be going to the Super Bowl, my fifth Super Bowl in nine years. We wanted to play the Steelers. We thought this time we would beat them. They were three-point favorites. Tom Henderson dominated the pre-Super Bowl coverage by saying that Terry Bradshaw couldn't spell CAT even if he spotted him the C and the T. That was all we needed to get Terry Bradshaw and the whole team riled up before the game. This was the most anticipated Super Bowl ever. We had both won two Super Bowls, and one of the two teams would be the first to win three Super Bowls. Tex Schramm really wanted this. As players, we needed to just win one game in the next few days. Then they could write history.

It was a festive event. A lot of people just came to Miami just to be there even if they didn't have tickets to the game. A couple of us took a cab to the stadium rather than wait for the bus. We got stuck in a traffic jam and barely got there in enough time to get taped and out the door for warm-ups. Friends of mine from high school and Don Dodson and C. A. Sanford from HEB were there. In the stands, it was the days of the Terrible Towel. They would wave that gold towel and sing a very unimaginative line. "Here we go, Steelers, here we go!" It was a humid, seventy-degree day with a light drizzle the whole game. The ball would be a little slippery. The Steelers were the first to score. Bradshaw hit John Stallworth for a twenty-eight-yard touchdown over the middle. Then Roger Staubach hit Tony Hill for a touchdown. Thomas Henderson and Mike Hegman nailed Bradshaw. Thomas grabbed Terry's other hand, and the ball was taken out of Terry's hands by Mike Hegman. He took it in thirty-seven yards, and we had a 14–7 lead. Then Bradshaw hit Lynn Swan for a seventy-five-yard touchdown to tie the game. Our offense drove the ball down to the sixteen-yard line, and then Mel Blount intercepted the ball. They scored with a seven-yard pass to Rocky Bleier to take the halftime lead 21–14.

In the third quarter, Roger passed to Jackie Smith into the end zone. There was no one around. Jackie dropped the pass and was in agony. Roger said he should have thrown it harder. We felt so sorry for Jackie. He had come over from St. Louis and was a great contributor during the season. We loved having him around. He would still be inducted into the Hall of Fame, but the blemish was there. We all had to live with the plays we missed making. When he dropped the ball, he stiffened his back in disgust and suspended himself one foot above the ground. That picture was on the wall at the Canton Hall of Fame. Instead of a touchdown, we had to settle for a Rafael Septien field goal. On the ensuing kickoff, Roy Gerela floated the ball in the direction of Randy White, who was on the kickoff receiving team. He had to wear a cast. The ball hit Randy, and Tony Dungee of the Steelers was able to recover the ball. They had good field position. On the next play, Franco Harris took it in up the middle for a twenty-two-yard touchdown. Now we were down 28–17. Then there was the pass interference call against Benny Barnes. They didn't have live replays. Benny argued he didn't touch him, but the referee called it different, and Pittsburg now had the ball on the eighteen-yard line. Terry hit Swan over the middle for a touchdown. This looked like the play that put the game away. It was now 35–17, with six minutes, fifty-one seconds to go. "Never say die!" Roger Staubach took the ball down the field and threw a seven-yard pass to Dilly Joe Dupree to close the lead to 35–24. Septien kicked the onside kick, and we recovered. Roger hit Butch Johnson with a four-yard pass. It was now 35–31, with twenty-two seconds left. Miracles don't happen twice in a game, so the onside kick failed. Rocky Bleier fell on the ball, and the game was over.

This was one of those games where too many things happened. Both sides commented on how physical the game was. Terry Bradshaw was the MVP of the game. He hurt his shoulder on the Thomas Henderson hit in the second quarter but sucked it up and kept going. This was the most attended, most watched, most entertaining game in history. To us it was still a loss. This was a "coulda, shoulda, woulda" game. Rather than blame anyone, I always took the approach that if I had done just a little better, maybe I could have made the difference to win the game for the team.

It was time to get back to full-time business. Tara Plantation was under development and soon to be ready to start houses by the spring. I hired Glen Schneider to find the builders and sell the lots. He was a licensed real estate agent that had worked for Stimmel Realtors, the number 1 local Realtor at that time. He was acquainted with some of the builders. It was his job to locate good-quality custom builders in the area. Our policy was that no builder could build the same exact house in the neighborhood. He would have to make elevation changes and some floor plan changes. Nobody wanted to walk into a custom house that was exactly like the one someone else just bought. Prior to building the houses, the builders would have to submit to us their floor plans and elevations to give our approval before he could get a permit. Before the first lot was closed, we needed to write deed restrictions as to size of house, restrictions on front-entry garages (only rear- or side-entry garages were allowed). We limited the number of pets.

Having strict deed restrictions was new to this area. We formed a homeowners' association to run the affairs of the neighborhood. We didn't require mandatory dues at that time. We felt that was a step too far. We found paying dues voluntarily was hard to do because only about 60 percent of the people were willing to pay something they didn't have to. The money was for mowing along the pedestrian trail and to manicure the entrances to plant new flowers every spring. In the future, we would make it mandatory.

We began construction of the covered bridge. After the grading was done, we could see how this would fit in perfectly. As you were coming down the hill at the entrance, you could see the full outline of the covered bridge. We tried to build it with wood but quickly figured it needed a steel frame. We painted the posts and the trim barnyard red, and then the balance of the siding in an off-white color, with the logo *Tara* on the face. We also set it up so the bridge was lit underneath. This way, at night you were welcomed home.

"Tara Bridge"

I put a lot of value in marketing. I had seen with the Dallas Cowboys and Vantage Companies the value of tying words and symbols together. We needed to get the attention of the public. We got a lot of free publicity from my football celebrity, but the picture of the bridge was enough for people to just come out there to see it. At the other entrance, I had a steel company in Gainesville, Texas, build an arched entrance with the full words "Tara Plantation" in the steel along with scrolls. That was unique too.

By the spring, we were able to close our first lots. Each time we closed a lot, I would pay the lender a partial release. Once the amount of the loan was decided, we would take the loan amount divided by the number of lots and multiply by 1.20. That would be the release amount. As each lot would close there would be about $5,000 a lot net difference that I could use for expenses. Once the loan was paid off, we would then be able to get all the proceeds, around $30,000 a lot for the last ten lots or so.

Our new office building was ready to move into. I hadn't had a real office since the Vantage Companies employment seven years earlier. It was an attractive one-story building. We had a reception room, a meeting room, offices for Linda and me and our new leasing agent, Julie Ansett, and a workroom area where our construction superintendent could sit down with the subs. The room that was the most appreciated was the conference room. I met with a lot of people about a lot of subjects, and this was a neutral ground rather than being opposite me at my desk.

In the spring, I received the Distinguished Service Award from the HEB Chamber of Commerce for civic leadership. When Jethro Pugh heard about this, he asked me if I would rather be a "big fish in a little pond or a little fish in a big pond." I guess this was his answer. My line coach, Ernie Stautner, came out and showed film of some of my best plays. That was kind of him to do that for the community.

In June, my hometown of Granite Falls, Minnesota, asked if I wanted to be the grand marshal of a parade they were planning to celebrate the one hundredth anniversary, the centennial year, of Granite Falls becoming a city. My great-grandfather came to this part of Minnesota in 1872 and settled in nearby Hanley Falls. I was honored to be the grand marshal. That town had been so good to me with great teachers, coaches, preachers, and just a lot of good people with common sense. I had an autograph session at the school; they were celebrating the opening of the refurbished Volstead Home. He was the man who sponsored the Alcohol Prohibition Act. That didn't work out so well, but he was instrumental in the establishment of co-ops, where farmers could collectively market their crops through their local grain elevators. That was essential to stabilizing the market. At the parade, they had a convertible. Linda sat in the front seat, and I and my two children sat on top of the back of the convertible. Mike was eight, and Christy was six. I dressed in a Western outfit with blue jeans, a cowboy shirt, and a Cowboys hat. I usually didn't dress like that for most events, but I had a little Hollywood in me to be visual. The event was very successful, and it was a chance to spend time with my mom and dad and for them to see their grandkids.

Grand Marshal parade.

We celebrated our tenth anniversary on June 21. We went to Edelweiss Restaurant to get that good steak that Bernd, the German owner, would pick out for us, and then his special German fried potatoes. I never did like sauerkraut, but it came with that anyway. After dinner, we went to the Ramadi Inn Hotel on Beach Street for the evening show. This night they had a band that played more country and Western songs. I was loosening up and was ready to go onstage. I sang "Luckenbach Texas" by Waylon Jennings. When it got to the lines "Ain't nobody feeling no pain," the crowd had a rise, and then when the line came where it said, "Four-car garage and we are still building on / I said still building homes," to personalize it to me, that got a rise. There are only a few songs I can sing where I can carry a tune.

When the band got to another song with the lyrics "Take this job and shove it," Linda thought I was singing about our marriage. I was frustrated that Ed Jones would be retiring or holding out from his contract negotiations. He said football wasn't that important to him. He would go into boxing. What? Was he serious? Yes, he was. That would unsettle the line. With Jethro Pugh retiring and Bill Gregory gone, we went from a deep bench to two guys, Larry Bethea and David Stalls, that had little experience and me. I was not happy about that.

When I headed back to training camp, the coaches were a little unsettled. They wanted to keep me playing left tackle because at this point in my career, this was my natural position. For that to happen, Larry Bethea would have to meet the challenge. Larry was stunned when Ed Jones didn't report to camp. That was because Ed Jones was his mentor. I don't think he was ready for the challenge. This year, Robert Shaw was the number 1 draft choice. He was a center from Tennessee. The other draft choices that contributed were Aaron Mitchell, defensive back; Doug Cosbie, tight end; Ron Springs, running back; and Bruce Thorton, defensive end.

Larry Bethea started the preseason games without making his move. I played left tackle all summer. By the last game of the preseason, Ernie told me I needed to switch to left end. I was not pleased. If I knew I would be playing there, I would have trained differently in the off-season, with longer steps and more edge pass rush moves. Nevertheless, that was the plan. David Stalls would take over at left tackle.

During the preseason, we played an exhibition game in Seattle. Their quarterback was Jim Zorn. He was in training camp a couple of years earlier. I was glad for him, that he was establishing himself as an NFL quarterback, because with Roger Staubach and Danny White, there wasn't any room for him. Also, Bill Gregory was there. I talked to him after that game. He seemed to be happy there to finally be a starter. One of his teammates was Nick Bebout, brother of one of my best friends, Eli Bebout. They won the game, and for us "bad fortune" happened. Charlie Waters got a major knee energy and would be out for the season. As he was our defensive leader, that would be a loss.

In spite of all this, we got off to a good start when the season started. We were 3–0, with close wins over St. Louis, San Francisco, and Chicago. Then we played Cleveland at Cleveland on *Monday Night Football*. It had been a while since we lost to Cleveland. Brian Sipe was their quarterback. He had led some come-from-behind-games wins, so both teams were undefeated. The stadium was sold out, with eighty-thousand-plus fans. They had Greg Pruitt and Reggie Rucker, who developed as a good wide receiver after leaving the Cowboys. Our run defense was soft. We lost 26–7. Our offense just couldn't get anything going.

We won the next four games. Roger Staubach and Tony Dorsett were having a great year. We had one of those bend-but-don't-break defenses. We were 7–1 going into the game against Pittsburg. Their defense was one of the best in history. Tony Dorsett gained seventy-three hard yards, but no touchdowns. We fizzled to a 14–3 loss. Losing to Pittsburg again was hard to take. Off the field, the Cowboys front office had been working to sign John Dutton of the Baltimore Colts. He was very disgruntled with the Colts and had played out his option year. He had not reported to camp. On October 24, the Cowboys signed a contract for him to play for them. I was delighted for this to happen. I could then return to playing tackle, and he would play left end. Larry Bethea would back him up, and Dave Stalls would back me up.

It took a few weeks for John to get in shape, so he played sparingly. We beat the New York Giants and lost the next two to Philadelphia and Washington. Washington would take the lead in the division race. John Dutton would start against the Houston

Oilers, with Earl Campbell as their new running back. He was the Heisman Trophy winner from the Texas Longhorns. This game had our Heisman Trophy winner against theirs. This was the Love Ya Blue days. He had debuted on *Monday Night Football* in a game against the Miami Dolphins, where he ran over people and gained 150-plus yards. This was a tough physical game. He was the hardest guy to take down that I ever played against. If you tackled him at his waist, he would just bounce off you. I would hit him, and if I didn't have help, he would drag me down after gaining five yards. I finally started tackling him beneath his knees. That would work better. They went on to win, 30–24. They won the Governor's Cup, the meaningless championship of Texas. We usually played them during the preseason, but this year we played during the season. Their nemesis was the Pittsburg Steelers, and so was ours. It had been a long time since the Cowboys lost three games in a row. Thomas Henderson left the team and didn't play against Houston. He didn't think he needed to practice. He said, "Just mail me the game plan. I will show up for the game." Tom Landry decided he was too much of a disruption, so he let him go.

We were now 8–5. And so were the Redskins. The next two weeks, we beat the Giants and the Eagles. The Redskins won their next two games also. Joe Theismann and John Riggins were starting to come into their prime. He had come over from the Jets. The big game was coming up in Dallas on December 17. The winner would take the division championship. The loser would go home.

Theismann got off to a good start and took the lead, 17–0. It looked like a blowout. Our pass defense wasn't very good. We missed Charlie Waters. There was confusion in the backfield and inexperience in the defensive line. John Dutton was new to playing the flex defense, but he was starting to pick it up. During his rookie year, Bruce Thornton started developing a pass rush. He and Larry Bethea would add some muscle to the pass rush. The rookie Ron Springs was coming into his own as a running back and a pass receiver. He scored first. Then Preston Pearson and Drew Pearson struck, and it was 17–14 at the end of the first half. It was a scoreless slugfest in the quarter. Robert Newhouse powered over the right side, and we took the lead, 21–17. That didn't last long. Then in the third quarter, Washington added a field goal and closed our lead to one point, 21–20. The Redskins got a flag and got the ball on the one-yard line. John Riggins powered over to give them a 27–21 lead. With about six minutes to go, Washington ran a perfectly executed outside sweep, where the fast running back John Riggins was able to turn the corner and take it in on a sixty-six-yard run. That extended their lead to 34–21. They were celebrating in the end zone. Roger Staubach went back to work and drove the ball down the field and found Ron Springs in the end zone for a twenty-six-yard touchdown. It was now 34–28, with two minutes and twenty seconds to go. Washington drove the ball to midfield and decided to run that same play they scored on earlier. It was third and second. If they got a first down, they could run out the clock. Instead, when they lined up, I noticed the lean of the lineman to the outside. I felt they would run the same play. If not, they would run it up the middle untouched. I gambled that I was right and adjusted my angle to the outside to miss the center's chop on me. I drove toward Riggins and caught him before he could get a first down. The crowd roared. It was like they made the tackle with me. Everyone on the team believed Roger could do it again. He did some short passes and runs. He got the ball down to the eight-yard line and hit Tony Hill in the end zone. He would connect.

It was now 35–34, with twenty-two seconds left.

Joe Theismann tried his own comeback to get the ball in field goal range. He got the ball to a distance that their kicker, Mike Mosely, had a chance, but time had run out.

We won!

This had become a bitter rivalry when Jack Pardee became coach. He accused Tom Landry of designing plays to hurt their receivers. They had done it to us earlier. This was a satisfying win. I remember walking off the field, looking at Tom Landry. He looked over to the other sideline for Jack Pardee to come over. He didn't. Coach Landry and I connected eyes. This is what Dallas Cowboys football is all about. I was proud to be a Dallas Cowboys. We were the most exciting team in the NFL. Charlie Waters was in the broadcast booth with Brad Sham. He gave the play-by-play with the words, "You have got to believe…" With all the critical plays in the last two minutes, twenty seconds, we reaffirmed that we were America's team.

The next week, we would play the Rams at Texas Stadium. Their record was 9–7. We were 11–5. Vince Ferragamo was their quarterback. The previous year, we blew them away 28–0 in the playoffs. They were not going to have that this year. We started the game with a safety by Randy White. We led 2–0. That would be our last lead. We were behind 14–5. Roger hit Jay Saldi at halftime. We closed the lead to 14–12. We went ahead 19–14 with a touchdown. Ferragamo hit Billy Waddy over the middle with a defensive break-down. He broke out in the open for a fifty-yard touchdown. We were in the game until the very end. This time we couldn't finish it. The Rams went on to beat Tampa Bay the next week and on to the Super Bowl. They were a better team by the end of the year than we gave them credit for. For us, this was a "duct tape" year. We were patching things together all year long. I was recognized for team leadership and received the Best Lineman award. This would be Roger's last game. What a career he had! He engineered fourteen come-from-be-hind wins. He set the standard in the NFL at that time.

On February 28, 1980, we held our grand opening at Tara Plantation. We had Bernd Schnerzinger, the owner of Edelweiss Restaurant in Fort Worth come out to serve lunch. This had been our favorite restaurant for many years. He also owned Cotton Barbecue and catered barbecue lunches. The food was great! We had a great turnout to put us on the map with local community leaders and Realtors. With the relocation of IBM and other companies to Las Colinas in Irving, it was only a twenty-minute commute to live in this wooded community in Colleyville. Instead of living in Plano or Carrollton, they would go the other way and live in Northeast Tarrant County on the other side of the DFW Airport. For those who traveled, being close to the airport was a big plus. During that spring, we sold enough lots and houses to pay off the phase 1 debt and start a second phase.

Roger Staubach had his emotional press conference as he announced his retirement. Most people don't understand how the emotions just come to the surface when you are such a competitor like he was. Danny White would be our new quarterback. He was well prepared and worked to keep up Roger's high standards. I was thinking about retirement again, but I just didn't want to end my career yet. Charlie Waters would be back this year. He wrote me a letter to encourage me to not retire. On the other hand, his good friend Cliff Harris decided to retire. I wrote him a letter in early April encouraging him to come back. His doctor was concerned about his long-term health. Those hits he initiated could potentially paralyze him. When Cliff hit you, you would feel it no matter what size you were. I remember watching Cliff hit Harold Carmichael in his back and he would collapse to the ground like a noodle. It toughened up Harold to move on to have a great career. Cliff decided it best that he retire. He had played in five Super Bowls in ten years. Few people can say that for themselves.

In June, five of us Cowboys got invited to participate in the *Family Feud*, the popular television show. Our team had Charlie Waters, Harvey Martin, Danny White, Tony Dorsett, and me. We would compete against five Cowboys cheerleaders. To avoid any "gossip columnist" stories, our wives were invited to be there so when the show was over, they brought them onstage. I think this was Tex Schramm's requirement. One of the wives refused to comply because he was making them do it, not asking them. The other wives thought it was cool to be seen on television. We were then given rooms at the Beverly Hills Hilton. They had a meeting room where the show was filmed. We were told to get together and practice before the show. We were confident we would do okay, but we totally underestimated how hard this was, to think so quickly on our feet. Before the show started, we did a practice round with the cheerleaders. We got skunked. Holy crap! We were going to embarrass ourselves on national television.

We then had another break where we got ourselves focused. The host was Richard Dawson. He liked to "slobber kiss" the cheerleaders and then the wives; however, he was a good show host. The contest started, and we kept even with them. I got the first questions right, but then I gave them a strange answer to the following question: "What makes an airplane fly?" I said air. Richard asked for a clarification of my answer; I told him in order for the plane to stay in the air, you needed air to travel over the top of the wing and then under the wing, to provide lift for the plane to stay in the air. I had learned that in my aeronautical engineering class in college. I then heard, "Brrrhhh! Ding! X! Wrong!" I got the next one right, and then the next question, "What vegetable can you stuff with fruit?" I said watermelon. The crowd started to laugh, and I was puzzled. When I was a kid, we grew watermelons in the same garden as the vegetables on our farm. The fruit trees of peach, apple, crab apple, and raspberry bushes were in the pasture. To me it was the same. This is where an analytical mind gets you in trouble. "Brhhhhh! X! Ding!" My kids were old enough to watch, as well as my nieces and nephews. They all laughed together every time I saw them for a couple of years. We got to the lightning round first. We were behind, but we could catch up and win if we got the last round right. We did. We won and felt relieved. The show has been run and rerun several times, at least once a year, to this day. We were in Hollywood and came through for the big show. I did my part for "comic relief," but that's show business. Just spell my name right.

I was getting ready to go to training camp for the 1980 season. A friend of mine showed me this year's Braniff Airlines football schedule card. This year it had my picture on the front of the card. Wow! I never expected that. On July 9, we got the word that Ed Jones would be back with the team. That was great news. We missed him the previous year. John Dutton was a good pickup. He had played right defensive end for the Colts, but as he got older, left tackle would be his natural position too. I would start at left tackle and play the first series, then I would come in on passing downs. At my age, I liked that setup. I could channel my energy into those plays to make a difference in my pass rush. This year rookie Bruce Thorton was starting to make a contribution. As in 1979, there was one too many defensive linemen on the team. After a couple of preseason games, David Stalls was traded to Tampa Bay. This would be his fourth year to establish himself as a starter. He never quite got there. He wasn't quite big enough to defend against the run in our system but was coming along on the pass rush. He went on to play for the Oakland Raiders and had a few more years to play.

We started the season against the Washington Redskins. We beat them 17–3. Our defense had stiffened up. Having Ed Jones in the lineup was so positive because the rest of us could fill in the gaps for the other positions. We knew it might take a while for the offense to gel under Danny White. The next week, we played the Denver Broncos and just fell apart and lost 41–20. We weren't quite as good as we thought. We moved on and won the next four games. The second of those games was against Phil Simmons, their new rookie quarterback. We were stopping him, but we saw how accurate and strong an arm he had. We weren't confident enough to let down to close the game. He would become a future star. The last of those was the San Francisco 49ers. They had a new quarterback, Joe Montana. We shellacked them, 59–14. He wasn't very effective, but he would remember this game in the future.

The next week, we went to Philadelphia. They were starting to establish themselves under head coach Dick Vermeil. They had added Wilbert Montgomery as their running back. He was from Texas Tech, so a few of us had seen him play in college football. We lost, 17–10. Then we played the San Diego Chargers. One of the all-time greats was Dan Fouts. During the first quarter, Dan said to me that Rick Hrdlicka said hi. Rick was the center on the Hawaii team in 1967 that we both played for. Rick seemed to know everyone from the days of him being a bartender at the Blue Goose. We got pressure on Fouts and won the game, 42–31. We then went to St. Louis and had one of those nail-biting games, and once again Harvey Martin applied the pressure to get the ball back for the offense. This time it was Danny White who engineered the comeback win. I ran down and trapped Jim Hart with nine seconds left to play as the clock ran out. The press loved it when I said that we were the two oldest players on the field and I was just trying to run out the clock because it took me so long to run him down in the open field. The following week, we played our rival, the Washington Redskins. It was a defensive battle. Joe Theismann left the game at the end of the second quarter with a pulled hamstring. We led at halftime, 7–3.

The third quarter was scoreless. Danny White had a rough game. He threw four interceptions, and the offense fumbled twice. In the fourth quarter, Mike Kruczek replaced Joe Theismann. He dropped back to pass. Randy White clobbered him. The ball came out and hit the front of my helmet. It bounced in front of me. I put my hands around the ball and headed for the end zone with no one in front of me. I needed to let the element of surprise spot me ten yards. I took the ball forty-three yards to the end zone. When I turned around, I saw Ed Jones come running right to me. I was determined to finish off with a spike. I didn't want Ed Jones to screw this up. I sidestepped him and wound up to spike the ball with my left hand. Then Ed and the others hugged me. The crowd roared with approval.

My touchdown run.

What I had learned in playing so long is that some plays never live that long if your team loses. Unlike last year's play against John

Riggins, I had to get back on the field to continue playing. It was an emotional event. As a veteran, I knew I needed to get my emotions under control and get back to work. We took the lead 14–3, but Danny White threw an interception. Monte Coleman ran the ball thirty-four yards to the eight-yard line. From there, Wilbur Jackson took the ball into the end zone on the next play. It was now 14–10, with six minutes to go. Ed Jones and Randy White then dominated that game with pressure on Kruczek. The game ended, and I headed for the locker room. For the first time in many years, the press wanted to talk to me in the pressroom. I took my time getting dressed. I got there and saw Frank Luska. He asked me why it had taken me so long to score another touchdown. I said, tongue-in-cheek, "Anybody can have an off-decade." I also said, "I was like an old dog. I just hung around for the scraps." On the interception play, Randy White and I had a stunt called the "cha-cha." I was effective in preoccupying the guard and center, which freed up Randy one-on-one. And then when I released them, I was behind Randy and in position to make the play. I took off as soon as I could because I needed the element of surprise to account for about ten yards of speed.

We won out the rest of the season and finished with a 12–4 record, but second to the Philadelphia Eagles for home field advantage throughout the playoffs.

We would host the LA Rams for the first game of the playoffs. We got our revenge from the previous year's surprise loss on the broken defense play, losing 21–19. We won, 34–13. We then played the Atlanta Falcons at their place. They had a 27–10 lead at halftime. Then they scored first in the third quarter and advanced their lead to 24–10. Robert Newhouse took the ball to the end zone and cut the lead to 24–17. Atlanta added a field goal. Now we were behind, 27–17. Our defense was starting to come to life. I didn't play much of the game. I got into the game in the last two minutes and trapped Bartkowski twice to get the ball back. Danny White found Drew Pearson over the middle for a fourteen-yard touchdown to close the lead to 27–23. Septien missed the field goal. With time running out, Danny White hit Drew Pearson for a twenty-three-yard touchdown. We survived and pulled out another comeback, but this time it was with Danny White. We would be going to the NFC championship again.

We traveled to Philadelphia to play that game. We split with them during the season. When you play teams in your division, they get to know one another quite well since they play one another twice a year. Ron Jaworski was having a good year. The score was 7–7 at the end of the first half. We kept them out of the end zone while giving up running yards. Wilbert Montgomery ran 194 yards. Coach Dick Vermeil had the offense take wider splits and ran the ball when we were in a pass rush defense. I wasn't able to close the gap between Ed Jones and myself, and Mike Hegman and Jones didn't close off the outside. We missed the quickness of Thomas Henderson. Mike was a very good player, but he wasn't Thomas Henderson. We also played the year without Cliff Harris. We lost the game, 20–7, but it felt worse. I didn't play very well. I knew going into the game that this would be my last game. As a pragmatist, I figured only twice in thirteen years that I was happy with the results when we won the Super Bowl. The other years would be what level of frustration you can stand. For me, losing to the Baltimore Colts in 1971 was the hardest. Losing to the Steelers in 1979 was Roger's most painful. I would wait until March to make sure I would retire and announce my retirement. In thirteen years I had only missed the playoffs once in 1974. How many people can say that? I counted my blessings and got back home to get on with my life without football. My body was looking forward to this.

I came back to the practice facilities for the last time to clean out my locker for the year. Aaron Kyle tried to tie me down to answer the question of whether I was coming back for next year. I knew, but I felt I owed it to myself to withhold my announcement until just before the off-season program and the draft. I drove off, never to return. The Cowboys were starting construction on a new facility in Irving, half the distance I was driving for ten years. Oh well.

In March, I was approached by my high school friend Carlton Werner and fellow high school football player about allowing myself to be "roasted." I enjoyed watching *The Dean Martin Celebrity* Roast, so I thought that would be fun.

The Arlington Ramada Inn was the corporate partner for the Easter Seals serving the handicap of Tarrant County. Carlton Werner managed the Fort Worth Ramada Inn. This event would be held at the Ramada Inn in Irving. The presenters would be my friends and teammates. I had Carlton Werner from high school, Mike Rengel from college, and Pat Toomay, D. D. Lewis, Charlie Waters, and Cliff Harris from the Cowboys. And also Brad Sham and Frank Luksa from the press; Don Dodson, Mayor of Bedford; and C. A. Sanford, former mayor of Hurst and local restaurant owner who was known for his wry, critical sense of humor. He was the master of ceremonies for many local chamber and charity events. He would spare no one. Bill Mercer of KLIF Radio would be the master of ceremonies. Since Mike Rengel and D. D. Lewis were my roommates, they had much information about being my roommate. Pat Toomay spoke on behalf of the Zero Club for Blaine Nye, who lived in California. They all did a good job and entertained the crowd. I responded to all of them or most of them. Boy, that was a lot harder to do than you think without any advanced notice of what they were going to say. At the end of the event, C. A. Sanford was given the job of presenting me a special award for the event. He pulled it out of his bag. It was a toilet seat. He showed the seat to the crowd and then opened the lid. Inside was a picture of me. The crowd roared. What should a member of the Zero Club expect? The event raised a lot of money. I was more than happy to have participated.

The next week I made an appointment to see Tom Landry. I had never been to his office before. He would usually just come over to my locker and tell me what was going to happen to me. I said okay. He was in charge. I had always wanted to retire on my own terms. The meeting with him took less than five minutes. We understood each other. He didn't try to talk me out of it. He had made the statement years before that when a player says it's time to retire, he has already retired in his own mind. He trusted I had thought this out. He knew how much work I had done to prepare myself for my next career. He told me that he would provide a full press conference at Texas Stadium. Wow! I never expected that. On Friday, March 27, 1981, the press conference was held in the pressroom above the stadium. I spoke first to make the announcement. I wanted to thank the Dallas Cowboys for drafting me in 1968. I then thanked Tom Landry, Clint Murchison, Texas Schramm, and Gil Brandt. I also then thanked my defensive line coach, Ernie Stautner. He had molded me into the player he wanted me to be. In later years, Charlie Waters asked Ernie, "Who was the most competitive guy I coached?" He said me. Not for my talent, but for my refusal to just give up and not fight back. That was an immense compliment. I would later be asked to be one of the six pallbearers at his funeral. I was honored. I then thanked the press, the fans, and all the people of DFW. Finally, I thanked the Washington Redskins. I then said they played a big part in my career. I gave four reasons that I was ready to retire:

1. I needed to throw all my energies into my business and cut the umbilical cord of another paycheck.
2. The second reason was for my family. My children were growing up and needed more attention. Mike was ten, and Christy was eight. I needed to watch their activities, not take time for mine.
3. I wanted to get out of football in one piece. I had never had surgery in twenty-three years of playing the game.
4. We had a meeting of the Zero Club. I was told to give up this publicity by April 1 or I would be kicked out.

I then went on to say, "One thing I've experienced is, the thrill of victory and the agony of defeat," made famous by Olympic and Football ABC Analyst Jim McKay. And I've had both. You just can't replace the feeling of winning the first championship in 1972 and then winning the second one in 1978. By the same token, you can't replace the heartbreaking losses we had to Baltimore and Pittsburg."

I then said, "I feel I've played in probably the most exciting era in pro football, coming in my rookie year, when the Jets upset the Colts, and then going through that era, when the Super Bowl was still relatively new. *Monday Night Football* was new, and they started building such fantastic stadiums."

"I just feel fortunate I got a glimpse out of the past at the old football, and a piece of the new."

It was now time for Tom Landry to speak. He said" I respect the person Larry is as I did Roger. When a player of this caliber makes that decision, I know it wasn't done for any other reason than what is best for him and his family. When you do that, I don't try to talk him out of it, even though I'd like to. We'll miss Larry Cole as a person more than anything else. I know that if I had forty-five guys like Larry Cole, I'd never retire, because they'd be a pleasure to coach. And I know they'd contribute greatly to the team."

Wow! What a great way to go out on top. Coach Landry said earlier in the fall about me. He said "He's been such a consistent player for us through the years. He's been kind of indispensable in that he's been able to play end and tackle."

I was so fortunate to play for only one head coach, Tom Landry, and one defensive coach, Ernie Stautner. Both men had a big influence on me. The fact that they both were also players made them real to me. The flex defense was to my advantage because so many players just couldn't pick up the techniques or didn't want to. I also think it saved my body from unnecessary physical blows because the point was to make the tackle, not ruin other people's bodies. I am forever thankful for the Coaches, Players, and the Trainers making this part of my life so meaningful and exciting. I received a congratulatory resolution from the Hawaii State House of Representatives signed by twenty-one of the representatives thanking me for the thirteen years representing the University of Hawaii in the NFL. Many others would follow me. I then received a letter from Dick Vermeil, head coach of the Philadelphia Eagles. He expressed his respect for the way I played the game and wished me good luck in the future. That meant a lot to me. I would only hope to inspire some young people out there to have a dream and follow it to wherever it would lead them. Football was a means to end, as my mother stressed. More than anything else, I loved being a part of a team and doing my part. I wish everyone all the best in forming and following their dreams.

CPSIA information can be obtained
at www.ICGtesting.com
Printed in the USA
JSHW041738260622
27361JS00003B/12